The Archaeology of Community Emergence and Development on Mabuyag in The Western Torres Strait

Duncan Wright

BAR International Series 2754
2015

Published in 2016 by
BAR Publishing, Oxford

BAR International Series 2754

*The Archaeology of Community Emergence and Development on Mabuyag in
The Western Torres Strait*

ISBN 978 1 4073 1415 0

BAR Publishing is the trading name of British Archaeological Reports (Oxford) Ltd.
British Archaeological Reports was first incorporated in 1974 to publish the BAR
Series, International and British. In 1992 Hadrian Books Ltd became part of the BAR
group. This volume was originally published by Archaeopress in conjunction with
British Archaeological Reports (Oxford) Ltd / Hadrian Books Ltd, the Series principal
publisher, in 2015. This present volume is published by BAR Publishing, 2016.

Printed in England

BAR
PUBLISHING

BAR titles are available from:

BAR Publishing
122 Banbury Rd, Oxford, OX2 7BP, UK
EMAIL   info@barpublishing.com
PHONE   +44 (0)1865 310431
FAX   +44 (0)1865 316916
www.barpublishing.com

Acknowledgements

There are many people who I would like to thank for their assistance with this book. A big eso to the Mabuyag community for their continued support of my research. In particular I acknowledge the role of the late Tim Gizu, also Edmund Bani, Cygnet Repu, Dimple and Gabriel Bani who have shared time, stories and songs with me. I thank the field crew over three field seasons: Beboy Whap, Thomas Whap, Shannon Sutton, Ben Watson, Cameo Dalley, Alice Bedingfield, Matt Coller, Sally May, Lewis Bani, Paula Whap for assisting with excavations. Thanks to Michael Field, Penelope Swales and Chloe Stapleton for volunteering to assist me sort over two tonnes of excavated materials. Also, Anna Shnukal, Rod Mitchell, B. Simpson, Ruaidhri Misteal for translating historical texts and Ian McNiven, Glenn Summerhayes, Alan Cooper, Ursula Pietrzak-Aniszewska, Peter Hiscock, Ken Aplin, Pamela Ricardi, Karlis Karklins, Jamey Allen and Bill Dickinson for assisting with artefact analysis. Great support and understanding was provided by my partner, Pamela Ricardi.

Thanks to Dr. Ian McNiven (Monash University) who introduced me (as my PhD supervisor) to the Goemulgal and has continued to provide excellent advice. Invaluable assistance has been provided by generous friends and colleagues who read drafts or offered advice: Tim Denham, Jim Peterson, James Flexner, Anna Shnukal, Mirani Litster, Geoff Clark, Alice Gorman, Lynley Wallis, Fiona Petchey, Sally May, Claire Smith, Ron Vanderwal, Matt Coller, Jeremy Ash, Alice Bedingfield, Liam Brady, Joe Crouch, Diana DeZilwa and Garrick Hitchcock. Many thanks Mirani for your excellent copyediting, and to Beth Cole who very kindly applied her considerable publishing skills to produce the page layouts. Your assistance is very much appreciated.

Thanks to the Australian Institute of Aboriginal and Torres Strait Islander Studies (AIATSIS) for fieldwork funding, regrettably one of the last grants before this important resource was put on hold, and AINSE for funding some of the radiocarbon dates. Monash Indigenous Centre also provided internal grant funding and support during my doctorate. A final thank you to editors of Quaternary International, Archaeology in Oceania, Australian Archaeology and Queensland Archaeological Research for supporting the inclusion of extracts which initially appeared in issues of their journals in this book. It is excellent that I am now it a position to put all this information into one place and repay all of you for believing in this research.

Contents

List of Figures

List of Tables

1

Introduction: Tracing the archaeology of 'community'

"We have been camping at the important village of Wagadagam for three days now. I am being introduced to the village and I think probably also taught the protocols of working here. At night we sit chatting around the fire and occasionally Edmund Bani tells stories and sings songs connected to this village. Such pride, even though it has not been occupied for a long time now. This morning, we were sitting on top of a small hill, the same place where men of the community used to sit and watch for enemy canoes coming around the headland."

(Authors field notebook extract, 15 November 2006)

The Mabuyag community (Goemulgal) is one of many self-differentiating social groups in Torres Strait. Others include the Saibailaig (affiliated with the North Western Islands); the Badulgal and Mualgal (on adjacent Western Islands); the Kaurareg (in the South Western Islands); the Kulkalgal (in the Central group) and the Meriam le in the Eastern Islands (Beckett 2004; Haddon 1904: 67; 1912: 97; 1935: 37; Moore 1984: 16). Numerous communities also exist across the adjacent mainlands in Southern New Guinea and Cape York Peninsula (Moore 1979; Tindale 1974). While Torres Strait communities affiliate themselves with residential island/s, there is an equally strong connection with sea territories, including reefs and sand banks. In a successful sea claim by Torres Strait Islanders, the trial judge, Mick Gooda acknowledged: "there is no land-sea dichotomy. The evidence clearly establishes that the estates are spatially projected out from the shores; they do not stop at the edge of fringing reefs or when deep waters are met" *(Akiba vs Commonwealth of Australia 2013).*

Both historically and ethnographically there is clear evidence that communities spent large amounts of time away from residential islands, with vibrant interrelations existing with other Islanders and communities from Papua New Guinea and Cape York, Australia. These were regulated through trade, exchange and family ties as well as ceremonies, warfare and head hunting (e.g., Beckett 1972: 311-13; Haddon 1890: 339-41; 1904: 293-97; Lawrence 1998: 17; MacGillivray 1852: 3, 35; McNiven 1998; Shnukal 2004). These links mean that contemporary community affiliation is not restricted to individuals on home islands but spans much of Torres Strait and adjacent Papua New Guinea/ far north Queensland. While ethnography supports fluid boundaries, connection to home islands continues to structure Torres Strait identities. Dimple Bani, the chief of Wagedoegam (a village on Mabuyag), currently resides on Thursday Island but ensures that he regularly returns to his ancestral home. With this in mind this book examines the long-term history of one Torres Strait Islander

community, the Goemulgal of Mabuyag in Western Torres Strait. Using a model of fissioning and regionalisation (discussed later in this chapter) this book will provide a detailed archaeological assessment of the emergence and development of ethnographically-significant villages around a single residential island. From this approach new information will emerge about the mid-late Holocene history of Torres Strait.

1.1 What is the archaeology of community?

The archaeology of social groups/ communities has emerged from over a century of theoretical discourse. Both evolutionary and culture history models perceived past cultures as temporally and spatially bound entities (e.g., Childe 1956). It was expected that regional patterns within archaeological assemblages could be used as a tool for "identifying and characterising cultural packages" (Shennan 1989: 5-14). Such "packages" might take the form of distinctive sites, material cultures and stylistic markers (Kroeber 1952; Renfrew 1978). It was recommended that artefacts and practices which were relatively resistant to change (e.g., pottery, ornaments and burial rites) were chosen for analysis rather than utilitarian artefacts (e.g., tools, weapons etc), which tended to diffuse rapidly from one group to another (Childe 1956: 129-131).

In the late twentieth century it became evident that there was a "potential lack of fit between the social configuration 'community' and … material remains" (Hodder 1978: 28). Material culture distribution could be influenced by environmental settings, trade ties, availability of resources, local traditions of craft production, status emulation, gender identities, intergroup marriage patterns and religious beliefs (Thomson 1939; Trigger 2006: 309). The dynamic, multilayered nature of human interaction was expected to disguise social groups, potentially creating homogenous material assemblages (e.g., Jones 2007: 47). A valuable method to mitigate this problem was comparisons between archaeological patterns and ethnographically-known sites and material culture (Binford 1962; Caldwell 1959; Trigger 2006: 320). Following the tenets of Middle Range Theory, if an artefact (or combination of artefacts) was found in contemporary societies this could be correlated to a particular form of behaviour or belief allowing for similar connections to be made based on archaeological assemblages (Binford 1962).

The prominence of ethnography (albeit with a greater emphasis on social actors) increased in the 1980s through Post-Processual archaeology (Hodder 1986; 1991; Shanks and Tilley 1987). Following Bourdieu (1977: 78-93), it was expected that "community" could be defined both in terms of shared residence or space and shared life experiences, knowledge, goals, habits, practices, memories, and sentiments (i.e., belonging). Isbell (2000: 249; see also Anderson 2006) suggested that these represent "natural" and "imagined" aspects of community. The "natural community" concept follows a culture history/ functionalist approach whereby community groups are bounded within time and space. This model moves beyond spatially and temporally bound patterns in sites and material culture, assuming that divisions may be removed in particular circumstances and places (e.g., formalised access/ trade routes). Boundaries may also be archaeologically recognisable through movement of goods and/or rock art styles (Minar and Greer 1969: 3; Yaeger and Canuto 2000: 11).

The "imagined community" concept follows an instrumental model in which communities are socially constituted and ever evolving (Anderson 2006; see also Isbell 2000: 249; Rowland 1994; Yaeger and Canuto 2000: 12). This fits with the picture of social dynamism and individual agency and it is expected that contemporary connections to place (even by people no longer living in this place) may be powerful tools for assessing past communities (e.g., Jones 2007). Settlements are assumed to go through multiple phases of growth, decline and even abandonment (Marcus 2000: 232). The archaeological record is therefore assumed to be diverse and changeable and the material domain is assumed to be "simultaneously the means, medium, and outcome of social reproduction" (Bourdieu 1977: 39; see also; Jones 1997: 117; Postone et al. 1993: 4; Soja 1989). Regional variations may also occur within communities. For example, nucleated villages in the Andes were closely connected to the architecturally dissimilar herders' corral sites higher up the mountain (Marcus 2000: 231). It is expected that both homogeneity and heterogeneity will occur within the material culture and settlement patterns of communities and that boundaries will frequently blur.

This social construction of community is "multi-layered" or "nested" (Alfred 1996: 18; see also Smith 1999: 126). Community may be viewed in holistic terms (i.e., a group with a common identity) or on a micro scale involving the archaeology of villages, households or family units (Orser 2007: 42). For example "in North America, 'Indian Country' defines one sense of community, a named nation such as the Navajo Nation defines another sense of community a named reserve defines yet another sense" (Smith 1999: 126). Similarly the Kahnawake identity in Quebec, Canada are conceptualised through "localised Kahawake, national Mohawk, broader Iroquois, and pan-Native" (Alfred 1996: 19). By layering "community" in this way it follows that broad regional patterns in the archaeological record would be expected, becoming increasingly blurred as the focus narrows (Barth 1969; Jones 2007: 51).

1.2 The archaeology of Indigenous Australian communities

Australia contains a multitude of self-differentiating Indigenous communities which are themselves divided based on clan and kin affiliation. For this reason, social

conceptions of community are prominent in this context. One model examines regional patterns in archaeology as part of an ethnographically-known social process of regionalisation and fissioning (McNiven 1999: 157 and discussed below). While this model is driven by a social conception of community (involving ethnographic analogy) it provides archaeological expectations that may be useful even when the case study is temporally or culturally remote from present-day communities. A second model (arguably centred on an imagined conception of community) centres on people's relationships with place. Native Title claims, for example, frequently examine sites (and/ or material culture) in order to establish correlations between oral histories and archaeology. This model enables a partnership (or community) archaeology perspective with contemporary communities brought to the heart of the research process (Clarke 2002; Greer et al. 2002; Marshall 2002: 216). It further "encourages us to ask questions of the past we would not otherwise consider, to see archaeological remains in new light and to think about how the past informs the present" (Marshall 2002: 218). While archaeology should be assessed independently from oral history (acknowledging the possibility that the two may disagree), a critical reading of oral histories can provide a more complete and nuanced understanding of archaeological communities. In the following section I review both conceptions of community before examining their application to the Torres Strait.

Bounded archaeological patterns - Group regionalisation and fissioning

Ethnographic studies suggest that social and/ or demographic pressures may cause social groups to fission into smaller groups with separate territories (Birdsell 1953). This simple premise has been applied to archaeological data, with fissioning expected to be archaeologically visible through shifts from one to multiple settlement sites (Dortch 2002: 13; McNiven 1999: 162, 2003: 331). As "new groups attempt to make a living from smaller and smaller territories" midden materials are likely to increase as settlements move from "dispersive" to "congruative" (McNiven 1999: 163; see also Hall and Bowen 1989; Dortch 2002: 4). It was expected that subsistence would also be influenced by this shift with efficient technologies required to accommodate growing food needs (Binford 1980; David and Lourandos 1998: 211; McNiven 1999). This would include "delayed return systems" such as fish-weirs or agricultural installations (Dortch 2002; Lourandos 1997: 319) and strict resource management/ restrictions (Barker 2004; David and Lourandos 1998: 211-212; McNiven 1999: 162). It was further predicted that new communities would become increasingly localised in their foraging/ hunting activities, restricted by a reduction in the size of clan territories (McNiven 2003; Pickering 1994).

Fissioning is likely to cause "regionalisation" of social/ political life, which may affect the archaeological record. This may include unintentional modifications (e.g., linguistic divergence) or intentional social markers (e.g., unique sites and cultural materials) (David and Lourandos 1998). Regional patterns may develop in mortuary practices (Pardoe 1995), rock art (David and Lourandos 1998; Taçon 1993), and site distribution (McNiven 1999: 163). A desire to maintain boundaries and boundedness may require altered relationships to land and sea and/ or the onset of a new political/ clan systems (Head 1994; McNiven 2003; Pickering 1994; Taçon 1994). These divisions could be regulated and maintained through songs, ceremonies and symbolic expressions (Morphy 1991; Taylor 1996). Connections between newly-formed groups and territories may promote development of formalised intergroup alliances and social gatherings associated with ceremonies and networks of trade/ exchange (David and Lourandos 1998: 198; Dortch 2002: 13; Lourandos 1997; McNiven 1999: 162; 2003: 331; McNiven and Feldman 2003: 171).

Regionalisation and fissioning events may have a number of archaeological expressions. Regional variation may occur in material culture distributions as exemplified by stone points in Western Australia (Hiscock 1994). Alternatively, distinctive sites and site combinations may occur (Barker 2004; McNiven 1999). This was the case for burial sites in South East Australia, South East Queensland and New South Wales (Hope and Littleton 1995; Pardoe 1998; Pate 1995; McNiven 1999: 158; Webb 1989). Furthermore, discrete distributions of shell midden were observed in the Great Sandy region of coastal South East Queensland (McNiven 1999: 163). Following the regionalisation model radiocarbon dates from middens identified "the locus of the fissioning process" on Fraser Island followed by three subsequent phases of expansion to the mainland (McNiven 1999: 163). A similar sequence has been observed between early-dated middens on Stradbroke Island and later middens on Moreton Island (Hall and Bowen 1989).

Clan groups and boundaries may also be stylistically inscribed through rock-art (David 2002; David and Lourandos 1998; Taçon 1993). This has been argued to be the case for late Holocene stylistic "groups" (e.g., Lourandos 1993; David and Lourandos 1998). For example on Cape York an expansive tradition of engraved geometric figures shifted to a dualistic division of painted motifs, closely correlating with two ethnographically-known regions (David 1991; David and Cole 1990; David and Lourandos 1998). This was observed in a number of other regions of Queensland (Lourandos 1993: 56) and Western Arnhem Land (Taçon 1993; 1994). Taçon (1994: 119) observed one case where a clan boundary could be recognised through a "47 metre non-engraved gap" between two sets of distinctive, totemic motifs. Such boundaries have also been identified through totemic and/ or ceremonial markers such as stone cairns (David et al. 2004b). It was acknowledged that clan differentiation may be obscured as clans frequently share food, ceremonies

and access to each other's land despite maintaining fixed clan boundaries (Taçon 1994: 119). The regionalisation model predicts that increased restrictions will occur as groups fissioned from the mother community (McNiven 1999). Cooloola provides an example of this with a shift from inland silcrete to locally available "arkose" used to explain a "dramatic cut in access to inland areas and inland resources" (McNiven 1999: 162; see also Guilfoyle 2005). In late Holocene Australia regulation of the landscapes may also be archaeologically visible through shifting fire regimes (Head 1994). However, evidence also supports an expansion of alliance formations "to overcome, among other things, the territorial and social constrictions of closure" (Lourandos 1993: 80). In South West Australia, it has been argued that trade links are archaeologically visible through increasing quantities of non-local stone in the cultural assemblages (Dortch 2002: 16).

The expectation that new forms of ceremonial behaviour would occur has been argued through the late Holocene emergence of stone cairns at Evans Bay, Cape York (McIntyre-Tamwoy and Harrison 2004: 41). As will become clear later in this chapter, this has also been argued for Torres Strait where dugong (*Dugong dugon*) bone and shell arrangements and mounds become prominent during a period of settlement expansion and increased midden activity (David et al. 2009; McNiven et al. 2009).

The regionalisation model may be strengthened when archaeological, ethnographic and/ or linguistic boundaries correspond. Key examples include a multi-disciplinary study of exchange networks/ territorial expansions in Cape York (David and Lourandos 1998). Skelly et al. (2010) provided a fascinating study of staggered village establishment in Papua New Guinea, structured around archaeological excavations at ethnographically-significant villages. Pardoe (1988) suggested that burial practices mirror ethnographically-known clan divisions. Regionalisation has also been argued using a combination of ethnographic and/ or linguistic information coupled with special variation in rock art (e.g., David 1991: 41; Taçon 1993; Ross 2013). Taçon (1993: 112) suggests that this "multi disciplined approach to the study of recent rock art in Western Arnhem Land is not only possible but also highlights the very close relationship between language, visual art, ceremony, traditional knowledge of the landscape and other aspects of culture". While these studies may use ethnography it is important to recognise that (in contrast to studies listed below) archaeological models and methods are the primary driver for research.

Ethnographically-known connection to place/ cultural practices/ artefacts

Indigenous and European histories recognise that discrete Nations (and communities) exist/ existed in Australia. This understanding has led to two major developments, the archaeology of Native Title and community based

3

(or partnership) archaeology. In the following section we briefly review these archaeologies. After Eddie Mabo's successful land claim in 1992, the *Native Title Act* was formed (in 1993). This process allows Indigenous groups to claim land back from State Governments by proving temporal and spatial connection to place (e.g., Veth 2000). It has been recognised that the identity of claimants within this context relies to a large extent on intangible heritage (e.g., ancestral histories, songs and natural boundary markers) something that is outside the normal parameters of archaeological studies (Beckett 1995: 20; Richards 2002: 111). For this reason it was necessary to develop a system by which oral histories and boundary knowledge could be used alongside archaeological or linguistic information (Godwin 2005: 74; Lilley 2000a: 20; McDonald 2005: 74; Richards 2002: 110; Veth 2000: 81, 86). One method by which communities identify correlates between the two epistemological domains is through archaeological excavations or surveys at known ceremonial, residential or historical sites (McDonald 2005: 30; Veth 2000: 82; Veth and O'Connor 2005: 7).

A number of Native Title studies advise that oral histories need to be contextualised with other "regionally unique signals" (Fullagar and Head 2000; McDonald 2000; Veth 2000; Veth and O'Connor 2002). These include homogenous patterns of settlement and subsistence between ethnographic and archaeological records (Veth 2000: 80). For example, permanent residential and infrequently occupied camps have been examined archaeologically based on expectations of seasonal patterns of subsistence identified in oral and written histories (Fullagar and Head 2000: 29).

Ethnographically and historically known ceremonial and totemic markers can potentially be traced archaeologically through a combination of stylistic indicators in rock-art and the formation of a totemic landscape of stone arrangements and artefact "caches" (Veth 2000: 80; Veth and O'Connor 2005: 7). Rock-art is expected to have "demonstrable connection to social signifying behaviour", providing corroborating information for linguistic or ethnographic boundaries (McDonald 2000: 58, 84; see also Harrison 2000: 43; McDonald 2005: 41; Veth 2000; Veth and O'Connor 2002). Many rock art sites are well-known to claimant groups, some of which continue to be painted by group elders (David *et al.* 2006; McDonald 2000: 82). Based on discussions with Indigenous people, Veth and O'Connor (2002: 124) also claimed that groups could be recognised through variable treatment of stone artefacts.

There is a distinction between community based (partnership) archaeology and the conception of communities mentioned above. Both are based on the sociological (imagined) conception of community, specifically contemporary people's connection to place. Clarke (2002: 251) has suggested that partnership archaeology must go beyond "consultation as the primary

and sole process of negotiating research" towards including "community members in decision making about research topics, research sites, analysis of data, curation and management of collections and the production of materials that are culturally appropriate and useful". It is expected that by bringing contemporary communities (many of which are intimately interconnected with ancestors) to the heart of research design enables decolonisation of methodologies, reducing the gulf between present and past (Moser *et al.* 2009: 220; Smith 1999).

This approach can be confronting for archaeologists, forcing them to alter research questions/ priorities based on Indigenous interests. It also encourages researchers to move beyond conventional scientific methods reflecting on their own practice and experience within place (e.g., Clarke 2002). For the same reason it can be rewarding, with new questions/ priorities enabling information to be generated that is meaningful and engaging to Indigenous and non-Indigenous peoples (Marshall 2002: 218; Smith 1999: 127). This model accepts that ethnography and archaeology will not always match; however, may initiate a process whereby cultural heritage can be negotiated (see McNiven and Russell 2005).

Australia represents one of the key areas in the development of community (partnership) archaeology, evident through an "Antipodean dominance" of a World Archaeological Congress special issue on the subject (Marshall 2002: 212). In part this may be explained through policy, with Indigenous involvement a requirement for cultural heritage work in the majority of states and territories. For example, in the Australian state of Victoria, significant power has been given to Native Title organisations in the practice and dissemination of cultural heritage (see for example the *Aboriginal Heritage Act*, 2006; also Australian Archaeology Association's code of ethics). This restructure of power relations is evident in a number of studies across Australia (Brady and Crouch 2010; Clarke 2002; McIntyre-Tamwoy 2001; McNiven and Russell 2005; Wright 2011c). Although outside the scope of this study, partnership archaeology is gaining momentum in Papua New Guinea: "Archaeology requires community support in order to continue and therefore it is the responsibility of archaeologists to make their research relevant to the local community" (Leaversley *et al.* 2005: 110; see also Byrne 2012; Skelly *et al.* 2010).

1.3   The archaeology of Torres Strait communities

For the sake of continuity this section will not include a review of all archaeological research for the region (although see Appendix 1, Barham *et al.* 2004 for additional context). After providing an introduction to the research area, this chapter will assess the extent to which archaeological research in Torres Strait has examined the emergence and development of communities.

The Torres Strait is an island-studded stretch of sea (approximately 48,000 km² in area), which extends 150 km between Cape York Peninsula and Papua New Guinea (Fig. 1.1). It links the Coral Sea in the east with the Arafura Sea in the west and remains an important (although shallow) international sea-lane. Traditionally, the islands within this region have been divided into three main groups: Western, Central and Eastern. The Western region is often further subdivided into Top Western, Mid or Central Western and South Western. These have a variety of distinctive topographies, geologies and ecosystems. Those closest to New Guinea are low-lying, formed by alluvial sedimentary deposits disgorged from the Fly and other subsidiary rivers. The Western Islands are the peaks of the northernmost extension of the Great Dividing Range and are therefore frequently hilly, steep and largely granitic (von Gnielinski et al. 1998). The Eastern Islands are extremely fertile, having volcanic origins while the Central region is less so, dominated by coral cays.

During the Last Glacial Maximum (26,500-19,000 years ago) the Western and Eastern high islands of present-day Torres Strait formed peaks and ridges which extended approximately 150 km between Australia and Papua New Guinea (Barham 1999; Willmott et al. 1973; Woodroffe et al. 2000). Based on sea level curves, swamp cores and coral dates this mountain range was breached sometime between 9000 and 7000 years ago (Chappell 2005: 525; Larcombe et al. 1995). After a sea-level highstand (approximately 6000 years ago) seas dropped to their current level within the past 4000-3000 years. Barham (2000: 291) predicted that the limited areas of platform/ fringing reefs (between 7500-6500 years ago) were destabilised further during a "high energy window" between 6500–5000 years ago. Beach progradation and sea-grass/ reef development occurred after 4000 years ago (Barham 2000: 290-92; Woodroffe et al. 2007). During this period (3500-3000 years ago) mangrove forests, which had expanded prior to marine transgression, decreased dramatically (Barham 1999; Rowe 2007).

The Indigenous inhabitants of the Torres Strait possess a distinctive culture and firm connection to place (both in terms of residential islands and surrounding seas). Torres Strait Islanders are "marine specialists", great hunters and navigators (Barham 2000; Beckett 2004; Haddon 1904; McNiven and Hitchcock 2004: 105). They covered large sea-distances in impressive outrigger canoes, which acted as "the bridge which spanned the world of the islands" (Sharp 1980: 41; see also Beckett 2004: 7; Brierly journals 1848-1850 cited in Moore 1979: 46; Haddon 1904: 305). Prior to the "Coming of the Light" (missionisation), trade networks stretched from Papua New Guinea to Cape York (Beckett 1972; Lawrence 1994; 1998; Moore 1979). McNiven (2003; see also McNiven and Feldman 2003) suggested that Torres Strait Islanders also developed complex cosmologies and ritual connections to the sea and seascapes. This was expressed physically through sites overlooking important fishing grounds involving

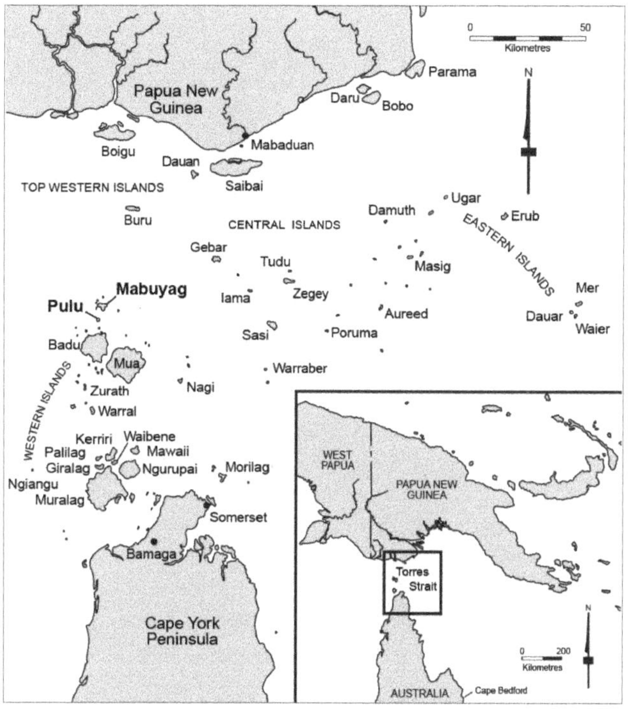

Fig 1.1. Map of Torres Strait with key areas discussed in this book highlighted in bold.

arrangements and mounds of dugong bone (McNiven and Feldman 2003: 169) and shells (David et al. 2005).

Archaeological research in Torres Strait (on a large/ inter-regional scale) supports fluid boundaries. This includes homogeneity in a plethora of occupation sites (e.g., rockshelters, shell middens, stone artefact scatters, oven stones); subsistence sites/ facilities (e.g., mound-and-ditch fields; stone fish traps); and ceremonial sites (shell arrangements, stone arrangements) (McNiven et al. 2004a). As will become clear later in this book, patterns in site types and material culture frequently transcend self-differentiating communities and do not always fit with ethnographic histories. Dugong bone mounds are an exception, restricted to the Western and Central Islands (McNiven et al. 2004a). Rock art also appears "not to have been influenced by social groupings of the late 1800s" (Brady 2005: 397; also Brady 2006: 370; 2010: 467). While statistically significant patterns were noted for motif form (and colour) on Pulu, Kirriri and Dauan the only sizable distinction appears to be a differing mode of artistic expression between painted traditions in the west and engraved traditions in the east (McNiven and David 2004). This corresponds with a linguistic division between Western and Central Islanders who speak Australian-derived Kala Lagaw Ya and Eastern Islanders who speak the Papuan Language, Meriam Mer (Ray in Haddon 1908; Wurm 1972). This artistic division may also reflect differing geologies between these regions (e.g., McNiven and David 2004). Brady (2010: 469) concluded that rock art "confirms the existence of an open communication network that incorporated the exchange of design forms" through Torres Strait. It was further noted that Dauan shared many designs with adjacent

Papua New Guinea, and that "Papuan decorative influence decreases in the mid-western and south-western parts of Torres Strait (Brady 2010: 378). Archaeological studies in Torres Strait are yet to test the potential for intra-island fissioning and subsequent regionalisation. To date, the most fruitful line of enquiry for examining Torres Strait communities has been through ethnographically-known sites (e.g., the ceremonial men's meeting place or *kod*-men's meeting places, *zogo*-sacred sites and villages) and practices (i.e., gardening and marine specialist activities). In the following section we will explore these potentials.

Archaeological research at ethnographically – known sites

Arguably, the most comprehensive study of an ethno-graphically-significant site in Torres Strait occurred at the Pulu *kod*, called *kwod* by Alfred Haddon (1904). Rich oral and written histories survive for this site, including descriptions of clan affiliation and ritual use of installations within this site (Haddon 1904: 3-5). McNiven *et al*. (2009) surveyed and excavated this site, providing archaeological data to contextualise ethnography. Archaeology supports site establishment after 300-400 years ago, followed by ongoing activity until approximately 150 years ago (McNiven *et al*. 2009). A dugong bone mound at this site was observed to be highly structured: "dugong ribs dominate [the] lower half of the mound while dugong skull fragments dominate the upper sections" (McNiven and Feldman 2003: 183). The lower ribs were observed to be "consistently arranged arching upwards and oriented perpendicular to the long axis of the mound" (McNiven and Feldman 2003: 183). This was interpreted as evidence for the ceremonial role of this site, further suggested by multiple "dancing" and "totemic" rock art figures (Brady 2006: 368-9). This site will be described in further detail in Chapter 2.

Despite the importance of *kod* sites for understanding the history of Torres Strait Islanders there are few comparable studies. Excavations of dugong bone mounds, potentially associated with ceremonial activity at Dhabangay (on Mabuyag) and on Tudu, also date to within the past 400 (and in the case of Tudu 100) years (McNiven and Bedingfield 2008; McNiven and Feldman 2003). A dugong bone mound (radiocarbon dated between 530 and 330 BP) was excavated at Koey Ngurtai, a small islet to the north of Badu (David *et al*. 2009; Skelly 2007: 55, 64). No oral histories were obtained to contextualise this site, however, the structured nature of all mounds (primarily ribs and skull fragments) and similar chronologies suggests shared ritual behaviour (McNiven and Feldman 2003: 186).

The Goemulgal (along with other Torres Strait Islanders) are ethnographically recorded to have formed arrangements of bu (*Syrinx aruanus*) shells (Haddon 1935: 56). These shells were used to identify totemic divisions (Haddon 1901: 138-9); to mark graves of culture heroes and for other ritual

purposes (Haddon 1935: 56; 360). They are particularly common on Badu, including alignments (e.g., Badu 21, 24) and isolated clusters (e.g., Badu 31) (David *et al*. 2005: 78-80). In keeping with ethnography some shells have trumpet holes (David and Mura Badulgal 2006: 135; David *et al*. 2005: 81). Shell arrangements have been radiocarbon dated to within the past 400-500 years and were apparently not used at the time of Haddon's arrival (David and Mura Badulgal 2006; David *et al*. 2005; 2009; McNiven *et al*. 2009). The formalised nature of bone mounds and shell arrangements and the synchronous nature of their development in Western Torres Strait have been used to argue for an alteration in socio-political and ceremonial relations during this period (David *et al*. 2005: 88; David *et al*. 2009; McNiven *et al*. 2009: 314).

A unique "story site" was discovered on Mua. This natural, granite boulder is located in the island's interior and called Turao Kula. A faded painting can be observed of an anthropomorphic figure clinging to the top of a coconut tree. This resembles a well-known story in which Badu warriors surprised Goba and his father with Goba escaping up a coconut tree (e.g., Lawrie 1970: 45-6). The boulder is reputed to be within 100 metres of the murder of Gobas' father (Brady *et al*. 2004: 32; David *et al*. 2004a: 163). Archaeological excavation at this site revealed the onset of occupation somewhere between 750 and 1400AD. The site was used much less intensively after this with a subsistence shift towards shellfish (David *et al*. 2004a: 167). Powdered ochre consistent with the rock painting was excavated within a layer dated to the past 500 years. The authors use oral histories and archaeology to argue reduction in site use may relate to an increase in head hunting raids such as the one recounted in this story (David *et al*. 2004a: 169).

In Torres Strait, "villages" are regarded as both residential areas and meaningful places connected with community/ clan identity (McNiven *et al*. 2004a; David and Ash 2008; Chapter 2). These have been recorded on 20 islands (amounting to 71 sites) in the Torres Strait with the majority (54) recorded within the Western and Eastern groups (McNiven *et al*. 2004a: 77).

Despite their prominence in oral and written histories, it was observes in 2006 that "not a single detailed archaeological site report has been published for any past or present village in Torres Strait" (David and Weisler 2006). Archaeological studies at villages frequently remained unpublished or were buried in the grey literature. This includes the work of archaeologists from University College London at Dhabangay and Goemu (on Mabuyag) and Sigan (on Mua; Barham and Harris 1987; Ghaleb 1990; 1998), also Mike Rowlands' (1985) excavations on Naghi and Mua and David Moores' (1979) excavation at Port Lihou on Murulag. This situation has changed in recent years following fieldwork by members of the Western Torres Strait Cultural Heritage Project (WTSCH Project) coordinated by Ian McNiven and Bruno David (David and McNiven 2004). Excavations have been conducted at the ethnographically-significant villages on Mua, including Totalai (on Mua) (Ash and David 2008; David and Ash 2008) and multiple villages on Mabuyag (McNiven and Wright 2008; McNiven *et al*. In press; Wright 2011a, 2011b, 2011c; This book). In addition, midden sites that may represent long forgotten village activities have been excavated at Kurturnaiwak on Badu (David and Weisler 2006), Tiger shark Rockshelter on Pulu (McNiven *et al*. 2006: 28) and Dauan 4 on Dauan (McNiven 2006). Results suggest that villages date within the past 1300 years, with the majority post-dating 800 years ago (Ash and David 2008; David and Ash 2008; Ghaleb 1990; McNiven and Wright 2008; Moore 1979: 15; Wright 2011a). As no large-scale studies have focused on the process by which ethnographically-known villages developed around a single Torres Strait island the antiquity and fissioning history of these sites remains uncertain.

Continuity of ethnographically – known practices

A number of researchers have looked at continuity between contemporary and past subsistence economies in Torres Strait. In Eastern Torres Strait, The Murray Islands Archaeology Project involved anthropological investigations of shellfish gathering on Mer, Dauar and Waier (Bird and Bird 1997; Bird and Bleige Bird 2000; Bird *et al*. 2002). Archaeological evidence suggested that there was considerable divergence between excavated materials and the anthropological record. On Mer "the most important shellfish prey types are virtually absent from the prehistoric archaeology, and conversely, prey that are relatively unimportant are quite common in the shell assemblages" (Bird *et al*. 2002: 467). This discrepancy was explained through the differential deposition of shellfish during the gathering process (Bird and Bleige-Bird 2000: 54).

A more general examination of subsistence patterns throughout the Murray Islands suggested "remarkable similarities between the composition of the archaeological species and the contemporary ethnographically marine based diet of the Meriam" (Carter 2006: 297). It was observed that shellfish, particularly those collected from nearshore, intertidal zones had been collected for 2500-3000 years (Carter *et al*. 2004: 178). It was further suggested that the numerous fish traps within this island group provided evidence for a period of intensified procurement of fish (Barham 2000). To date, there have been no systematic attempts made to obtain a chronology for these sites. It was observed, however, that they cluster around ethnographically-known villages and therefore are expected to date to within the past 1000 years (Harris and Ghaleb 1987: 32; see also Rowland and Ulm 2011: 8). While Haddon (1912: 158-59) did not believe that their construction survived in living memory, the maintenance of these appeared in songs collected by Haddon that relate to "the Saw Fish dance" (see Barham 2000: 263). This being the case it is not unreasonable to suggest fish

traps led to alterations in management strategies and the development of present-day maritime specialist activities (Carter 2006: 300). Ethnographic histories suggest that gardening was a principal subsistence strategy for Eastern Torres Strait Islanders (e.g., the Meriam). Once again, archaeology "only partially matches the pattern predicted from ethnographic accounts" with relict mound and ditches (elsewhere associated with horticultural practices) not recorded for the Eastern Islands (Barham *et al*. 2004: 46). Microfossil results from both Sokoli and Ormi provided evidence for the introduction of banana and coconut after 2000 BP (Carter 2002b: 6-7). A shift from native grasses (*Thermeda australis*) to the more fire resistant taxa *Imprita cyclindrica* also implies widespread clearance during this period (Parr and Carter 2003: 140; Carter 2006: 298, 300). Archaeological assemblages from this region frequently contain large quantities of fish bone, while the majority of fish traps are located in the Eastern Islands (84 out of 115) (McNiven *et al*. 2004a: 77). This suggests fishing was comparable, if not more important (in terms of dietary importance) to horticulture in the Eastern Islands (Barham 2000: 264).

In Western Torres Strait advanced maritime specialist activities/ technologies have been noted for contemporary Torres Strait Islanders (e.g., Beckett 1972). This provides a starting point for studies examining the emergence and development of these maritime focused communities. Extensive middens (often consisting of large vertebrate bone and incorporating a wide variety of fish species) have been excavated at numerous sites on Mabuyag/ Pulu (Ghaleb 1990; 1998; Harris *et al*. 1985: 16; McNiven and Hitchcock 2004: 110; McNiven and Wright 2008; McNiven *et al*. 2008: 20). In particular, the excavations at Goemu identified a number of similarities between the ethnographic and archaeological fishing records with inshore taxa such as Scarids and Labrids dominating (Ghaleb 1990: 286). The small quantities of fish bone were seen to be at odds with the prominence of these for contemporary Islanders. This was attributed to taphonomic and sampling biases (Ghaleb 1990: 172). Midden dugong bone was radiocarbon dated within the past 600 to 800 years suggesting that these food groups were widely established within the late Holocene (Ghaleb 1990; 1998).

A similar focus on marine resources has been suggested for Badulgal, however the Berberass excavation revealed procurement of dugongs, turtles, sharks, rays and fish from approximately 4000 years ago (Crouch *et al*. 2007: 60). Midden bone and shell on Mua, Badu and Dauan (in North Western Torres Strait) provides evidence for an 800-year history of fish, dugong, shellfish and turtle exploitation (David *et al*. 2008; McNiven 2006; Rowland 1985: 126-7).

Horticulture (gardening) is described in ethnographic and historical accounts for Western Torres Strait (Haddon 1904; MacGillivray 1852). Barham *et al*. (2004: 47) identified oral histories for two types of horticultural boundary markers (stone cairns/ arrangements and linear and curvilinear mounds). Mound-and-ditch field systems were not explored in the Haddon archives (1904), although significant details were provided about land tenure and maintenance. Ethnohistorical and archaeological data suggests the age of the mound-and-ditch fields on Mua, Badu and Mabuyag may be recent (Barham *et al.* 2004: 47). Archaeological results from excavation mound-and-ditch field systems in Saibai suggest these date between 800-1200 BP and (based on ethnohistorical and genealogical information) must predate 400 years ago (Barham 1999: 101; Barham *et al.* 2004: 48; Carter 2002a).

Amity and enmity

Ethnography suggests that relationships between Islander communities were frequently driven by enmity or amity (e.g., McNiven 1998). Examples of this include close links between Goemulgal and Badulgal, who were both frequently embattled with Mualgal (e.g., Haddon 1904). There is little substantive archaeological support for this; however, parallel temporal and spatial developments (e.g., bone mounds, *bu* shell arrangements at Pulu, Mabuyag, Koey Ngurtai and Zurath) may support social connectivity. As these sites are also found on Mua the relationship between communities and material culture appears more complex than a simple reading of oral or written histories suggests.

Excavations of Totalai on Mua suggest significant decrease in midden materials after 926-1068 cal. BP. It has been argued that this represents a period of village abandonment possibly resulting from increasing tension between Mua and the other Western Islands (Ash and David 2008). As reported earlier in this chapter the Goba site may also fit this pattern. A final occupation period at Totalai, approximately 141-228 cal. BP, appears to involve increased predation of shellfish as opposed to dugong/ fish. This is mirrored by a number of other Mualgal sites e.g., Gerain, Urakaraltam and Turau Kula which all provide evidence for altered subsistence immediately prior to/ after European arrival (David *et al.* 2008). The authors suggest that this shift may be explained through ethno-historically recorded tensions between the Mualgal and their island neighbours. This is expected to have caused restrictions in access of hunting grounds, requiring targeting of safer inshore regions.

Enmity and amity may also be evident in rock art. Brady (2005: 165, 397; Brady 2010: 377) observed motifs (e.g., the "triangle" or "triangle variants") that were restricted to Pulu, Badu and Mua. The bird has only been recorded on Pulu and Badu. Brady (2005: 410; 2010: 164) points out that frigate bird and cassowaries are totem animals for both Badulgal and Goemulgal. A connection may also be established between the two, allied islands through use of red and yellow pigment. This combination has not been found elsewhere in the Torres Strait (Brady 2005: 401-2). Rock-art may provide corroborating evidence for the close

relationship between the Kuarareg and the Gudang people of Cape York (Brady 2010: 377). A number of motifs are shared including E shapes, crescents, enclosed grid patterns and comb shapes (Brady 2005: 397). A similar connection between the two communities was observed through pigment colouration with a combination of mulberry, white, red and black used in both regions (Brady 2005: 402; 2006: 27). Despite these comparisons, Brady (2005: 398; 2007: 27; 2010: 377) concluded that rock-art at Somerset (Cape York) has many more differences suggesting that the Gudang were always on the fringe of the island systems. One such variant is the canoe which at Somerset is consistently depicted through simple motifs as opposed to those recorded in the South Western Islands where canoes have distinctive elements such as central platforms, flags, bow ornaments etc. (Brady 2006: 27).

1.4   Summary

Earlier in this chapter, two methodologies were presented for examining the archaeology of communities. The fissioning and regionalisation model provides a large number of criteria that can be traced archaeologically. These include regionally distinct sites/ artefacts/ subsistence practices, increasing insularity, and the emergence of new social/ ceremonial activities. It also assumes that boundaries and trade routes may be physically inscribed through material distributions and rock art styles. The second uses ethnographically-known cultural practices, sites and material culture to explain and even predict archaeological patterns. These models are not mutually exclusive and indeed have been combined on mainland Australia to provide strong evidence for past communities. In Torres Strait, archaeological sites and rock art provide little evidence for regionalisation between contemporary, self-differentiating communities. In a region that is ethnographically and historically known to have been dynamic both in terms of trade and exchange and family ties this should not surprise us. To date, the most fruitful line of enquiry for examining Torres Strait communities has been on a smaller/ regional scale, through ethnographically-known sites (e.g., villages and the ceremonial kod) (McNiven *et al.* 2004a). These sites are historically-documented, ethnographically-known, and intimately connected with contemporary Torres Strait communities. While this has been successfully trialled for *kod* complexes (McNiven *et al.* 2009), archaeological studies are yet to comprehensively test the emergence and development of ethnographically-known villages around a single residential island, including how the archaeological record corresponds with oral historical accounts of settlement fissioning. In the following chapter this potential is explored through an ethnographic and archaeological assessment of Goemulgaw[1] villages.

---

1 Goemulgaw is the possessive form of the noun Goemulgal in Mabuyag orthography.

8

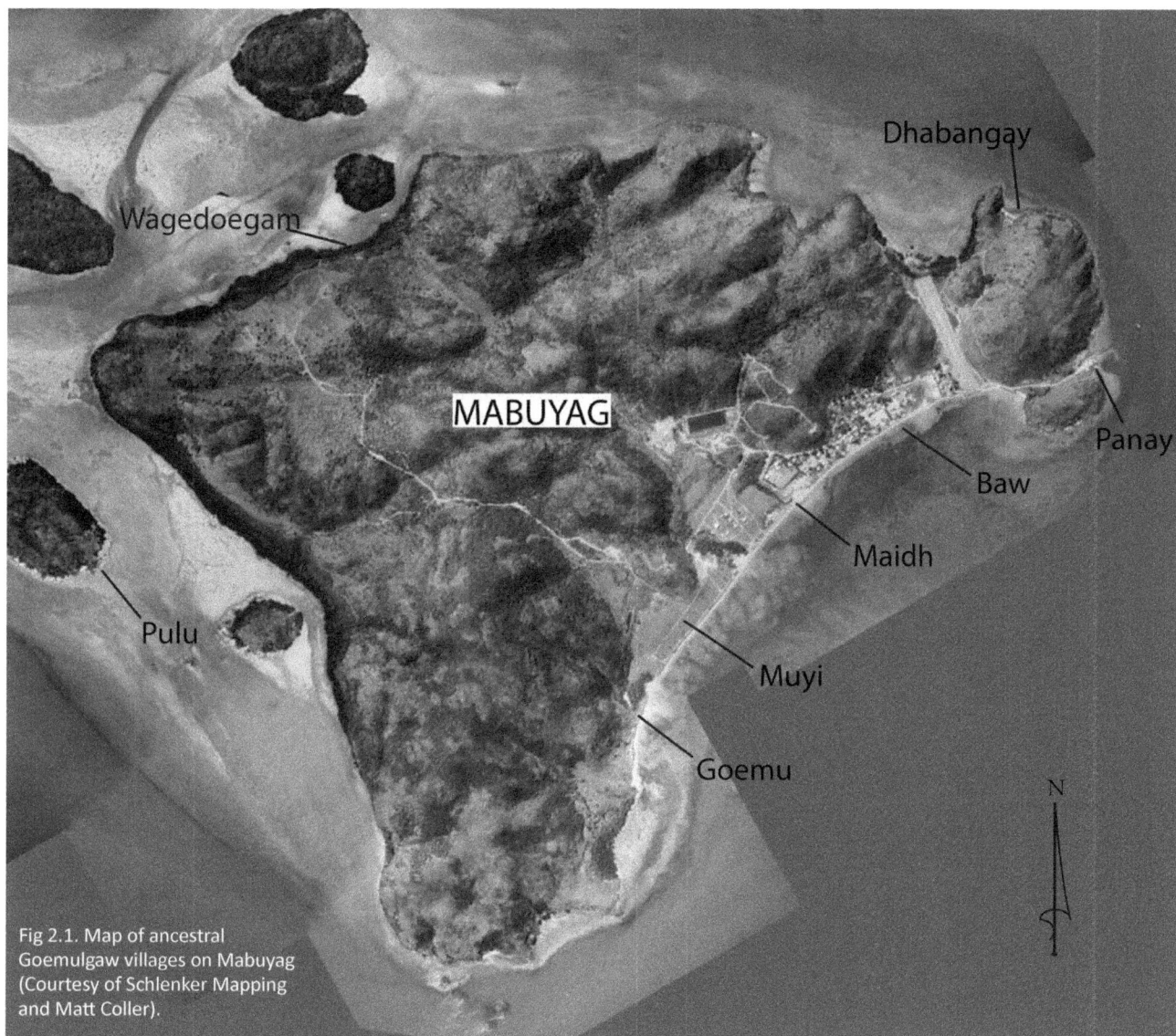

Fig 2.1. Map of ancestral Goemulgaw villages on Mabuyag (Courtesy of Schlenker Mapping and Matt Coller).

2

Expressions of the Goemulgaw community

In the previous chapter I reviewed the archaeology of community, specifically models that had been success-fully applied to Indigenous Australian contexts. It was suggested that a model of fissioning and regionalisation was useful, strengthened further when coupled with a social, community-based approach (involving archaeological research at ethnographically-significant sites). It was recognised that the combination of these approaches was yet to be systematically applied to Torres Strait and that two site-types, the ceremonial *kod* and traditional village, were appropriate for doing so. While social archaeology projects had successfully assessed the former (e.g., Pulu *kod*), very few excavations had targeted villages, with none concentrating on late Holocene fissioning around a single island. This chapter provides ethnography and archaeology for one self-differentiating Torres Strait

community, the Goemulgal. The chapter starts with a broad assessment of ethnographic research before narrowing the focus to traditional villages. It then explores existing archaeological research for Mabuyag, excluding recent excavations by the author at each of the villages.

2.1 Goemulgaw ethnography

The Goemulgal claim jurisdiction over Mabuyag (an 8 km², granitic island at the northerly point of the mid-western chain; Fig. 2.1), its surrounding seas, fishing grounds, reef systems and adjacent islets (Tom cited in Haddon 1904: 285; Tim Gizu, pers. comm., 10 November 2006). Haddon (1890: 301) suggested their territory includes "the islands between the last [Badu] and New Guinea". Davis and Prescott (1992: 121-22) were informed that Goemulgaw territory stretched some 40km north of Mabuyag, encompassing Turnagain (Buru) and Deliverance (Warul Kawa) Islands, six reef systems and at least two sand banks. This included large swathes of rich, fishing grounds (including Ormans' and Jervis Reef) where both turtle and dugong congregated in large numbers. The Goemulgal did not possess Badu or Mua although they shared a sea border with both Badulgal and Mualgal (Davis and Prescott 1992: 121). As opposed to many communities who name themselves after residential islands (e.g., Badulgal, Mualgal), the Mabuyag people are named after a single village (Goemu). According to Tom of Mabuyag (cited in Haddon 1890: 302; 1904: 67) this was because Goemu was "the place of Kwoiam", an important cultural hero belonging to this community. Kwoiam brought the knowledge of war and head taking to the Torres Strait and may also have been involved in the establishment of Pulu as a sacred site (Haddon 1890: 302, 324; McNiven et al. 2009). Before his death he made two crescentic, turtle shell ornaments (kutibu, giribu) into which he put his strength and courage (Haddon 1904: 153; Wilkin cited in Haddon 1904: 312). These artefacts were housed in the Awgadhal kula cave on Pulu and used by the Goemulgal in battle (Haddon 1904: 153, 311; Moore 1984: 48-9; Whap cited in Philp 2001: 32).

The primary residence of the Goemulgal is Mabuyag, the location of multiple ethnographically-significant sites (as explored in detail later in the chapter). Important Goemulgal sites were also located on Pulu (an islet 300 metres to the west of Mabuyag). This was a spiritual hub for the Goemulgal, where clan representatives met at a "national Kwod" (Haddon 1904: 3). The leaves on the trees at Pulu "represented the Mabuyag men and if the former were burnt men would be killed in the next battle" (Haddon 1904: 327). Every year the markay or "death dance" was held at this kod and skulls from head-hunting raids placed in the nearby Awgadhal kula cave along with items associated with Kwoiam (Haddon 1904: 368). Annual visits to the Pulu kod were also required to initiate young warriors, and to perform dugong and turtle increase ceremonies (Haddon 1904: 252; McNiven et al. 2009). Pulu continued to be an important refuge for Goemulgal after the sighting of European ships (Haddon 1935: 55).

Oral and written histories suggest that the Goemulgal were/ are marine specialists particularly known for their skills in dugong hunting. Mabuyag is described by Haddon (1890: 351) as "the headquarters of the fishery of this Sirenian" with the Western Islanders associated with culture heroes who introduced new fishing techniques to the Torres Strait (Gelam, and Sesere). Sesere used the skull of his father to divine a method of capturing the dugong by building wooden platforms over sea-grass beds (Haddon 1904: 40-2). Ghaleb (1990; see also Haddon 1904) suggested that Islanders developed technologies (and provided names) for approximately 450 species of marine animals. This includes a dugong harpoon (wap) with detachable head, thick buoyant line made of vines

and a long hard-wood pole (Haddon 1890: 339, 387; 1904: 293-4; Moore 1984: 23, 43; Appendix 2). Fish were speared with multi-pronged fish-spears or scooped up in bamboo tubes (Moore 1984: 23). Anna Shnukal (pers. comm February 2015) suggests that the latter technique was adopted from the Eastern Islanders. Fishing was also conducted using fine vine and barbless turtle shell fish-hooks or through stone-walled fish traps.

Although gardens were tended prior to the arrival of Europeans, little ethnographic information has been collected from Mabuyag. Haddon (1904: 289) was convinced that horticulture was comparatively unimportant "among a people so much addicted to fighting, fishing and trading as the Gumulaig", with gardens quickly abandoned after arrival of Europeans. Land was cleared using stone axes, with branches strewn over the ground and then set alight to clear a patch for yams which were planted using a digging stick (Haddon 1890: 354; Moore 1984: 22). Coconut trees and other fruit were also associated with gardens both on Mabuyag and elsewhere in the Torres Strait (Haddon 1890: 354; Macgillivray 1852: 230). Few of the western island culture heroes are associated with gardening, although Yawar of Badu is reputed to have taught people how to cultivate yams (Haddon 1890: 355; 1904: 31; 1935: 375).

The Goemulgal developed a complex system of sacred totems shared by Mabuyag and adjacent islands. Although the word Awgadh has been used to describe the cult hero, Kwoiam, for the most part it represents a dualistic division between the Koey Awgadhaw Khazi (children of the big Awgadh) and the Moegi Awgadhaw Khazi (children of the small Awgadh) moieties. These are divisible into land and sea animals with the former including koedal, samu, thabu, and umay[2], and the latter: dhangal, kaygas, baidam, tapumul, soelwal/waru and gapu[3] (Haddon 1904: 172; Rod Mitchell pers. comm., February 2015). Haddon (1904: 172) also mentioned dhoebu, wadh, maywa, kursi, sapur and wawmer[4] although he was unable to collect details about these clans and suggested they had all but died out by the time he arrived on the island (Haddon 1904: 154). Descent was patrilineal; however, children inherited a subsidiary totem from their mother's family. Therefore two or more clans could have the same chief totem along with a different subsidiary totem (Haddon 1904: 159).

Material expressions based on the totem groups appear to come in two forms, those that mark people and personal property and those belonging to place (frequently connected with clan ceremonies). Haddon (1904: 158) was informed that clan emblems were occasionally cut into the loins or upper body of the Goemulgal. Although he only found evidence of this amongst the older women,

---

2 crocodile, cassowary, snake, dog.

3 dugong, shovel nosed shark, shark, sting ray, mating turtle pair and sucker fish.

4 king-fish, fish with blue spots (possibly blenny), giant clam, hammer-head shark, flying fox and frigate-bird.

he was told that totems were also cut on the right shoulder of men (Haddon 1904: 159). Badges were worn by clan members, fashioned out of a piece of skin from the totem animal (Haddon 1890: 392-3). Totems were also carved onto personal belongings such as bamboo pipes, combs and drums (Haddon 1904: 163-5, 169). According to Gizu of Mabuyag they were also painted onto skulls taken in war and arranged "so that each clan had only to glance into *Augudalkula* to know whether its reputation for prowess was well sustained or otherwise" (Wilkin cited in Haddon 1904: 305).

Totemic objects were used in a number of ceremonies on Mabuyag, either in the form of carved representations, rock paintings or cairns erected to represent/ or attract/ honour the totem animal. Turtle increase ceremonies at Goemu and Pulu utilised carved effigies of turtle and sucker fish (used in turtle hunting) during turtle increase ceremonies (Haddon 1904: 336; Moore 1984: 48, 333). Effigies were also carried in canoes to increase the likelihood of a catch (Wilkin cited in Haddon 1904: 333). Totemic objects used in dugong hunting magic ceremonies were equally prevalent including dugong models shaped from stone, bone, tusk and wood (Haddon 1890: 352; 1904: 183, 333, 338; Moore 1984: 48-9; Appendix 2). On Pulu, Haddon (1904: 4) identified pictographs representing totem animals such as cassowary. Totem animals (shark/ dugong) were painted on Pulu as recently as 2001 (Beckett 1963: 54; David et. al. 2006: front cover; McNiven *et al.* 2002: 69). As will be explored later in this chapter, cairns of stone shaped like totem animals (dugong, turtle and shark) continue to be maintained and built at totem centres on Mabuyag. Oral and written histories suggest that the Goemulgal maintained a strong alliance with Badu (as explored above), with both islands reputed to belong to a single group, the Maluigal[5] (Haddon 1890: 301, 353; Moore 1984: 16). An extract from a missionary's letter gives further insight into this relationship:

> "While sitting among the Jervis [Mabuyag] islanders, in their gipsy-looking camp, a little ugly idol was produced, which is affirmed to be the principal god of the Mulgrave and Jervis [Badu and Mabuyag] islanders." (Gill cited in Haddon 1912: 171)

Inter-marriage occurred on a regular basis between the two islands resulting in frequent visits. The social links forged by marriages were cemented through resulting land ownership on both islands (Haddon 1890: 357, 396; 1904: 229-30). Tom of Mabuyag informed Haddon (1904: 289) that he owned land on a number of islands including Badu. Family members tended these plots when Tom was not on the island. This situation continues to the present, with the north coast of Badu reputed to be a "garden place" for the Goemulgal (Dimple Bani pers. comm., September 2006). A further method of maintaining

ties involved a customary practice of exchanging names (*natham/ takuiap*), a frequent occurrence for Goemulgal and Badulgal (Haddon 1904: 282; Moore 1984: 17). In one case *natham* occurred between Gizu of Mabuyag and Kanai, the chief of Badu (Haddon 1904: 282). Haddon (1890: 332) witnessed "sports" by which large numbers of Badu men came over for "friendly contests" including javelin hurling. This sport clearly had more serious undercurrents as Mabuyag and Badu frequently united during times of war.

Aggressive behaviour took two forms: head-hunting raids and ceremonial fights (Haddon 1904: 298). Head hunting raids occurred regularly and were often aimed against neighbouring Mua (Wilkin cited in Haddon 1904: 312). Legend suggests that a continuing feud between Mua and Badu/ Mabuyag occurred after Mabuyag people were caught stealing fruit from a garden on Mua and were attacked. In retaliation "Mabuiag took vengeance and burnt all their houses and destroyed their gardens" (Wilkin cited in Haddon 1904: 308). Attacks on Mua brought transferral of land to Mabuyag, retained until "the establishment of a white government in Torres Straits" (Haddon 1904: 288). On return from a successful battle, canoes went to the *kod* on Pulu where there was a *kawaladi* or war dance (Haddon 1904: 301). Warriors would then continue to Goemu, blowing *bu* shell trumpets to herald their arrival and another *kawaladi* would be held, this time involving women. The men would later return to Pulu to partially cook the skulls in earth ovens with cheeks and eyes eaten by the newly initiated warriors to teach them to be brave and fearless. The heads were then painted with red ochre (often with totemic designs) and deposited at *Awgadhal kula* on Pulu or in the skull houses on Mabuyag (Haddon 1904: 301).

Goemulgaw villages

The Goemulgaw community is structured through totemic affiliation with four principal ancestral "villages": Wagedoegam and Dhabangay on the north coast and Maydh and Goemu on the east coast (Haddon 1904: 266, 1935: 56) (Table 2.1). Smaller settlements exist at Muyi and Udhay (east coast), Dhogay (south east coast) Saw, Awbayth and Koedhakal (north coast), Ii and Sopolay (west coast) and Dhadhakul and Maytan (interior) (Harris and Ghaleb 1987: 7, 27; Vanderwal 1973: 178). These were viewed as small, seasonal camps. The outer islets of Woeydhul, Pulu and Redfruit may have also been the location for small settlements (Haddon 1904: 217; Lawrie 1970: 85-7; McNiven *et al.* 2009). Geographically the two moieties occupy distinct regions on Mabuyag, the bulk of the *Koey Awgadhaw Khazi* coming from the north west side while the *Moegi Awgadhaw Khazi* were spread along the bulk of the south, east and north east side of the island

---

5 "the people of the sea"

Village	Primary Totem 1	Subsidiary Totem 1	Primary Totem 2	Subsidiary Totem 2	Primary Totem 3	Subsidiary Totem 3
Wagedoegam	crocodile	sucker fish	snake	dugong	turtle	frigate bird, fruit bat
Goemu	turtle	crocodile, dog	–	–	–	–
Maidh	snake	turtle, sucker fish	–	–	–	–
Dhabangay	dugong	crocodile	–	–	–	–
Pulu	dugong	sucker fish	cassowary	dugong, snake	dog	turtle

Table 2.1. Totemic affiliation (from sketch map drawn in 1898 by Ned Waria cited in Haddon 1904:163).

Fig 2.2. Culture hero, Waiat at the Woeydhul *kod*. Drawn by Gizu for Alfred Haddon (1904: 52).

(Haddon 1904: 172). *Kod* sites were connected with all the main villages on Mabuyag as well as the smaller village of Awbayth (Haddon 1904: 3; 1935: 58-9; Gill 1876: 203; Wilkin cited in Haddon 1912: 98). Further *kod* sites were recorded at Kuykusogay (or Redfruit Island), Woeydhul and Pulu (Haddon 1904: 3; Fig. 2.2). These sites appear to have been the hub of the social and ritual life of the men with no women or uninitiated boys permitted to visit (Haddon 1904: 365; 1912: 9). They were central to turtle and dugong increase ceremonies, initiation, and the *markay* (death dances). They were also used for storing masks and effigies relating to ceremonies (Haddon 1904: 365).

Totemic affiliation structured the behaviour, practice and spiritual/ ceremonial roles of people belonging to each village. Each clan member had empathy with his/ her totem animal and with the exceptions of dugong and turtle was banned from killing them (Haddon 1890: 309, 393; 1904: 186). Such affinities gave each clan a certain amount of power over these animals, which could be harnessed through ritual activity (Haddon 1935: 355). In line with its primary totem, Dhabangay is reputed to be the place of great dugong hunters including Sesere, a culture hero who brought the dugong platform to Western Torres Strait (Haddon 1904: 40-4). Dugong hunting was mediated by ceremonies, one of which "had for its object the constraining of the dugong to come towards the island to be caught" (Eseli *et al.* 1998: 74; Haddon 1904: 40-44,

1935: 182-183). Such magic involved "proprietary offerings" of dugong bones placed in the trunk and roots of large banyan trees (Moresby 1876: 131). The people from Goemu were "largely concerned with turtle fishing" and like the turtle are perceived as peaceful and humble (Haddon 1904: 183; Gabriel Bani, pers. comm., 21 September 2006). Success in turtle hunting was ensured through a number of key ceremonies at the Goemu *kod* and a shrine consisting of tall thin stones (*adhil*) surrounding a large water-worn cobble (*wiway*: Haddon 1904: 164, 330-335; 1935: 59, 353). Community identities further developed through association with culture heroes. For example, Kwoiam (reputed to have brought warfare to the Torres Strait) is connected with many of the landmarks at Goemu, including boulders representing the heads of his victims (Haddon 1904: 285; Lawrie 1970: 99).

The significant conceptual and spatial distinctions between villages were carefully maintained and regulated. To move between villages it was necessary to follow paths that were kept open through reciprocal gift exchange (Haddon 1904: 99; Landtman 1917: 152; Lawrie 1970: 99). The people of Wagedoegam, for example, provided *biyu sama* (mangrove) to people on the east coast who provided dugong meat in return. Abuse of this system resulted in serious punishment for the perpetrator and the risk of closing down paths (Haddon 1904; Lawrie 1970: 119). Access was also restricted to *kod* sites and markay mudh (ceremonial house in Maydh) (Dimple Bani, pers. comm., 10 September 2006; Haddon 1890: 399, 1904: 208-209). A rare exception was "the national Kwod" of the Goemulgal on Pulu (Haddon 1904: 3). This was the only *kod* in the Torres Strait where women and children were permitted to attend (McNiven *et al.* 2009: 293). It was also the location for ceremonies relating to all Goemulgaw clans, with fireplaces, bone mounds and *bu* shell arrangements inscribed (and spatially organised) based on totemic affiliation (Haddon 1904: 3-4, 208-209, 266, 1935: 56-57) (Table 2.1). Every year the *markay* or "death dance" was held at this *kod* and skulls from head-hunting raids placed in the *Awgadhal kula* skull cave along with items associated with Kwoiam (Haddon 1904: 368). Annual visits to the Pulu *kod* were also required to initiate young warriors, and to perform dugong and turtle increase ceremonies (Haddon 1904: 252; McNiven *et al.* 2009).

Village knowledge, skills and stories were carefully guarded but in exceptional circumstances these restrictions could also be lifted. This is illustrated in a recent narrative about village relations:

"One day a man from Goemu accidentally speared a crocodile rather than a dugong when he was hunting at night time. He realised he had done wrong and brought the body of the crocodile around to the people of Wagedagam. Those people [the people from Wagadagam] cried for that crocodile. Then they made a crocodile out of tortoise shell and gave it to the man [from Goemu] and told him that he could carve new things" (Tim Gizu, pers. comm., 1 October 2006; see also Lawrie 1970: 120).

A similar example exists for *kuthibu* and *giribu*. While these objects were protected by the *Koey Awgadhaw Khazi* (big totem clans), it was recorded that *kuthibu* was carried by a warrior from the *Moegi Awgadhaw Khazi* (small totem clan) while the *giribu* was carried by a warrior belonging to the *Koey Awgadhaw Khazi* during conflicts (Wilkin in Haddon 1904: 318, 372). In this sense, the socio-political and ceremonial life of the Goemulgal involved the selective protection and passage of knowledge, skills, artefacts and stories.

A study of oral and written histories provides insight into the appearance of Torres Strait villages (David and Ash 2008). Criteria include: relative permanence of settlement, multiple houses, paths, midden materials, specialised activity areas including earth ovens and dancing areas, also bamboo groves, coconut trees and close proximity to the sea. Building on this study Mabuyag villages may be characterised based on natural and cultural sites. They were frequently described to be coastal, "in places with a wangay tree…also where there is good water" (Tim Gizu pers. comm., 1 October 2006). They may be near good fishing places and boat landings (Edmund Bani pers. comm., 30 September 2006). Haddon (1912: 131-32) claimed that "kitchen-middens are not formed now, nor did I come across traces of ancient refuse heaps". He (1912: 132)

goes on to suggest that any bone mounds constructed were for "ceremonial purposes or merely to keep count of the number of animals caught in any one season". As we shall see later in this chapter this runs contrary to archaeological results from Mabuyag. Huts were described as "simple, oblong, low structure[s] built on the ground with a roof sloping on each side to the ground, or in some there were very low side walls" (Haddon 1935: 26, 299; see also 1912: 98; Fig. 2.3). Such houses "varied in length and were generally not more than 1.8m (6 ft.) in height. The floors were white sand covered with layers of grass and mats, hence the bed, *toie*, was sometimes called *apa-sik* (*apa* = garden bed)" (Haddon 1912: 97). The roof was constructed out of large grass or tea tree bark mats (*waku* or *moder*) flung over mangrove poles or paddles (Haddon 1890: 392; 1912: 97; Tim and Louisa Gizu pers. comm., 1 October 2006).

Elsewhere I have suggested that Torres Strait villages may be better understood based on a social, "imagined" conception of community (Wright 2011c: 124). These sites are meaningful places connected with socio-political (clan) identities but were not always residential centres. On Mabuyag, for example, passage into Maydh is ethnographically known to have been deliberately restricted (Aaron Whap pers. comm., December 2006; Haddon 1904: 323). This was an important socio-political centre, the location of the Maydh *kod* and a place where the *Maydhallgal* (or magic men) performed rituals. Wagedoegam (along with all other ethnographically known villages) continues to be conceived by the resident Mabuyag population as a village (in the present rather than the past) despite the physical relocation of the Goemulgal away from this site at least 150 and possibly 550 years ago. These different ideas about what constitutes a village contribute to a broader understanding of what is "significant" about these sites and emphasise the importance of examining oral histories before assessing Torres Strait cultural heritage (Wright 2011c: 124).

Ethnography suggests multiple phases of community fissioning. Wagedoegam is considered the ancestral village, with all other villages founded by the sons and daughter

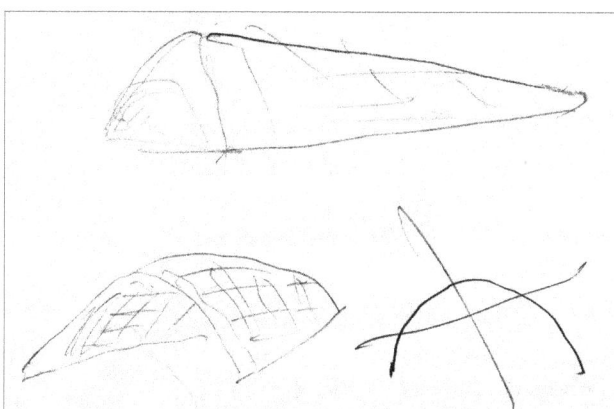

Fig 2.3. Drawing by Tim Gizu of traditional house (1 October 2006).

of Bari, first chief of Wagedoegam (Haddon 1904: 164, 236, 267; Mooke 1972: 1; Edmund Bani pers. comm., 12 November 2006). The dualistic division between moieties and further overlay of multiple clans provides insight into multiple phases of community emergence. Haddon (1904: 164), further noted that Maydh was the only traditional village owned by the *Koey Awgadhaw Khazi* moiety on the eastern side of the island, suggesting this may represent a later fissioning event at which point Maydh and Awbayth split from a single, unknown village. Following "The Coming of the Light" (i.e., arrival of the London Missionary Society, LMS) to Mabuyag in 1872, residents of the various, discrete villages and hamlets amalgamated into the single settlement of Baw. The scale of this shift is uncertain with historical records suggesting that Goemulgal did not abandon ancestral villages. In 1877, the LMS were continuing to push for community relocation to Baw (Eseli *et al.* 1998: 25). In August 1920, Reverend Done (1987) records that the Goemulgal had spent four of the last eight weeks "camping at Wagedugam and Sipungur making gardens". In 2006, village custodians were observed to frequently visit ancestral sites.

2.2   Goemulgaw archaeology

At the time of project commencement minimal archaeological research had been completed in Goemulgaw territory. Initial research involved incomplete survey and test excavation of Pulu and Mabuyag by Ron Vanderwal (1973). Expansion of Baw village necessitated survey of this area (including Maydh) by Cultural Heritage consultants (Neal 1989). Systematic research began on Mabuyag through a University College London (UCL) project targeting multiple Western Torres Strait islands. Coordinated by David Harris, later also Tony Barham, results are documented through multiple unpublished site reports (e.g., Barham and Harris 1987; Harris *et al.* 1985), two articles (Ghaleb 1998; Harris *et al.* In press) and a PhD thesis (Ghaleb 1990). After a hiatus of approximately 20 years, the WTSCH Project coordinated by Ian McNiven and Bruno David reignited interest in the region, involving survey and excavations on Mabuyag and surrounding islands (e.g. David and McNiven 2004; McNiven and Bedingfield 2008; McNiven and Wright 2008; McNiven *et al.* 2006; 2008; 2009). In the following sections archaeological research is presented, with the exception of research by the author at Gowmulgaw villages (see Chapters 3-7).

Archaeological research on Mabuyag

Surveys of Mabuyag identified an abundance of archaeological sites, including middens, fish traps, stone-edged trackways, stone rectangles and circles, mound-and-ditch systems, surface arrangements of *bu* shells, dugong bone mounds, burials, rock art and wells (Harris and Ghaleb 1987: 5). A review of cultural sites across Torres Strait

concluded that Mabuyag had a site diversity second only to the much larger island of Mer (13 and 17 site types respectively) (McNiven *et al.* 2004a: 77). Goemu was reported to be the most archaeologically spectacular village on Mabuyag, with a landscape significantly altered through substantial midden and mounding activity (Harris and Ghaleb 1987). The quantity of shell and bone midden was considered unprecedented on the island. In 1984, detailed archaeological survey revealed over 100 midden features including unique platform and ridge mounds of dugong bone and earth (Harris and Ghaleb 1987: 12). The map that was produced during this fieldwork and updated in 2005 can be found in Chapter 4. Circular mounds were particularly common, with smaller numbers of linear (platform) and rectangular (ridge) mounds. The majority of circular mounds (number in 1984 = 95) clustered in the southern side of the village, with seven linear ridge and platform mounds in the northern part of the village (Harris and Ghaleb 1987: 12). This site also contained arrangements of *bu* shells, a grave littered with ceramic and glass fragments and a house platform attributed to a shelter built for the Paipai family in 1947 (Ghaleb 1990: 160-161, 181-185; Harris *et al.* 1985: 44, 48). Further inland from Goemu at Udhay, Harris *et al.* (In press) observed stone lined trackways and "many large linear and circular stone piles" in association with wild yams and the remains of several types of shellfish. A turtle shaped stone arrangement was also recorded on a hill overlooking Goemu (Harris and Ghaleb 1987: 10). It was observed that there were two fish-traps either side of the rocky headland near Goemu (Harris *et al.* In press).

Dhabangay, "with its abundant and varied archaeological features, appears to be the next most potentially rewarding area, after Gumu, for future archaeological research on Mabuiag" (Harris and Ghaleb 1987: 28). It was observed that this village had a locally-unique system of stone-lined tracks (approximately 1m in width) connecting the beach to the Koedhakal double fish trap (west of Dhabangay) and the hills inland (Harris *et al.* 1985: 27). Other features include a large, oval-shaped dugong bone mound associated with a stone naturally shaped like a dugong, 30 stone-bone-shell mounds and five stone "cairns" (Harris *et al.* In press). The village was further associated with multiple mound-and-ditch fields, along with "rectangular units which may represent old occupation areas or former fields" (Harris and Ghaleb 1987: 48). Totemic stone arrangements included a crocodile and dugong at Dhabangay and crocodiles at both Koedhakal and Saw to the west (Edwards and Edwards 1997: 3-5; Harris *et al.* 1985: 26-27).

Other villages on Mabuyag (Wagedoegam, Maydh, Awbayth) were surveyed but revealed little evidence of cultural activity. The only conclusive evidence of former occupation at Wagedoegam was several relict mound-and-ditch fields in the north eastern quarter of the valley (Harris and Ghaleb 1987: 28; Ghaleb 1990: 158, 163). In the same area was observed "a large grove of tall bamboo growing around a water hole" (Ghaleb 1990:

158; McNiven 2008: 453-454). Ghaleb (1990: 158; see also McNiven 2008) suggested that this type of bamboo (*Bumbusa arundinacea*) belongs to a South-East Asian species which arrived prior to mid 19th century. Previous surveys in the area overlooking Maydh identified a stone arrangement shaped like a crocodile, and fragments of *bu* and *akul* (*Polymesoda erosa*) shells, also mound-and-ditch fields, "rectangular stone arrangements" and stone piles/ buttresses in the dhadhakul valley (Harris and Ghaleb 1987: 32; Ghaleb 1990: 157). Survey of this area by Neal (1989), confirmed large field systems and recorded an old grave with cement headstone. The Awbayth/ Saw region (an embayment on the north coast, west of Dhabangay) contained a small number of relict fields and (at the former) two stone arrangements one of which may be an animal effigy (Ghaleb 1990: 156; Harris *et al.* In press). Based on data from the Queensland Department of Environment and Resource Management Indigenous Cultural Heritage Database (ICHD), Rowland and Ulm (2011: 7) identified two fish traps between Wagedoegam and Awbayth and an additional one at the north eastern most point of Baw village. Barham and Harris (1987) made the interesting observation that fish traps were absent on the west coast of Mabuyag, with their distribution along the east and north coast. This suggested close connection with former settlement areas: Goemu, Dhabangay, Koedhakal, Maydh and Wagedoegam.

The initial survey phase by UCL (1984-1985) was followed by excavations (primarily at Goemu) in 1985. This involved sub-surface assessment of discontinuous midden, circular and ridge midden mounds (Ghaleb 1990: 213-220). Five 1 m x 1 m test pits were spaced across platform and ridge midden mounds (Squares E, GH, M, T and Y). A radiocarbon date of 658-498 cal. BP (Beta-21385) was obtained from the base of midden deposit (Ghaleb 1990: 221). Another sample (Beta-21384) was obtained from the same stratigraphic context but came back as "modern". This was interpreted as anomalous and intrusive. A final date of 1050±100 (Beta-21386) was obtained from fragments of charcoal underlying the midden. This calibrates to 724-1096 BP at two sigma (henceforth σ) and was believed to predate mound construction (Ghaleb 1990: 221). The midden feature included shellfish, turtle, dugong, fish and lithics and was therefore considerably more diverse than the mound (see below). Similarly, there was a high variation in fish and shellfish, all of which can be found today in the immediate vicinity (sandy foreshore, lagoon, fringing reef, mangrove and rocky headland; Ghaleb 1990: 272). In addition to dugong skulls and ribs (37 % of the total) there was a significant quantity of vertebrae and limb bones (63 % of the total) suggesting a much less structured formation (Ghaleb 1990: 251, 257; 1998).

A circular bone mound at the northern end of Goemu (#87) was dominated by dugong skull parts, ribs and lesser quantities of vertebrae and limb bones (Ghaleb 1990: 251). Although no dates were obtained from this feature, glass was observed throughout indicating deposition within

the past 200 years (Ghaleb 1990: 234). A further mound "dissected" in the southern part of Goemu was reputed to have been the location of the *wiway*, turtle ceremony. A minimum number of six dugongs were recorded along with shellfish, a few fragments of turtle carapace and fish bone (Ghaleb 1990: 364-65). As previously reported, Ghaleb (1990) identified continuity between past and present Goemulgaw diet, specifically the prominence of dugong and turtle (Ghaleb 1990: 336-337). Archaeological and ethnographic histories for shellfish and fish gathering strategies were less compatible (Ghaleb 1990: 339). Ghaleb (1990: 174-179, 365-7) further attempted to trace ceremonial elements of the Goemulgal, concluding that the *wiway* mound provided only "superficial" evidence for connection with the turtle ceremonies or ritualised construction. This mound lacked subsurface structure, contained very little turtle bone and integrated numerous material additions that would not be expected if this were a site focused on turtle increase (Ghaleb 1990: 364). The one mitigating factor was the observation of a single, sub-surface arrangement of dugong ribs around a lump of coral shaped like a "head" (Ghaleb 1990: 364). In contrast, Mound 87 with its large quantity of dugong bone (ribs and skull fragments) may have been formally constructed (Ghaleb 1990: 227-29, 255, 365).

Two additional test pits were completed by the UCL team at Maydh and Dhabangay. The former, excavated at an undisclosed location, was described as "culturally sterile" (Harris and Ghaleb 1987: 32). The latter tested a mound-and-ditch field observed to underlie the edges of stone-bone-shell mounds. This suggests that field systems may pre-date village midden, however, excavation did not produce datable material to test the age for either site-type.

A 70 cm x 70 cm excavation was conducted into the large dugong bone mound at Dhabangay (McNiven and Bedingfield 2008). This tested the proposition that this mound was constructed as part of ceremonial activities associated with the *kod*, revealing dugong bone (primarily ribs and skull parts) to a depth of 90 cm and an MNI count of 115 dugong (McNiven and Bedingfield 2008: 512). The mound appeared to have been carefully structured with four layers of complete dugong skulls in the upper portion, capping a level dominated by dugong ribs (McNiven and Bedingfield 2008: 508). Marine shell from the base of the bone mound provided a date of 479–278 cal. BP (WK-16365). Glass and metal in the upper layers suggested continued deposition within the past 150 years, although Christian missionisation was expected to have led to the abandonment of ceremonial activities at this site. The mound was apparently not being used by the time Haddon arrived in 1898 (1904: 183, 341-2).

Archaeological research on offshore islets

Pulu, an island approximately 700 m west of Mabuyag with a circumference of roughly 500 m, has interested

European researchers for over a century. The islet (and most prominently, the *kod*) was described in detail by Alfred Haddon (1904: 3-5; discussed above). A subsequent visited by Ron Vanderwal (1973) suggested presence of midden bone and shell, also shell and stone artefacts and a small fragment of a stone club head (*gabagaba*). In 1984, when UCL archaeologists visited this island they observed the same features recorded by Haddon, including a large dugong bone mound, arrangements of *bu* shells (*Syrinx* sp.) and painted rock art (Harris and Kirby In press). According to Harris *et al.* (In press) it was "the only location where we observed a close association between a midden mound, shell arrangements and pictographs". Most recently, academics from Monash University conducted archaeological research across the island, suggesting a remarkable variety of sites including the most extensive rock art complex so far recorded for the Torres Strait (Brady 2006: 368-9; McNiven *et al.* 2009). Survey revealed *bu* shell arrangements (which in Goemulgaw ethnography were called *Koey Awgadhaw Kupay, Moegi Awgadhaw Kupay, Koey Math, Moegi Math*), a dugong bone mound (*Moegi Sibuy*), a stone arrangement (*Aadhi*) and unnamed midden areas (McNiven *et al.* 2009).

Excavations on Pulu include a small test pit (50 cm x 50 cm) dug in "a shallow part of the Pulu [*kod*] site, adjacent to some midden debris and off to the right of the large stone shown by Haddon" (Vanderwal 1973: 178-180). Cultural materials from this test pit consisted of bone, shell and flaked quartz artefacts, with "sterile soil" reached at 50 cm below the surface. Two drilled shell artefacts were recovered during excavation (Vanderwal 1973: 180).

As part of the WTSCH Project, detailed survey and excavation was completed at the *kod*, Mask Cave and Tiger shark Rockshelter (McNiven *et al.* 2006; 2008; 2009). Tiger shark Rockshelter, on the southern end of Pulu, was excavated in 1999. Four, 50 cm x 50 cm squares tested a cave floor characterised by black, organic sandy sediments littered with marine shell, large tiger shark teeth and marine bone (McNiven *et al.* 2008: 17). No oral traditions were collected for this site. Radiocarbon dates from Squares A and C supported intermittent occupation between 500 and 1300 BP with intensification in site use around 500-700 years ago (McNiven *et al.* 2008: 15, 28). At this point there was a dramatic increase in sedimentation rates and the density of shellfish and other faunal remains (e.g., fish, bird and large vertebrate bone) (McNiven *et al.* 2008: 20). The presence of bottle glass (some of which had been flaked) suggested minor activity in the late 19th and early 20th centuries. The faunal remains represented at the site suggest opportunistic targeting of sharks and small-sized fish (McNiven *et al.* 2008: 22). Large vertebrate (mainly turtle) bone made up 70 % of the total bone assemblage indicated that deep-water hunting also occurred. Flaked dugong bone and shellfish artefacts were observed, also unmodified ochre excavated from layers dated to 500-700 years ago (McNiven *et al.* 2008: 25-27). This may provide an age

for rock-art motifs on the granite boulders above (Brady 2006; McNiven *et al.* 2008: 27).

Monash archaeologists were subsequently invited to join senior custodians of Pulu to survey, excavate and radiocarbon date a number of the archaeological features at the Pulu *kod* (McNiven *et al.* 2009). Excavations revealed the oldest installation of the *kod* to be a small mound of dugong bone (*Moegi Sibuy*), which dated to 670±44 BP (1550-1660 cal. AD at one σ) *Koey Awgadhaw Kupay* also dates to this period (1610-1710 cal. AD). McNiven *et al.* (2009) argued that the *kod* complex developed over a 300 to 400 year period, with *Moegi Sibuy* and *Koey Awgadhaw Kupay* continuing to be constructed until approximately 300 years ago, while many shell arrangements (e.g., *Koey Math; Moegi Math; Koey Awgadhaw Kupay*) were dated to within the past 300 years (McNiven *et al.* 2009). *Moegi Sibuy* contained large quantities of dugong bone (approximately 97 % of the total) many of which were ribs and rear skull parts. Oral histories suggested that this reflected the desire of the hunter to utilise "radar bones" (ear ossicles) to communicate with dugong (McNiven and Feldman 2003: 186). As noted in Chapter 1 the mound of dugong bone was highly structured, interpreted as evidence for its ceremonial role at the site. Underlying midden material was located during excavation of the *Adhi* shell and stone arrangement (Square C) and again during excavation of Squares B and D. A single radiocarbon date of 1396±41 BP (AD c.600-700) was obtained from the base of this deposit. McNiven *et al.* (2009) believe that this was consistent with a former village site on Pulu cited in Lawrie (1970: 87).

Mask Cave, immediately beyond the *Awgadhal kula* skull cave, was excavated in 2002 (McNiven *et al.* 2006). A number of rock paintings, including a red ochre face or mask were recorded on the large granite boulder and supporting bedrock "pillars". On the surface of the cave floor was a lag deposit of flaked stone artefacts, shellfish, turtle bone and a number of European items including a broken bottle, a match tin and a possible knife. Two fragments of plain ware and red slipped pottery were also observed.

Two trenches were excavated in the west and east margins of the shelter (McNiven *et al.* 2006: 53). Broad stratigraphic similarities were observed between the two, also localised burrowing and/ or tree root activity. An intrusive "channel" feature was also observed in basal deposits (McNiven *et al.* 2006: 54). The radiocarbon sequence suggests four occupation phases. A major division exists "between lower levels dated 3000-3800 years ago and upper levels dated within the last 2500 years" (McNiven *et al.* 2006: 10). After 2500 years ago there was a considerable increase in bone discard as well as the first appearance of red slip pottery (McNiven *et al.* 2006: 58). A second phase of pottery manufacture (consisting of ten petrographically identical sherds to those found in older deposits) was dated to 1500-1800 BP, coincident with a further increase in cultural material (McNiven *et al.* 2006: 63-4). McNiven *et al.* (2006: 58) suggested that this represents a "major pulse of activity". The final period (1000-1500 cal. BP) was marked by sharp reductions in all cultural materials (McNiven *et al.* 2006: 57). Faunal remains support the targeting of offshore resources (turtle and to a lesser extent dugong) and near-shore low tide reef pools (small fish). Shallow water/ reef species dominate the fish bone record (e.g., Scarids and Puffers). Major quantitative changes occurred with a dramatic increase in bone discard in Phase 2 dated to 2100-2600 years ago (McNiven *et al.* 2006: 62). No birds or terrestrial mammals were recovered from the excavation suggesting a diet dominated by the surrounding rich marine resources.

Artefacts recorded at the site include 842 stone flakes and cores. A dramatic increase was observed in bipolar reduction within the past 1700 years. This appeared to be contiguous with a shift away from the use of granite/ rhyolite for artefact manufacture to quartz (McNiven *et al.* 2006: 62). All materials are known to be located on the adjacent islands of Mabuyag, Mua and Badu (McNiven *et al.* 2006: 63). A petrographic analysis of ceramics from both 'phases' is indicative of local manufacture (McNiven *et al.* 2006: 66).

Woeydhul, to the north of Pulu, off the north west coast, was reported to be the location of a *kod* and a "garden" area (Haddon 1904: 3; Wilkin in Haddon 1904: 290). Vanderwal (1973: 178) recorded a midden, also stone artefacts and cooking stones. UCL researchers observed a large (11 m x 7 m) oval, dugong bone mound and a fish trap at the northern tip of the island and on the tiny offshore islet of Sarabar a single and double fish trap (Harris *et al.* 1985: 46; see also Rowland and Ulm 2011: 7). A further two fish traps were recorded on the islets, Pururay (200m from Wagedoegam) and Aypus (immediately to the north of Pururay) (Harris and Ghaleb 1987: 6; Lawrie 1970: 82; Rowland and Ulm 2011: 7).

Kuykusoegay (Red Fruit), is a small islet to the north east of Aypus. Haddon (1904: 3) was informed that that there was a *kod* on this islet. A linear dugong bone midden and a circular dugong-bone mound was observed in the centre of the island, surrounded by rock outcrops.

2.3   Summary

This chapter has concentrated on the ethnography and archaeology of the Goemulgal, specifically four main villages: Wagedoegam, Dhabangay, Maydh and Goemu. While it has been established that villages were not always large residential centres they were (and remain) unique socio-political and ceremonial centres for the Mabuyag clans. Each village had well-orchestrated roles both in the physical and ceremonial well-being of the community with decisions made within the men's meeting house or *kod*. Haddon (1904: 306) suggested that villages and *kods* "differed materially" from one another. Archaeological surveys identify some compatibility between archaeological records for each village, frequently (although as evidenced by Maydh and Wagedoegam not always) associated with midden materials. They are also all associated with fish traps and mound-and-ditch garden areas. Conversely, oral history and archaeology support village individuality. Goemu provides a unique landscape of mounded midden (including platform and ridge midden mounds), while Dhabangay incorporates stone lined paths and stone piles/ turrets. In addition, all villages are associated with stone arrangements in the shape of related totem animals and culture hero sites (e.g., the *wiway* shrine at Goemu). Whether regional variation becomes more or less archaeologically visible with further surveys and excavations of Goemulgaw villages is a key consideration in this book. It may also be possible to establish "at what point Mabuiag became a residential island and a separate people (i.e., the Goemulgal) with their own identity" (McNiven *et al* 2006: 75). Excavation of villages is likely to provide a fissioning history for human settlement, which can then be compared with Goemulgaw ethnography. In the following section archaeological results, spanning three field seasons of research (2005, 2006, 2011) are presented for each of the Goemulgaw villages, as well as the small sites of Muyi, Baw and the Wagedoegam *kod*.

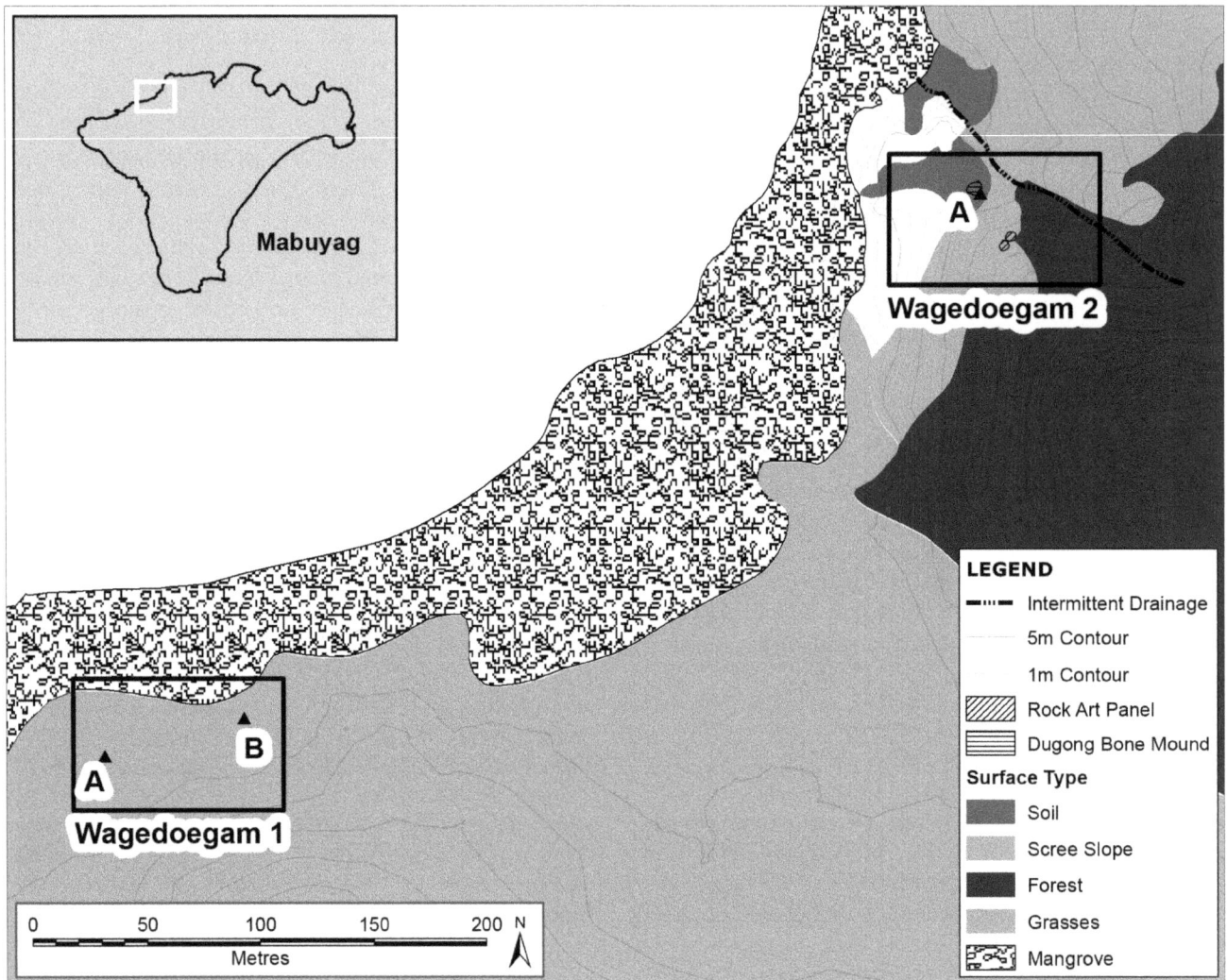

Fig 3.1. Wagedoegam including areas excavated in 2006 ("Wagedoegam 1") and 2006/ 2013 ("Wagedoegam 2"). Topographic data courtesy of "Schlenker Mapping", with illustration by Aaron Fogel.

3

Wagedoegam

Wagedoegam is located on the north west side of Mabuyag, encompassing inland hills (an area known as "Bari"), coastal margins (Wagedoegam proper) and abutting the Dhadhakul valley (a traditional garden area and route between villages on the west and east sides of the island) (Haddon 1904: 99; Landtman 1917: 152; Lawrie 1970: 99). Lawrie (1970: 105, 108) suggested that there were once two large villages in the region, Wagedoegam and Urabal Gagait. These lie adjacent to one another with the former at the end of the current road, next to Dhadhakul, while the latter was further to the west. Despite its current inaccessibility (with no passable road) this continues to be a significant place for the Goemulgal and was regularly visited by custodians during fieldwork by the author on Mabuyag.

This village was the focus of activities relating to the *Koey Awgadhaw Khazi* moiety of which *koedal* (or crocodile) was the main totem and reputed to be the

Fig 3.2. Rock art boulders at the Wagedoegam *kod*. The main rock art panel (containing images depicted below) can be seen on the nearest boulder.

ancestral village of the Goemulgal. Oral and written histories suggest Wagedoegam continued to be regularly visited after missionary arrival, including a period of reoccupation during World War Two (Dimple Bani pers. comm., 21 September 2006; Ghaleb 1990: 134).

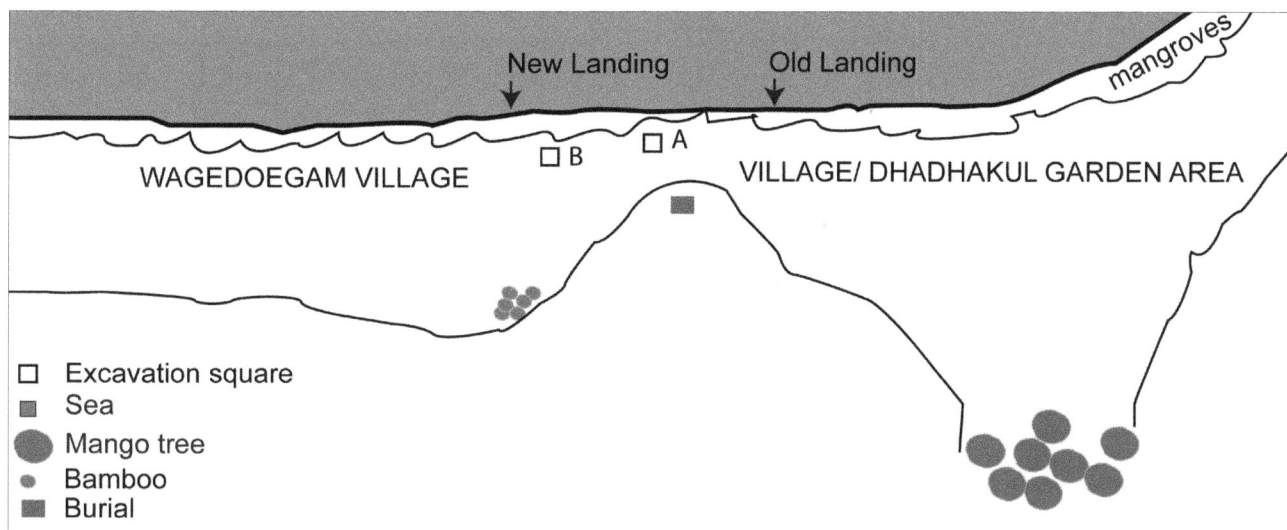

Fig 3.3. Map (not to scale; aligned west) of Wagedoegam derived from 2006 survey results and a sketch by Tim Gizu (see Wright 2011c).

Haddon (1935: 58) was informed that a *kod* existed at Wagedoegam and also believed that the original skull house of the moiety was located in this village. It was speculated that this site was used to make decisions about warfare and headhunting raids and for initiation ceremonies (Haddon 1936: 56; Douglas Bani pers. comm., October 2013). Until 2006 the location for this site remained unpublished. In the following section archaeological results are presented from excavations of Wagedoegam village and *kod*.

3.1   Surface survey and excavation

Prior to this study no excavations were conducted at Wagedoegam and (as has been covered earlier) little surface materials or sites had been recorded. Surveys of this area in 2006 confirmed a paucity of archaeological sites in Bari and along the Wagedoegam foreshore. In addition to features reported in previous studies, a burial was observed on a raised granite platform between Dhadhakul and Wagedoegam (Fig. 3.1). This consisted of two large piles of stones and *Syrinx* shells, with site boundaries apparently delineated by standing stones and small cairns. Careful observation revealed that the stone mounds covered 19th and/ or early 20th century European ceramics and human skeletal remains. According to Cygnet Repu (pers. comm., September 2006) the grave belonged to a "Chinaman" who worked on pearl-shelling boats. In addition, and plausibly for the first time, the Wagedoegam *kod* was shown to and recorded by a non-Indigenous researcher. This site is located on raised granite bedrock, approximately 300 m north of the Dhadhakul valley. Incomplete survey revealed two large boulders with at least two panels of red ochre rock art (Fig. 3.2), a large dugong bone mound and eight stone arrangements. Stone arrangements included linear and curvilinear lines (occasionally surrounding trees/ groups of trees) and intricate designs on exposed bedrock. Maitui Whap (born in 1975) informed us that he was shown this site by his grandfather when he was young.

While rock art analysis had not been completed at the time of this project two images are of importance for understanding site history. The first appears to be a "bird" motif (Fig. 3.4), positioned immediately underneath two human figures, invisible without use of colour modification in Adobe Photoshop (Fig. 3.5). While all paintings were damaged by water erosion, they support ceremonial (and potentially totemic) activities at the Wagedoegam *kod*. The size differentiation of the two figures may also provide insight into initiation ceremonies ethnographically recorded to have occurred at *kod* sites in the Western Islands (e.g., Haddon 1904). The headdress is reminiscent of the traditional "*dhoeri*", a key marker of Torres Strait identity (see the Torres Strait flag), the significance of which will be explored later in this book.

In 2006, two excavations (Wagedoegam 1, Squares A and B) were excavated on the coastal fringe, at the end of a dirt track into the village and near the "New Landing" (Fig. 3.1, 3.3, 3.6; also Wright 2011c). Bulldozing activity during road construction had caused disturbance in upper layers of Square A. This square (1 m x 1 m) was substantially disturbed so results are only presented for Squares B (70 cm x 70 cm). A small test pit (Wagedoegam 2, Square A) was also dug into the dugong bone mound associated with the *kod*.

3.2   Square B

Square B was positioned four metres from the mangrove line on an elevated platform surrounded by a natural stone barrier (see Fig. 3.3 and 3.6). This unit was excavated to a maximum depth of 63 cm below surface, henceforth cmbs (18 XUs), with bedrock reached in some sections after only 33 cm. Excavation units (XUs) were guided by natural changes in stratigraphy and averaged 3 cm in depth, not including the preliminary sweep of top-soil (XU 1). All sediment was wet sieved through a 2.1 mm mesh.

Fig 3.4. Bird motif recorded at the Wagedoegam *kod* (enhancement by L. Brady).

Fig 3.5. Two anthropomorphic figures on the main rock art panel at Wagedoegam (enhancement by L. Brady).

The weight of each XU was logged and depth elevations were recorded for the corners and centre of each square at the start and finish of each XU, also for unique artefacts and samples of charcoal for radiocarbon dating. Due to the large quantities of non-cultural rock (>5 cm) this was weighed and discarded on site (included in backfill).

Sediment samples were air dried in the Archaeology Laboratory (GES, Monash University) and then tested for acidity (pH) and colour (Munsell). Samples were prepared for pH testing using a ratio of one to 5 soil/distilled water and tested using an electrode array. MNI counts for dugong bone were obtained based on a fixed set of criteria relating to ear bones (see Appendix 3). The MNI for shellfish utilised conventional methods with the left and right umbos were counted for bivalves over 1.5 cm in diameter. The columella, opercula and spires were counted for gastropods. The same methodology was used for all other village sites.

Stratigraphy

Little stratigraphic change was observed in this excavation. Sediment was consistently dry, silty and mildly acidic throughout (Table 3.1). A slight change in

SU	XU	Sediment description
1	1-3	Very dark grey (7.5YR = 3/1), mildly acidic (5.46-6.17), silty sediment. Consolidated throughout, with a high organic component (rootlets and leaf litter). Very little cultural material observed
2	4-11	Black (7.5YR = 2.5), silty sediment with a tendency to form into clumps. Mildly acidic (5.84-6) and contains root and insect holes. Small quantities of cultural materials and fire damaged rocks observed.
3	11-18	Black to very dark grey (7.5YR - 2.5-3) sediment with texture identical to SU 2. The pH is acidic (5.88-6.11) and there is a greater quantity of large vertebrate bone. Also increasing numbers of large rocks.

Table 3.1. SU description, Square B.

colouration was observed at the base of SU 1 (between 3 and 6 cmbs) from very dark gray to black. At this point a shift occurred from consolidated, organic rich to increasingly friable and unconsolidated sediment. Patches of more consolidated sediment were recorded in SUs 2 and 3, with the transition between SU 2 and 3 (between 27 and 30 cm) involving substantial increases in rock, pumice and cultural materials (Fig. 3.7). Although the sediment was similar in texture to SU 2 it gradually reverts in colour to very dark gray.

There was no evidence for substantial disturbance in this excavation, however minor admixture was noted throughout in the form of fibrous roots. This was particularly prominent in the upper two SUs, with the lower portion of SU 2 also disturbed by two large roots (>3 cm diameter) and numerous insect holes. Further post-depositional disturbance may have occurred through a rodent burrow isolated in SU 3 (XUs 12 and 15).

Fig 3.6. Excavation at Square B with Square A, stone outcrop and Dhadhakul in the background (to the north) and excavators Alice Bedingfield and Ben Watson.

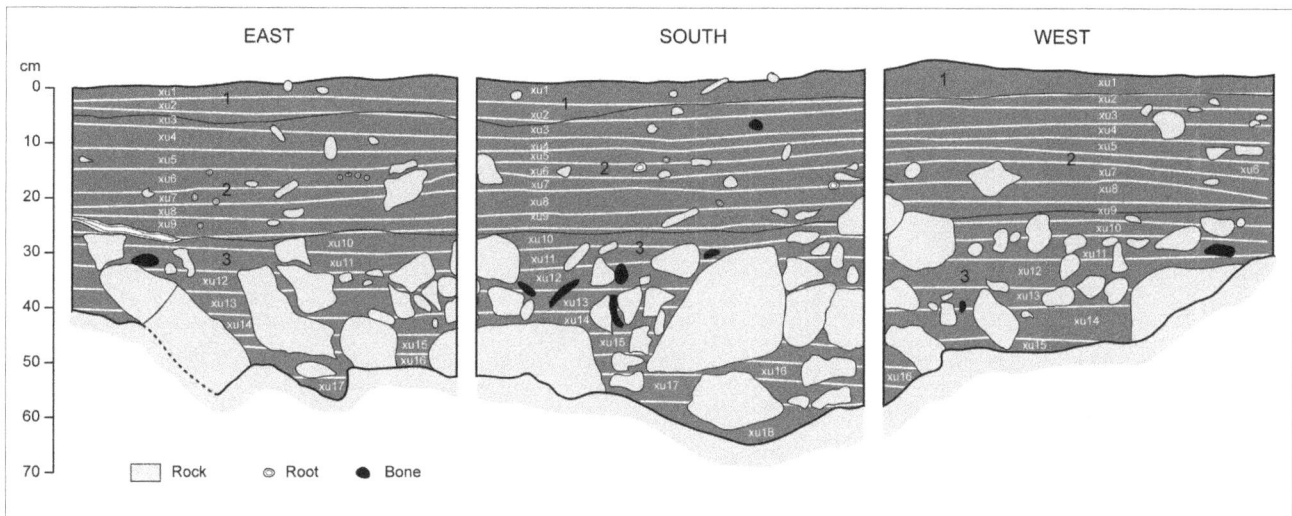

Fig 3.7. Stratigraphic drawing, Square B.

Laboratory Code	XU	Depth below surface (cm)	Sample weight (g)	C13‰	C14 Age (bp)	Calibrated Age BP 2 sigma
WK24932	4	7-11	0.43	25.7±0.2	486±30	464 – 535
WK24933	10	30-32.5	0.38	24.4±0.2	1050±40	800 – 890 896 - 968*
WK24934	16	53-56	0.14	25.3±0.2	1134±30	932 - 1018* 1022 - 1056
WK24935	18	60-63	0.5	25.3±0.2	1140±30	934 - 948 951 - 1057*

Table 3.2. Radiocarbon dates from Square B charcoal samples. * = highest probability of calibrated ranges.

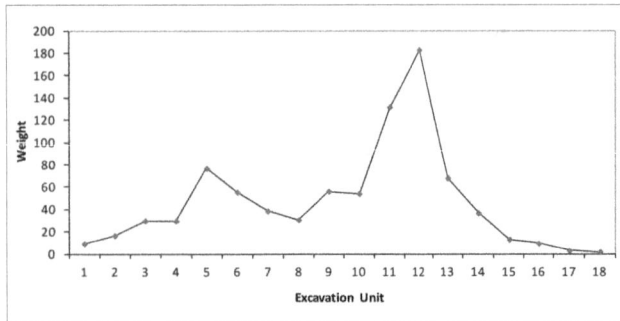

Fig 3.8. Vertical changes in marine vertebrate bone, Square B (grams per 10 l deposit).

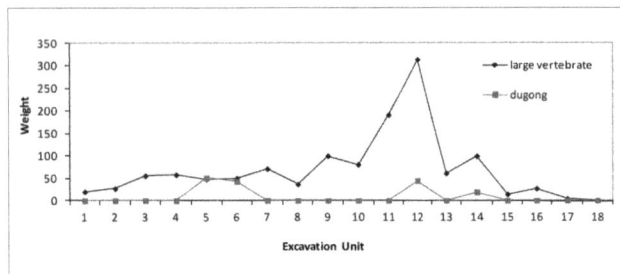

Fig 3.9. Vertical changes in large vertebrate/dugong bone, Square B (grams per 10 l deposit).

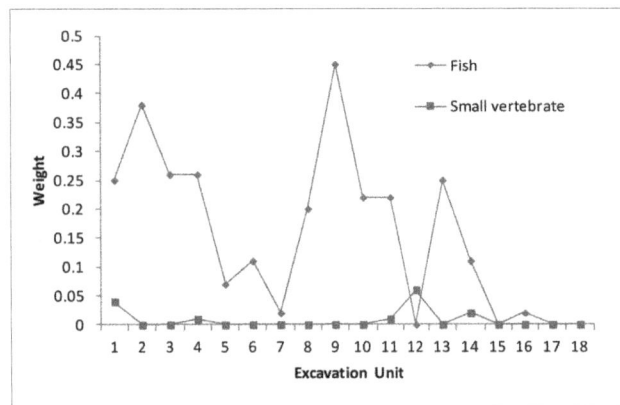

Fig 3.10. Vertical changes in fish and small vertebrate bone, Square B (grams per 10 l deposit).

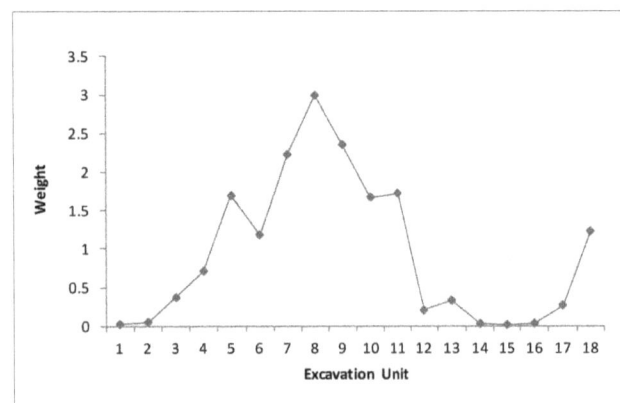

Fig 3.11. Vertical changes in charcoal, Square B (grams per 10 l deposit).

Radiocarbon dates and chronology

Four samples of charcoal were submitted for AMS dating to Waikato dating laboratory, New Zealand. These tested major shifts in natural and cultural material distributions, in particular a substantial reduction after SU 3. Waikato charcoal samples were prepared in a bath of hot 10 % HCl and then further treated with hot 5 % NaOH before being filtered, rinsed and dried. Calibration of radiocarbon dates was completed using OxCal 4.1 (Bronk Ramsey 2009) with Southern Hemisphere dataset (ShCal04) (McCormac et al. 2004) applied to charcoal dates.

Large marine vertebrate bone and the majority of lithics (igneous and quartz) clustered in layers radiocarbon-dated to 1057-464 cal. BP (Wright 2011c: 121; Table 3.2). The former was particularly common in layers that predate 800 years BP. Ten fragments of non-diagnostic glass were recovered from the upper 4 XUs (five in the top two XUs) suggesting human activity continued at this site during the "Period of European Contact" (henceforth PEC). There was no evidence for activity during the intervening period (after 464 cal. BP). Layers associated with European-manufactured objects contained small quantities of fish bone, also glass and quartz flaked artefacts, suggesting continuation of traditional economies during the PEC.

Cultural materials

The acidic soils and low sedimentation rates appear to have led to the poor preservation of cultural materials at Wagedoegam. Large vertebrate bone was frequently highly eroded falling to pieces during excavation. It is expected that less robust materials (such as small vertebrate bone) may have disappeared altogether from the site. Predictably, little cultural material survived to the analysis stage. The bulk of the assemblage comprised of unidentified large vertebrate bone (1.3 kg) with dugong and turtle adding a further 159.2 g. Economic shellfish and terrestrial vertebrates were entirely absent while fish (3.0 g) and small vertebrate (0.1 g) were rare. Although not always identified in situ due to the dark sediment colour there was considerable quantities of charcoal (40.3 g). The bulk of stones were unmodified, apparently part of natural rock fall, a common feature of the Wagedoegam landscape. The contents of this excavation are now assessed in detail.

Marine vertebrate bone
Marine vertebrate made up the bulk of the Wagadagam cultural assemblage (1.4 kg), of which the majority was unidentified large vertebrate (88.5 %) and dugong bone (11 %). The remaining turtle and fish made up less than 0.5 % of the total. Marine vertebrate bone was present in small quantities within SU 1 (55.5 g per 10.0 l) increasing in SU 2 (286.7 g per 10.0 l). The majority; however, comes from the top of SU 3 (XUs 10-14) at which stage there is 472.7 g per 10 l of deposit (Fig. 3.8). After this point

the quantity of marine vertebrate bone drops considerably (26.3 g per 10.0 l). It was observed during excavation that this transition was matched by a significant drop in bone size beneath XU 14, consistent with trickle down into culturally sterile layers.

The fragmented and eroded nature of the large vertebrate bone has meant that only three bones can be confidently identified as dugong or turtle (Fig. 3.9). During excavation it was noted that dugong bone was often so brittle that it fell to pieces upon removal. In XU 12 a number of post-cranial (i.e., rib and vertebrae) dugong bones were observed, however these did not survive transportation to the laboratory. Those that did survive consist of two Parietalia (skull) fragments from XUs 5 and 6 and a rib from XU 12. As no ear bones were excavated the estimated MNI is a notional one for the site. Only one fragment could be confidently identified as turtle bone. This was excavated from XU 7 and weighed 0.7 g.

Less than 2 g of fish bone was excavated from Square B with no evidence for cartilaginous types such as shark or ray. Fish clustered between XUs 7 and 14 with a second more consistent peak in the top four excavation units (Fig. 3.10). A similar trend was identified in the small vertebrate bone which was restricted to XU 12 and the top four excavation units, suggesting fish bone makes up the bulk of the unidentified small vertebrate bone.

Charcoal
The dark, silty sediment negated charcoal identification *in situ* with all but five samples collected during the subsequent sort. Charcoal was recovered in all XUs up until XU 12 (Fig. 3.11). A significant increase occurred between XUs 7 and 11, accounting for 73 % of charcoal (17.0 g per 10 l deposit). There was a further minor peak in the basal two XUs. It remains uncertain whether this is a genuine pattern or was due to natural bioturbation of small fragments on to the underlying bedrock.

Material culture
Square B contains a total of 3136 flaked stone artefacts and seven definite (+3 probable) glass flakes. Quartz was the prominent material used to make flaked artefacts (n=3043), followed by igneous (n=93; Fig. 3.12). The remaining non-flaked artefacts consisted of two fragments of ground ochre and a single stone implement with use impact. The bulk of artefacts (by number) come from the upper 12 Excavation Units (broadly correlating with SUs 1 and 2). This accounts for 96 % of quartz and 92 % of the igneous flaked assemblage (Fig. 3.13). While quartz artefacts were consistently present throughout these layers, the bulk of igneous flaked artefacts were recovered between XUs 6 and 12 (75 %). Flaked glass was found in the upper four XUs, with the proportion reducing significantly below XU 2 suggesting potential bioturbation events. It is intriguing that the average weight of glass flakes is higher below XU 2 (between 0.23 and 0.22) than above it (between 0.10-0.11). Although average weight is

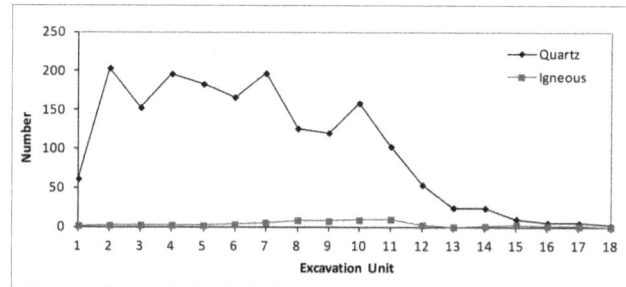

Fig 3.12. Quantity of quartz and igneous artefacts, Square B (number per 10 l deposit).

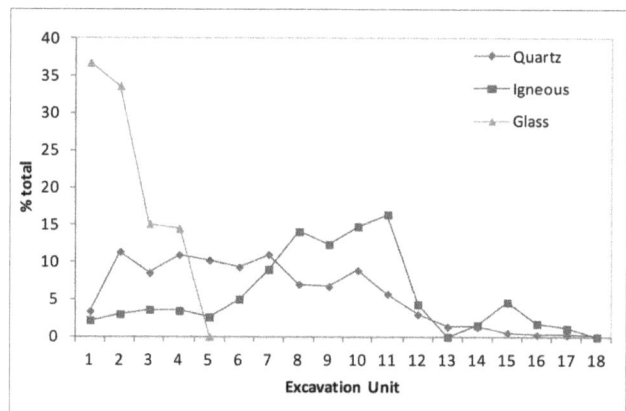

Fig 3.13. Proportion of flaked lithic and glass artefacts, Square B (percentage of total number for each material type per 10 l deposit).

not always an accurate method for ascertaining flake size it is proposed that significant disturbance events would be required to explain this distribution should they not be *in situ*.

The mean weight of quartz flaked artefacts drops below XU 11. While the same caution is required when interpreting such data, this potentially suggests bioturbation of smaller artefacts into lower deposits. An interesting reversal occurs with the igneous assemblage which becomes larger and heavier between XUs 9 and 15. The mean weight above XU 9 is 1.8 g, increasing to 19 g between XUs 10 and 15 and then dropping again to 1.2 g in the last three XUs.

3.3   Wagedoegam 2, Square A

It only remains to present results from a small test excavation into the dugong bone mound (Fig. 3.14). This is reputed to have been an important installation of the Wagedoegam *kod* (Edmund Bani pers. comm., November 2006), with archaeological research restricted to a 40 x 40 cm unit on the mounds periphery. This was recorded as "Wag2 Sq A" in 2006 (Wright 2010), with a subsequent field season of research in 2013 as yet unpublished. This chapter concentrates on initial results to be expanded in future publications (Wright *et al.* In prep). Excavation and sampling methodologies have

Fig 3.14. Wagedoegam bone mound (photographer is facing north west).

with sediment matrix consisting entirely of white bone dust (Munsell = 7.5YR 6/1 to 6/2). There were no observable shifts in pH levels which were consistently mildly acidic (PH = 5.68-6.18). SU 1b varied only through the large quantities of small rootlets (possibly a form of lichen) immediately above bedrock which had stained the surrounding bone dust.

The extent to which this site has been disturbed remains uncertain. The mound appears to have been subject to subsidence across the bedrock surface. Such a scenario would explain its large size (11 m x 7 m) and low depth (>10 cm). It also may also explain a modern radiocarbon date (128±105 BP; 1962-1982 cal. AD at 2 σ; WK-20615) obtained from a burnt seed collected in the basal excavation unit. Attempts to date dugong bone collagen were unsuccessful leaving the antiquity of this mound unresolved.

been reported elsewhere with two exceptions. Firstly, all XUs were collected as bulk samples to offer some protection during transit for the extremely brittle dugong bones. For the same reason excavated materials were dry (as opposed to wet) sieved using a 2.1 mm mesh.

Stratigraphy and radiocarbon dates

Square A was excavated to a maximum depth of 12 cm (eight XUs) with granitic bedrock reached in some sections after only 7 cm (see also Wright 2010: 206; Fig. 3.15). Excavation Units averaged 2 cm in thickness and did not exceed 2.5 cm. Little stratigraphic variation was observed

Cultural materials

Large vertebrate and dugong bone made up over 99 % of the total cultural assemblage (1.4 kg; 1.0 kg = "unidentified large vertebrate" and 384.3 g = "dugong"). It is likely that these categories are one of the same, as indicated by the high MNI count of eight dugongs for this small pit. The remaining marine vertebrate bone consisted of a single fragment of fish bone from XU 6 (Table 3.3). In addition, small quantities of charcoal (0.3 g), ochre (0.8 g) and quartz artefacts (0.1 g) were recorded. While ochre appeared similar to the colour of rock-art panels there was no evidence for use wear.

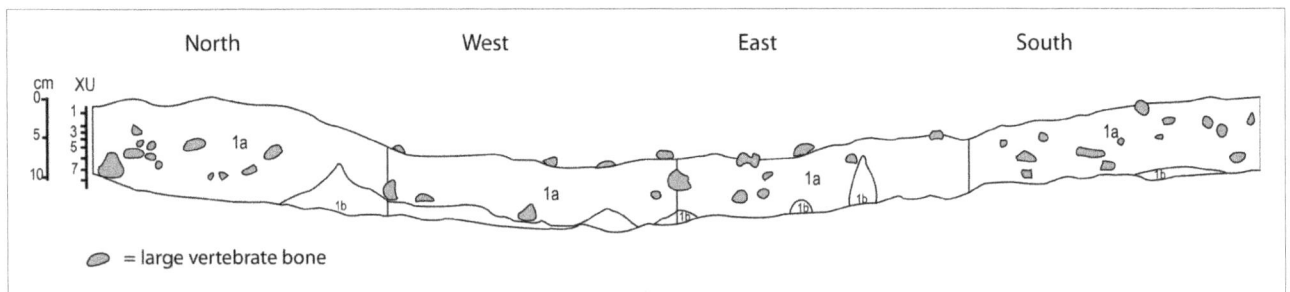

Fig 3.15. Stratigraphic drawing, Square A.

SU	XU	pH	Total weight (g)	Marine vertebrate (g)	stone (g)	quartz (g)	ochre (g)	charcoal (g)
1a	1	5.95	200	120.6	21	0	0.2	0.4
1a	2		600	103.3	0.8	0	0.1	0
1a	3	5.9	800	102.7	0.7	0.02	0.1	0.01
1a	4		1900	227.3	1.0	0.01	0	0.03
1a	5	6.0	1000	260.3	2.5	0	0.1	0.03
1a, 1b	6		1600	282.1	1.8	0	0	0.02
1a, 1b	7	6.18	2600	246.8	1.8	0	0.1	0.03
1a, 1b	8		1800	51.8	0.6	0	0	0

Table 3.3. Raw excavation data, Square A.

XU	Ribs	Skull	Ear	Fore limb	Scapula	Non diagnostic	Burnt bone
1	240.0	0.0	118.0	0.0	28.0	1444.0	0.0
2	262.0	0.0	184.0	0.0	0.0	2.0	0.0
3	52.0	0.0	82.0	0.0	0.0	0.8	0.7
4	288.0	18.0	248.3	0.0	14.5	29.2	1.3
5	76.8	13.6	120.3	2.2	0.0	170.8	0.0
6	56.4	0.0	51.3	0.0	0.0	16.6	0.0

Table 3.4. Vertical changes in dugong bone elements (NISP).

While the assemblage is likely to be significantly disturbed, cultural materials demonstrate non-random distribution; for example, the bulk of the dugong bone clustered in the top excavation unit and dropped significantly in subsequent layers (Table 3.4). A narrow range of elements was identified, with ribs (298.1 g) dominating the lower portion along with a single fragment of skull (19.2 g) and ear ossicles present throughout (68.8 g) but most common between XUs 1 and 4. The majority of the charcoal came from XU 1; however, recent burning activities in the vicinity of the site may explain this pattern. Small fragments of unmodified ochre were present throughout the assemblage with the majority excavated in the upper three XUs. Two small (<4 mm maximum dimension), quartz flakes were recovered from XUs 3 and 4.

3.4   Summary

Excavations at Wagedoegam provide insight into the sacred and secular history of a Goemulgaw village. The main period of human activity within the vicinity of the new landing appears to date between 1057-800 cal. BP. During this period people hunted large marine vertebrates (primarily dugong) and used a variety of quartz and igneous flaked artefacts. After 800 BP the site appears to experience continued visitation although there is reduced quantities of all cultural materials. Quartz and igneous artefacts continued to be made, while quantities of large marine vertebrate bone/ dugong bone substantially drop. Between 800-464 cal. BP there is evidence for increased burning, also continued fin-fishing. By 464 (and quite possibly considerably earlier) there was a substantial drop in the quantity of igneous stone artefacts being used at the site, while quartz continued to be used in high numbers. This supports a potential technological/ economic shift in activities after 800-464 years ago away from large igneous artefacts. After 464 cal. BP there is no evidence for sustained human activity with little dugong bone or charcoal observed in associated deposits. Fishbone and

lithics do continue in upper layers, also European materials suggesting that Wagedoegam continued to be visited immediately prior to, during and after LMS and pearl shelling activity was initiated. While further excavations are required to ascertain whether this is representative of broad chronological patterns on the north west coast of Mabuyag, the scarcity of surface midden and sites within the Wagedoegam district suggests that any later settlement phase was not on the scale observed at either Goemu or Dhabangay.

The Wagadagam *kod* consists of a large number of archaeological features, including stone arrangements, stone-lined platforms, bone mound and rock-art. Excavations revealed high quantities of dugong bones, with a focus on ribs and skull parts (particularly ear ossicles). While no direct chronology can be obtained for this feature, the rock art and a formal comparison with other known *kod* sites in Western Torres Strait (see McNiven *et al*. 2009) suggests that it dates to within the past 400 years. Further research is currently underway to identify whether or not this is the case. If this is correct then Wagedoegam may have experienced a significant shift from a residential to ceremonial area within the last 400 years. The distinctive rock art images provide insight into these ceremonies, supporting initiation and potentially totemic activities at this site. The presence of the Torres Strait headdress (*dhoeri*) provides remarkable insight into the origins of material culture objects that continue to structure Goemulgaw and broader Torres Strait islander identities.

Returning to models of fissioning and regionalisation it is interesting that archaeology supports an early phase of human activity at Wagedoegam (1057-800 cal. BP). During this period, economies were reminiscent of those currently practiced by the Goemulgal, including fin-fishing and dugong hunting. Later chapters will examine whether the reduction in cultural activity at Wagedoegam after 800 cal. BP (and again after 464 cal. BP) coincided with establishment or intensified activities at other villages. As new villages formed, the regionalisation model predicts new socio-political and/ or ceremonial activities. The Wagedoegam case study suggests that ceremonial activity (evident through rock art and bone/ stone installations at the *kod*) may succeed settlement, suggesting deliberate reuse of an important ancestral site after abandonment. The reinterpretation of Wagedoegam as a culturally significant and sacred site is likely to have been reinforced by this shift. While regional patterns in sites and/ or material remains are hard to ascertain for Wagedoegam the rock art at Wageodoegam arguably provides insight into site specific events, ceremonies and/ or totemic activities.

4

Goemu (Sipi Ngur)

Goemu (in the region known as Sipi Ngur) is located on the south east coast of Mabuyag. This open site has its foundations on prograded shelly-sand and is backed by the largest hill on the island (Kwoiam antra). Vegetation is dominated by grass, interspersed with coconut palms and mangroves. As the ancestral home of Kwoiam, centre for the *Moegi Awgadhaw Khazi* and namesake of the Mabuyag Islanders (Goemulag-translated as "people of Goemu") this site was considered an important place for archaeological research. This was emphasised through UCL research which recorded a substantial landscape of middens, mounds and stone/ shell arrangements. During the PEC site activity is expected to have reduced at Goemu as village residents moved to the centralised village of Baw (Shnukal In press). Haddon made no mention of occupation at Goemu during visits in 1888 and 1898.

Fig 4.1. Ian McNiven standing over Square A (photographer facing north towards Baw village).

4.1　Surface survey and excavation

In 2005 archaeologists from Monash University, led by Dr Ian McNiven, surveyed Goemu and updated the UCL map. Results confirmed Goemu as a major settlement area with platform and ridge mounds considered unique to this part of the island (see also McNiven *et al.* In press). New features were observed; however, it was noted that bulldozing had removed 70 % of the original surface features (McNiven and Wright 2008; Fig. 4.2). A stone arrangement in the shape of a turtle, recorded by Harris and Ghaleb (1987: 10), was identified as a marker of the region's primary totem (Tim Gizu pers. comm., 1 October 2006).

Two excavations (Square A and B) tested bone and earth mounded features at Goemu. Square B results have been presented elsewhere (McNiven *et al.* In press). In this chapter results are presented from a 1 m x 1 m excavation into a platform mound in the northern portion of the village (Square A).

4.2　Square A

Square A was positioned on the eastern edge of a 28 cm-high linear platform mound. This runs parallel with (and approximately 40 m from) the current high tide line and lies in an undisturbed crook of a bulldozed road into the village. The surface of the mound was densely packed with large vertebrate (predominately dugong) bone (Fig. 4.1). Excavation reached a maximum depth of 202 cm (34 XUs), continuing into culturally sterile beach sand. Excavation Units averaged <4 cm thick in midden levels with excavation and sampling methodologies identical to those reported for Wagedoegam.

Stratigraphy

Two major and seven minor stratigraphic units were recorded (Fig. 4.3). SU 1a was restricted to the upper 25-30 cm (16 XUs) and contained dense midden materials including dugong, turtle and fish bone. These were couched within dark, loamy grey-brown sediment and were associated with considerable amounts of rock, pumice and ochre. Small quantities of glass and metal were also observed. SU 1b (35-40 cm) is a layer of slightly lighter coloured soil with a visible reduction in cultural materials. The quantity of foraminifera-rich beach sand increased in the 10 cm below this unit (SU 1c) and shifts to a coarse-grained shelly sand (SU 2a). This sediment was associated with very little cultural materials although ash-rich capping of SU 2b may represent a fire pit. An alignment of six stones in SU 2c (95-100 cm below surface) may also have a cultural origin.

Radiocarbon dates and chronology

Eight charcoal and six *Paphies striata* samples were sent to Waikato Radiocarbon dating laboratory for AMS dating (Table 4.1). Results from charcoal, AMS samples suggest the mounded ridge feature (SU 1a) dates to within the past 545 years (WK-21516), with an expansion in midden activity within the past 150 years. The latter is supported by *Paphies striata* AMS dates from associated layers which cluster within the past 464 years (WK-29691). Increased activity within the recent period is suggested by sustained presence of glass and metal during the upper seven XUs.

Radiocarbon ages from the base of SU 1b and SU 2a (WK-21517 and WK-21518) were stratigraphically inverted.

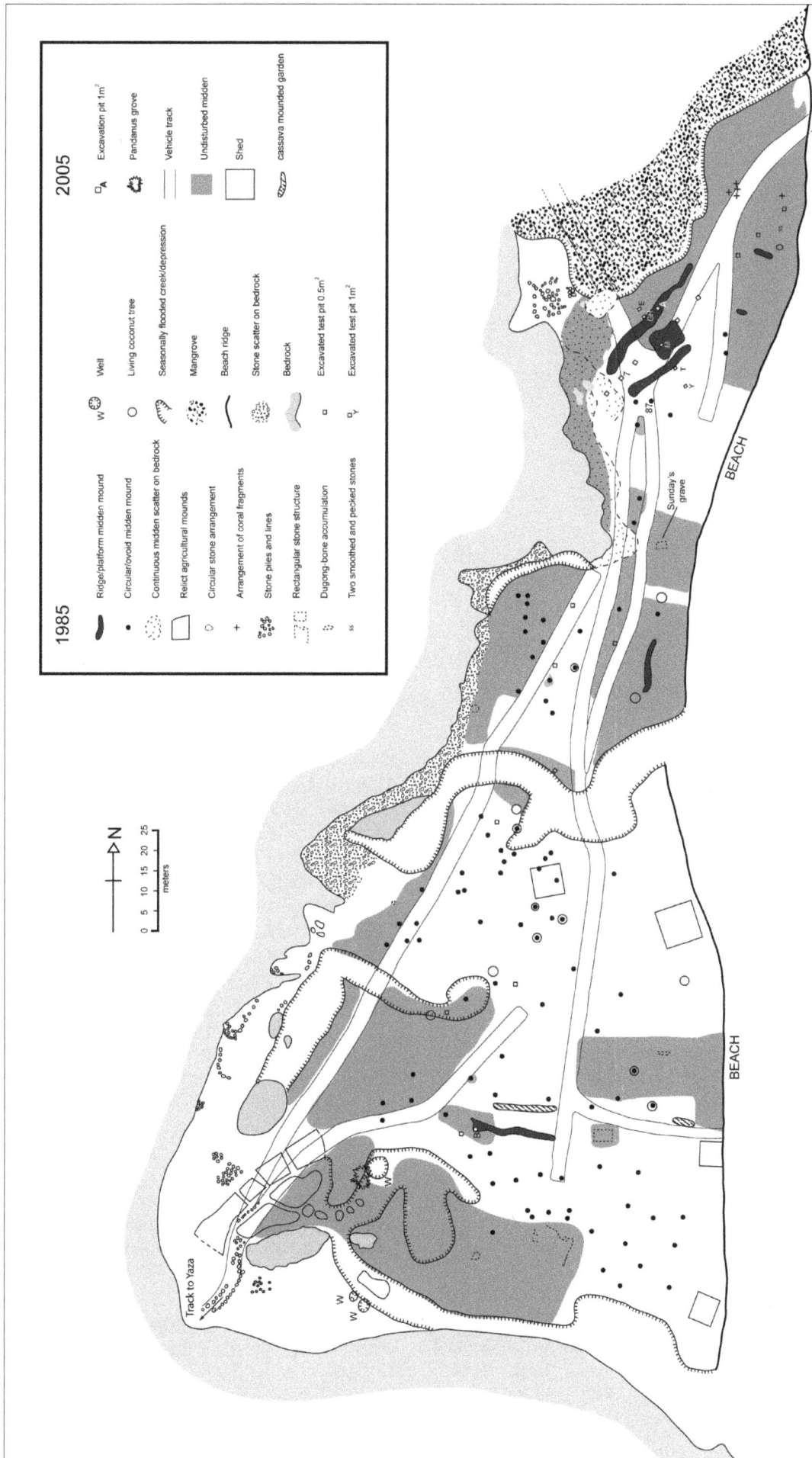

Fig 4.2. Dumpy level map of the archaeological features at Goemu village (from McNiven et al. In press).

1985

Ridge/platform midden mound	
Circular/ovoid midden mound	
Continuous midden scatter on bedrock	
Relict agricultural mounds	
Circular stone arrangement	
Arrangement of coral fragments	
Stone piles and lines	
Rectangular stone structure	
Dugong-bone accumulation	
Two smoothed and pecked stones	

2005

Excavation pit 1m²	
Pandanus grove	
Vehicle track	
Undisturbed midden	
Shed	
cassava mounded garden	

Well	
Living coconut tree	
Seasonally flooded creek/depression	
Mangrove	
Beach ridge	
Stone scatter on bedrock	
Bedrock	
Excavated test pit 0.5m²	
Excavated test pit 1m²	

N

0 5 10 15 20 25
meters

Track to Yaza

BEACH

BEACH

Sunday's grave

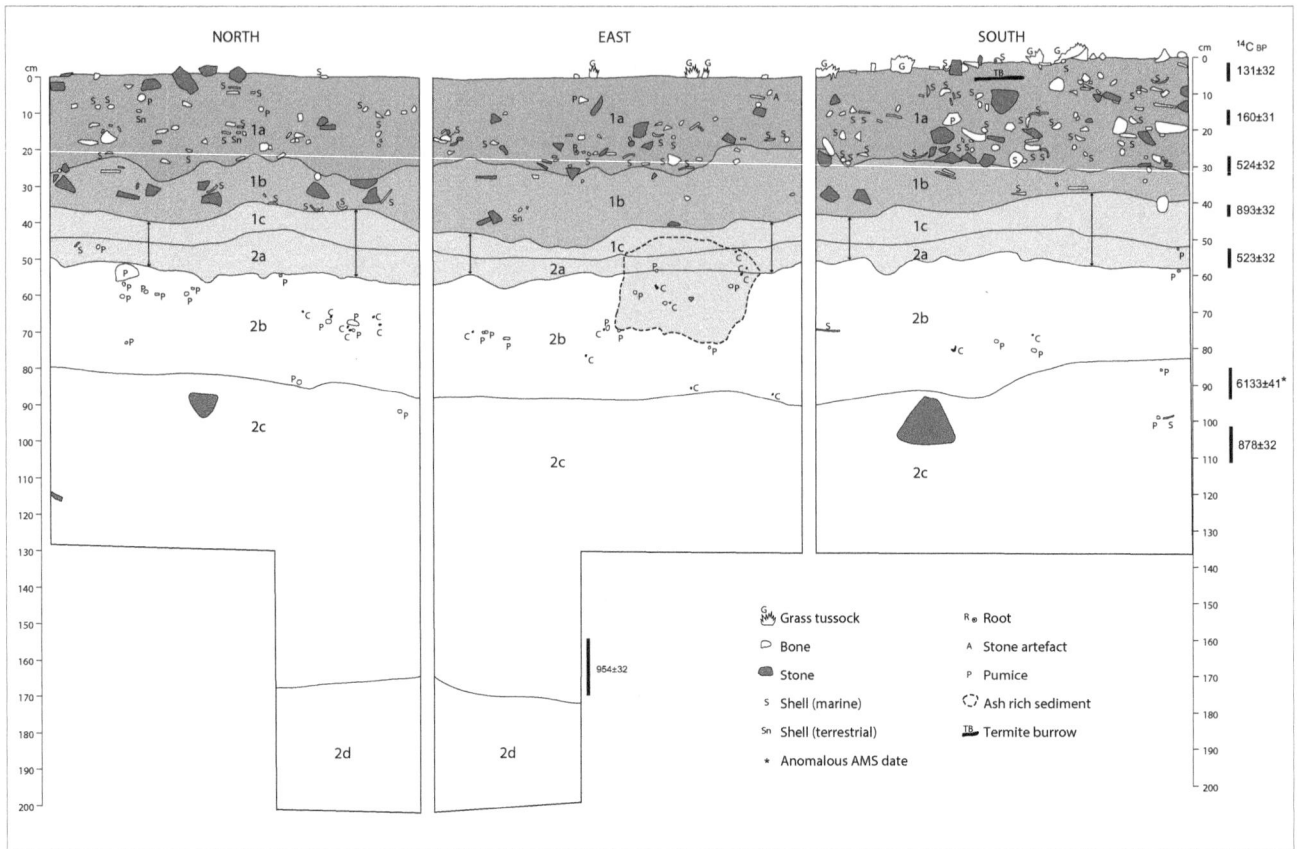

Fig 4.3. Stratigraphic drawing, Square A (from McNiven *et al.* In press).

A charcoal/ shell pair in XU 15 overlapped (683-888 cal. BP) suggesting that WK-21518 is intrusive. Taphonomic issues continued with depth, an anomalous age of 6792–7029 cal. BP obtained from charcoal that was bracketed between two *Paphies* samples which span 706–986 cal. BP. The latter range is expected to provide a maximum age for the "ashy pits" and possible stone arrangement (see McNiven *et al.* In press). The antiquity of human activity at the site is problematic due to disparity between shell and charcoal calibrations (Table 4.1). Based on charcoal samples culturally sterile deposits, underlying cultural materials date to within the 745–909 cal. BP (WK-21521). A greater antiquity is suggested by AMS dates using a *Paphies* valve. This was excavated at least 50 cm above the charcoal age and dates to 1528–1894 cal. BP. Elsewhere (McNiven *et al.* In press), have argued that *Paphies* sp. provides a more "internally consistant sequence". It is evident that fragments of charcoal have experienced substantial post-depositional movement. Ultimately, resolution to the chronology of this site requires further research.

Cultural materials

Goemu, Square A was dominated by marine vertebrate bone (46.3 kg) and economic shellfish (14.8 kg). There were also 969 flaked artefacts, fragments of worked shell (112.8 g), worked stone (3 ground pieces) and charcoal (62.8 g).

Marine vertebrate bone

As noted above, marine vertebrate bone made up a sizable proportion of the Goemu assemblage. Dominating this category was large vertebrate bone (38.1 kg) and dugong (6.9 kg). Turtle bone was present in small quantities (450.0 g), alongside unidentified small vertebrate (397 g), fish (331 g), shark/ray (46.2 g) and terrestrial (bird, snake/ lizard bone = 51.9 g). The bulk of marine vertebrate bone was excavated above XU 11 (43 kg; Fig. 4.4). The large size and weight of most of the large vertebrate bone and the clear correlation with dugong suggested that much of this was also dugong. Diagnostic turtle bone also fits within this broader pattern (Fig. 4.5). Density of marine vertebrate bone was particularly high in the upper two XUs, containing 4.5 kg (2.4 kg per 10 l deposit). This drops significantly (to 166.3 g per 10 l deposit) between XUs 12 and 17 and finally to only 1.5 g per 10 l deposit below this. The latter is marked by a stratigraphic change from dark, organic SU 1 to increasingly sandy SU 2. There was a slight increase (0.8 g per 10 l deposit) in marine vertebrate bone at the base of the excavation (between XUs 31 and 32).

Dugong bone elements represented are diverse, with little evidence for selective deposition of particular bones. This includes 1.2 kg of vertebrae; 4.3 kg of ribs and 1.1 kg of skull bones (including ear ossicles and tusks/ teeth). There were also smaller quantities of limb bones (268.4 g) including scapula (see Fig. 4.6). There was little pattern to vertical distribution, only a steady increase in all categories (with the exception of skull fragment which peak in XU 6). Ribs were prominent throughout, with a single rib fragment found in XU 31.

Approximately half of the small vertebrate bone excavated was classified as fish bone, with the other half likely also to belong to this category based on the near identical trajectories of vertical distribution (Fig. 4.7). While fish and unidentified small vertebrate were present in small quantities to XU 32, a period of consistent growth in discard occurs after XU 17 and in particular between XU 12 and the surface (8.8 g per 10 l deposit). This reaches a peak between XU 9-12 with quantities remaining moderate until a secondary peak after XU 2 (8.6 g per 10 l deposit; Fig. 4.7).

There was also a small component of terrestrial/ other vertebrate bone. This included 6.1 g of reptile bones

(snake, skink, goanna and crocodile) and 0.4 g of bird bone (see McNiven *et al.* In press for details). This clustered within the upper 11 XUs, with a substantial peak (0.75 g per 10 l deposit) in XU 6.

Marine invertebrates
A total of 14.8 kg of economic (and 949.8 g of non-economic) shellfish was excavated from Square A. Shellfish was dense within the upper 11 XUs (12.4 kg in total and 352.5 g per 10 l deposit; Fig. 4.8), with the surface XU containing 686 g (857.5 g per 10 l deposit). Below XU 12 the weight – excavated sediment ratio drops to 24.4 g per 10 l deposit.

There were 28 taxa represented at Goemu. These were dominated by *Paphies striata* (64 % of the total MNI) and *Nerita* sp. (15.6 % by MNI), with *Chama* sp. making up a further 5.4 % and Trochidae 4.5 % (Table 4.2; see also McNiven *et al.* In press). As well as shellfish there were

Laboratory Code	Excavation Unit	Depth below surface (cm)	Sample and 14C Technique	Sample weight (g)	C13%°	C14 Age (BP)	Calibrated Age BP 2 sigma
WK 21514	3	1.5 - 3.4	Charcoal	0.01	22.7±0.2	131±32	0-146* 222-263
WK 29690	3	1.5 - 3.4	*Paphies Striata* (Single valve)	1.23	1.7±0.2	710±25	301-493
WK 21515	7	9.5 - 12.5	Charcoal	0.01	9.8±0.2	160±31	0-153* 173-177 208-277
WK 29691	7	9.5 - 12.5	*Paphies Striata* (Single valve)	1.24	2.3±0.2	654±28	270-464
WK 21516	11	24.1 - 28.3	Charcoal	0.06	25.2±0.2	524±32	496-545
WK 21517	15	37.5 - 41.1	Charcoal	0.06	26.8±0.2	893±32	683-801* 875-882 887-897
WK 29693	15	37.5 - 41.1	*Paphies Striata* (Single valve)	1.02	1.7±0.2	1163±25	672-888
WK 21518	18C	49.8 - 54.9	Charcoal	0.02	25.6±0.2	523±32	496-545
WK 29693	18C	49.8 - 54.9	Paphies Striata (Single valve)	0.95	1.5±0.2	1213±25	706-921
WK 21519	23	81.6 - 90.1	Charcoal	0.07	25.1±0.2	6133±41	6792-7029* 7045-7069 7079-7085 7106-7156
WK 29695	23	81.6 - 90.1	*Paphies Striata* (Single valve)	0.06	2.0±0.2	1273±25	747-986
WK 21520	25	98.3 - 104.7	Charcoal	0.04	27.8±0.2	878±32	681-794
WK 29695	25	98.3 - 104.7	*Paphies Striata* (Single valve)	0.62	1.7±0.2	2018±25	1528-1894
WK 21521	32	156.2 - 171.2	Charcoal	0.02	26.5±0.2	954±32	745-909

Table 4.1. AMS radiocarbon dates, Square A. Calibrations calculated using Calib 5.0.2 (Stuiver and Reimer. 1993). * = highest probability of calibrated ranges.

a number of other invertebrates. Chiton clustered in the upper 10 XUs but continued to be present until the base of Layer 1c. Barnacles, limpets and crabs were recorded throughout the excavation with crab particularly prominent in SU 2b.

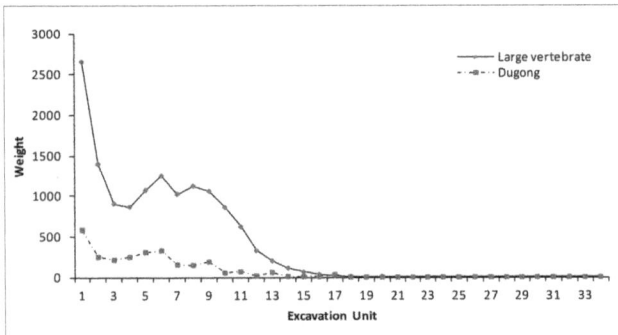

Fig 4.4. Vertical changes in large vertebrate and dugong bone, Square A (grams per 10 l deposit).

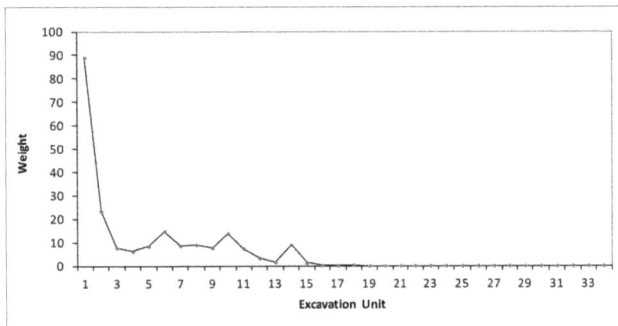

Fig 4.5. Vertical changes in turtle bone, Square A (grams per 10 l deposit).

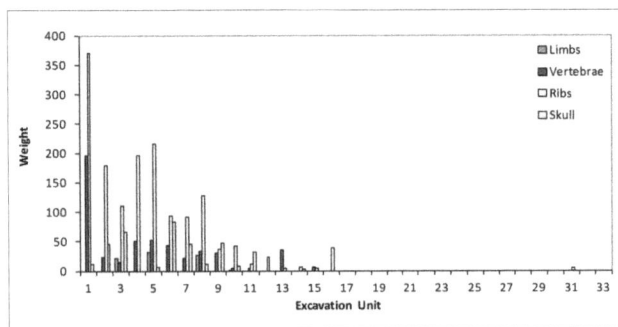

Fig 4.6. Vertical changes in dugong elements, Square A (grams per 10 l deposit).

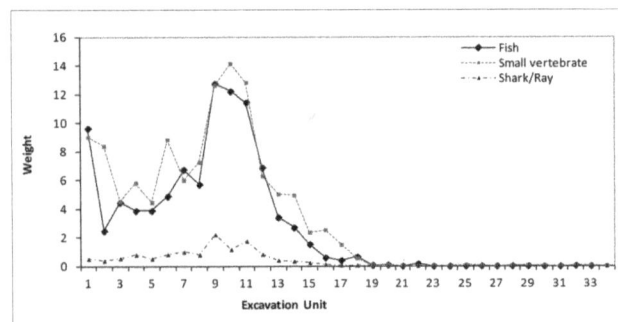

Fig 4.7. Vertical changes in fish, shark/ray and small vertebrate bone, Square A (grams per 10 l deposit).

With the exception of SU 2d, shellfish were recovered from all stratigraphic units. The majority came from SU 1a (76 % of the total) and SU 1b (19 % of the total). Both sub-layers are roughly on parity in terms of density of deposit with an average MNI of 198 per XU for SU 1a and 165 per XU for SU 1b. The density drops significantly in SU 1c (2.7 %), SU 2a (0.6 %) and SU 2a (0.3 %) before increasing slightly in SU 2b (1.2 %).

Only *Paphies striata* was represented throughout the assemblage. Most other shellfish were restricted in the upper layer (SU 1). In this layer there were 26 taxa represented as opposed to SU 2 which only contained six taxa. *Fragum unedo* and Hamminoidae offer the exception to this rule, restricted largely to SU 2. While the latter may be due to the natural mobility of these shellfish the former suggests a shift in focus for shellfish gathering. A divergence in subsistence strategies is also suggested for basal layers which are dominated by shellfish from the easily accessible littoral (sandy) zone (e.g., *Paphies* sp. and *Fragum unedo*). The upper layer contains shellfish from brackish lagoons, mud-flats, reef tracts, sand beds and rocky zones (Table 4.2). Particularly notable is the increasing focus on brackish lagoons and mud flats (e.g., Cerithidae; *Strombus* sp., *Terebralia* sp., *Polymesoda* sp., *Saccostrea* sp. and *Chama* sp.). There were also a number of deep water species (Nautilidae, *Syrinx aruanus*). Considering the distance of this excavation away from the high water mark, the focused nature of the assemblage and the large size of shellfish it is considered unlikely that these were natural accumulations. More likely is a shift away from opportunistic gathering in the immediate region to a much wider and more diverse strategy targeting a number of different ecological niches.

Charcoal

Considerable quantities of charcoal were recovered from this excavation (62.8 g). Distribution was marked by a shift from sparse deposits below XU 23 and significant increase after this point (Fig. 4.9). Between XUs 19 and 20 there was a major peak in charcoal (2.9 g per 10 l deposit), with quantities remaining high (1.0 g per 10 l deposit) until they drop off within the upper five XUs (0.3 g per 10 l deposit).

Material culture

The majority of artefacts belong to a flaked assemblage, with flaked quartz, igneous and glass represented. There were also five shell artefacts including flaked clam (n=3) and pearl shell (n=2, one in XU 7 and 9 respectively) and a single shaped and perforated proximal section of *Strombus* sp. (in XU 5). A single large hammer stone was excavated from XU 5, also a ground stone (possibly an axe fragment) in XU 6, and a volcanic bevelled-edged implement in XU 11. In addition, 47.3 kg of rock rubble was excavated. Although stone continued to the base of this excavation the bulk of it came from SUs 1a and 1b. The quantity of stone increased further in the upper four XUs at which point there was evidence for fire fractured and heat effected cobbles. A

Taxon	Tidal zone	Substrate	Total MNI							Total	Ranking
Gastropods			SU 1a	SU 1b	SU 1c	SU 2a	SU 2b	SU 2c	SU 2d		
Nerita spp.	littoral	rocky	288	101	8	0	0	3	0	400	2
Trochus niloticus	littoral	rocky/ coral reefs	102	12	1	0	0	0	0	115	4
Turbo sp.	supra—littoral	rocky/ coral reefs	3	0	0	0	0	0	0	3	15
Melo amphora	littoral + sublittoral	sand/ mud	10	1	0	0	0	0	0	11	10
Cerithidae	mangroves/ lagoons	esturine sandy/ muddy	3	13	1	0	0	0	0	17	8
Strombus sp.	littoral and sublittoral	muddy, sandy, rubble	1	0	0	0	0	0	0	1	17
Syrinx aruanus	littoral + sublittoral	sand/ coral reefs	1	0	0	0	0	0	0	1	17
Cyprae sp.	littoral + sublittoral	coral reefs	4	2	3	2	0	0	0	11	10
Terebralia sp.	mangroves/ lagoons	mud	4	13	1	0	0	0	0	18	7
Nautilidae	continental shelf	rocky/ coral reefs	2	0	0	0	0	0	0	2	16
Murricidae	?	?	1	0	0	0	0	0	0	1	17
Haminoeidae	Mobile	mobile	0	0	1	0	1	7	0	9	12
Littoraria sp.	Demersal	sandy	1	0	0	0	0	0	0	1	17
Bivalves											
Chama sp.	littoral + sublittoral	rocky/ coral reefs/ lagoons	71	48	17	1	0	1	0	138	3
Pinctada sp.	littoral + sublittoral	rocky/ coral reefs/ lagoons	19	11	2	0	0	1	0	33	6
Paphies striata	littoral	sand	1411	270	30	12	5	7	0	1735	1
Polymesoda erosa	littoral (intertidal)	mud/ mangrove	8	4	0	0	0	0	0	12	9
Anadara antiquita	littoral	sand/ mud	18	0	0	0	0	0	0	18	7
Fragum unedo	littoral	sand/ mud	0	1	0	0	0	9	0	10	11
Gafrarium sp.	littoral	sand/ mud	2	0	1	0	0	3	0	6	13
tridacna squamosa	littoral	coral reefs	1	0	0	0	0	0	0	1	17
Dosinia sp.	littoral	sand	0	0	0	0	1	1	0	2	16
Telina scobinata	littoral	sand	22	7	4	1	1	0	0	35	5
Davila plana	littoral	sand	4	8	0	0	0	0	0	12	9
Mactra sp.	littoral	sand/ mud	1	1	0	0	0	0	0	2	16
Saccostrea	littoral + epipelagic	rocky/ mangrove/ lagoons	4	0	0	0	0	0	0	4	14
Timoclea	littoral (intertidal)	sand/ mud	0	0	0	1	0	0	0	1	17
Asaphis violasens	littoral (intertidal)	sand	1	2	0	0	0	0	0	3	15

Table 4.2. MNI of shellfish excavated from Square A (zonation of taxa from http://www.sealifebase.com.org).

linear arrangement of six large, cobbles was excavated at 95-100 cm below the surface.

Flaked artefacts clustered in the upper 11 XUs (n=716; 20.3 per 10 l deposit; 74 % of total). Glass flakes and shell artefacts were restricted to the upper nine XUs (mainly SU 1a). In the subsequent XUs (between XUs 12

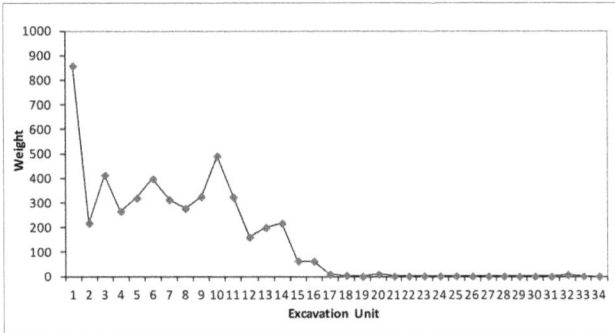

Fig 4.8. Vertical changes in economic shell, Square A (grams per 10 l deposit).

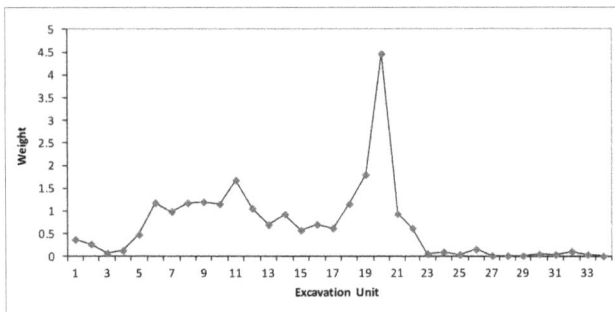

Fig 4.9. Vertical changes in charcoal, Square A (grams per 10 l deposit).

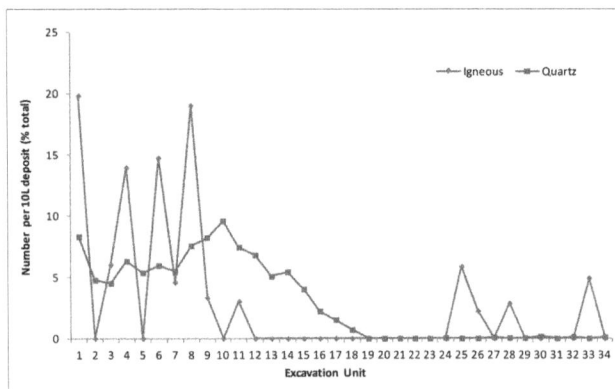

Fig 4.10. Vertical changes in stone artefacts, Square A (number per 10 l deposit).

and 17) flaked artefacts dropped to 0.5 g per 10 l deposit and then further still (0.1 g per 10 l deposit) between XUs 18 and 25 (Fig. 4.10). A second, smaller peak occurs between XUs 26 and 32, accounting for 2.8 % of the total before artefacts disappear completely below this. Both quartz and igneous flakes are present in small numbers in basal layers (i.e., below XU 25). For the first time, however, the latter is the most prominent material type.

4.3   Summary

This research confirms previous studies which attribute the majority of cultural (midden) activity at Goemu to the past 800 years. Radiocarbon dates from Square A provide a 550 year antiquity for the onset of midden activity, with evidence for human activity from at least 747-986 years ago and possibly closer to 1600 years ago. Continuity of activity after European arrival on the island is evident through radiocarbon ages and the consistent presence of European manufactured materials in the upper deposit of Square A. The Goemu excavation further supports the complexity of mound construction. This linear, ridge midden-mound contained a large variety of materials (including significant quantities of shellfish and turtle/ dugong bone), also a large variety of dugong, skeletal elements. This corresponds with platform midden mounds excavated by UCL archaeologists, but appears very different from circular mounds which contain a high proportion of dugong bone, predominately skulls and ribs (Ghaleb 1990: 251; McNiven and Wright 2008: 142).

As the namesake of the Goemulgal, excavations provide important information about community emergence and development. Specifically, we learn that significant activity (involving maritime specialist subsistence and possibly also structured-ceremonial treatment of dugong bone) occurred within the past 550 years. During the succeeding period of mound construction archaeological and ethnographic research suggests that distinctive, totemically-inscribed stone arrangements and mounded features were added to the site. The presence of earlier, ephemeral activity suggests continued visitation of Goemu many hundreds (possibly thousands) of years before establishment of this site as a residential centre.

5

Dhabangay

Dhabangay lies within the Panay district in north eastern Mabuyag. This region encompasses Panay village, "Kiyay, Thoekaral Kiyay, Snake Hill and the land near the shore called Kawzar Nab, which starts from Ghost Creek" (Eseli *et al*. 1998: 84). Oral histories identify its significance to *dhangal* (dugong) and *koedal* (crocodile) clans, totem groups that often provided chief men on the island (Haddon 1904: 162; Chapter 2). Dhabangays' importance was further cemented when this beach was used as the first meeting place between the London Missionary Society (LMS) and Goemulgal during "The Coming of the Light" (Missionisation). The following chapter documents two field seasons of archaeological research (2006 and 2011) at the back of the Dhabangay embayment to resolve the nature and chronology of human activity at this important village.

5.1   Surface survey and excavation

A survey was completed at Dhabangay in 2006, recording numerous archaeological features. These included stone arrangements (including two "turrets" and crocodile and

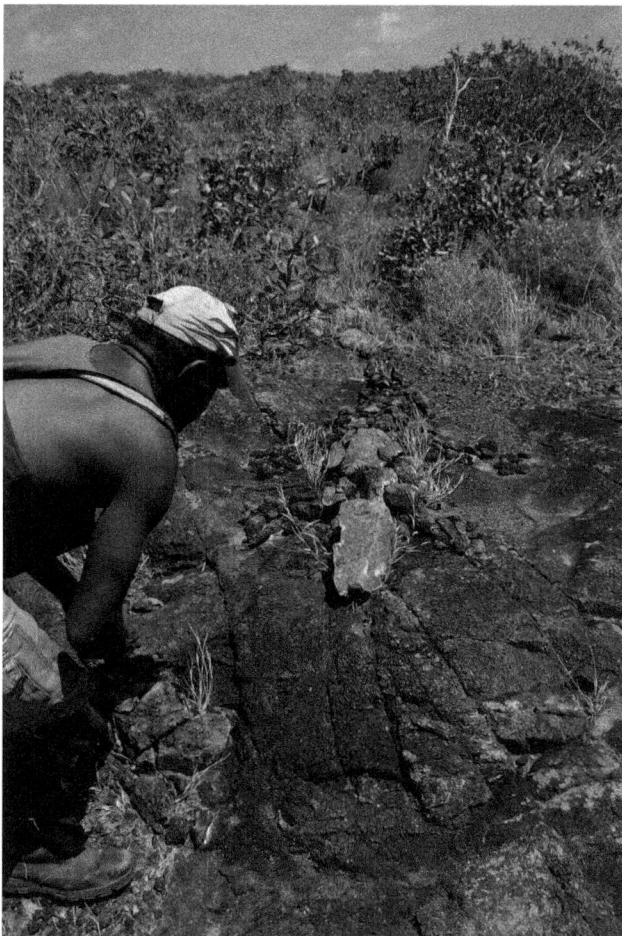

Fig 5.1. Beboy (Maitui) Whap clearing stones away from the crocodile stone arrangement at Dhabangay.

dugong arrangements; four mounded structures of earth shell and bone; two low mounds of dugong bone, isolated *Syrinx* shells and two paths lined with small stones (1.3m across). According to Beboy (Maitui) Whap, the totemic stone arrangements continue to be maintained in the contemporary period by site custodians (Fig. 5.1). Two turtle-shaped cairns were described (but not visited) in the vicinity of Dhabangay (Cygnet Repu and Maitui Whap pers. comm., November 2006). Of the 26 surface features recorded in 2006, only 11 survived bulldozing related to the excavation of a substantial waste dump in 2007 (Wright *et al*. 2013; Fig. 5.2). Cultural materials at this open site included midden large vertebrate/ dugong bone, turtle shell and shellfish (*Baler*, *Bu* and *Akul* predominating), also bottle glass, metal and clay pipe bowls and stems.

In September 2006 a single 1 m x 1 m excavation was conducted 55 m inland from (and 12 m above) the present high water mark in an area of level bone and shell midden (Wright 2011, Figs 5.3, 5.4). This was located 3 m north west of a sewerage trench and at the edge of a waste dump. The area was chosen, as it was well outside the storm wash zone and due to observed distributions of midden materials. The topography changed markedly inland from this point, climbing into rock scree and low scrubby vegetation. In November 2011, two additional 1 m x 1 m excavations were completed to locate undisturbed deposits and better understand human activity across the Dhabangay embayment (Wright *et al*. 2013)

5.2   Square A

Square A was excavated to a depth of 92 cmbs (35 XUs) at which point the excavated area was reduced to 40 cm x 40 cm in the north east corner. This reduction was necessary due to increasingly concreted sediment and a desire to avoid areas of disturbance. Excavation continued for a further 67 cm to a maximum depth of 169 cm before being discontinued when confined space made it impractical to continue. The excavation did not reach culturally sterile deposits. Excavation and sampling methods followed those reported in Chapter 3 with the average XU depth 3.2 cm. All materials were collected, sorted and analysed using methodologies provided earlier, with the exception of areas of termite disturbance (B deposit). These were excavated and bagged separately and have not been included in the list of archaeological materials.

Stratigraphy

Two major and six minor stratigraphic units (SUs) were identified in Square A (see Fig. 5.5; Table 5.1). The upper 30-40 cm (SUs 1 and 2/ XUs 1 to 14) features a very dark grey, humic soil (7.5 YR 3/1) with the exception of the top-soil which is black (7.5YR 2.5/1). Sediment was neutral to slightly alkaline (6.06-6.61), becoming

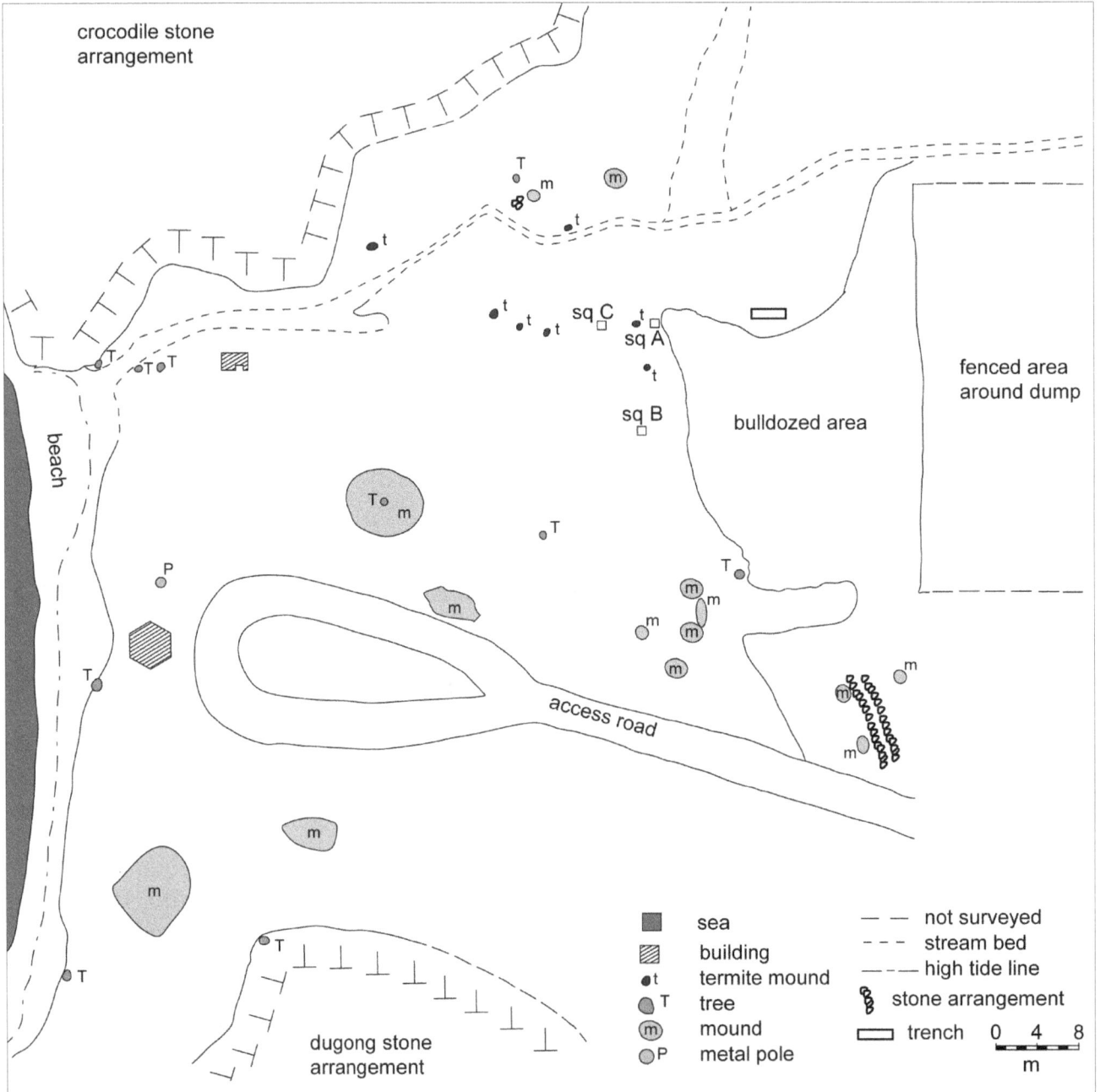

Fig 5.2. (above) Dumpy level map of Dhabangay including excavation squares from 2006 (A) and 2011 (B and C) fieldwork.

Fig 5.3. Aerial photograph of Dhabangay (courtesy of Ian McNiven).

increasingly loose/ friable with depth. At the base of SU 2 was a "pit feature" (SU 3) which contained extremely fine, brownish yellow (10YR 6/6) silty soil and a large quantity of burnt fishbone (Fig. 5.6). The pH levels were similar to surrounding deposits (6.66-6.78).

A mixed zone (SU 4) underlies SU 2 and surrounds the "pit feature" (SU 3). This SU continues to a depth of approximately 60 cm (XUs 14 to 24) grading from dark grey (7.5YR 3/1) at the top to brown at the base (7.5YR 5/2). There is no change in the pH levels throughout this graduation (6.01-6.75) and the sediment is patchy, varying from loose, silty soil to more consolidated sandy sediment. Basal SUs 5 and 6 became consistently lighter and sandier (brown to pinkish grey–7.5YR 5/4-6/2) with depth. After XU 28, patches of cemented sand ("cockina") increasingly became a feature of the excavation. This is likely to have been caused by the through flow of calcium carbonate rich water into old shell beds, which crystalizes, cementing clumps of sediment (Professor Jim Peterson pers. comm., 10/2/09).

Disturbance (termite activity) was observed throughout SUs 1 to 5a with soft, darker soil trickling down through tunnels into lower SUs (Figs. 5.5 and 5.6). Tunnels were isolated and excavated separately along with a 3 cm-wide buffer. SUs 5b and 6 contained no evidence of post depositional movement with sediment observed to be cemented into a calcite conglomerate. Intact lenses of charcoal (XU 36), stone (XU 39) and pumice (XU 41) were recorded in SUs 5b and 6.

Radiocarbon dates and chronology

Eight *in situ* charcoal samples and one fragment of burnt large vertebrate bone were selected to provide a chronology for stratigraphic changes and to test the extent of site disturbance (Table 5.2). AMS dating was undertaken at The University of Waikato and Australian Institute for Nuclear Science and Engineering. Methodologies for Waikato have been reported in Chapter 3. At ANSTO the charcoal was treated with HCl (2M, 60°C) for 2 hours, NaOH (3 %, 60°C) for 2 hours and HCl (2M, 60°C) for 2 hours. Samples were washed thoroughly with Milli-Q water and dried before combustion and conversion of the resulting carbon dioxide to graphite for AMS analysis. Calibration of radiocarbon dates was completed using OxCal 4.1 (Bronk Ramsey 2009) with Southern Hemisphere dataset (ShCal04) (McCormac *et al.* 2004) applied to charcoal dates and marine calibration dataset (Marine09) for the marine bone date (Reimer *et al.* 2009). The calibrated age for the marine bone was corrected for a local marine reservoir effect, using data obtained from the 14CHRONO Marine Reservoir Correction Database (Reimer and Reimer 2001). A weighted mean average $\Delta R = 50\pm45$ was obtained from three separate ΔR values determined for the Torres Strait (Gillespie and Temple 1977).

Fig 5.4. Field team around Square A (Left to right, Ben Watson, Maitui Whap, Cameo Daley, Thomas Whap).

Two settlement periods can be observed based on quantitative and qualitative shifts in cultural materials (Table 5.2). Phase 1 is represented by five AMS dates which bracket SUs 5b and 6 between 7239 and 4901 cal. BP (at 2σ) accumulating at a rate of 3.54 g / year. These dates were associated with highly consolidated sand and in the case of OXM309 a lens of charcoal. Samples of turtle and fish bone were submitted to Waikato for dating, to ascertain whether or not faunal remains were intrusive. A fragment of calcined large vertebrate bone (probable turtle) was chosen by Waikato for AMS dating. This confirms the *in situ* provenance of large vertebrate bone in SU 6. No chronological inversions occur in the AMS dates from SUs 5b and 6.

A late-Holocene settlement phase (XUs 1-34, 313-0 cal. BP) was marked by a significant increase in cultural materials. A single radiocarbon age from XU 9 (WK-24928) supports deposition within the past 150 years. This radiocarbon date overlaps with calibrated ages of three samples (50 cm below the aforesaid calibration) suggesting either rapid, recent sedimentation rates (41.32 g/ year) or significant bioturbation events. If the former is correct then, midden activity (shellfish, fish and small and large vertebrate bone) may postdate European activity at the site. Considering the lack of European materials below XU 9 (with the exception of a single glass flake in XU 18a) it is expected that the majority of midden materials were deposited over 140 years ago, however termite disturbance and slight inversions in radiocarbon dated samples means that taphonomic factors could not be eliminated.

Cultural materials

The Dhabangay excavation contained a wide variety of cultural materials. Flaked stone artefacts dominate the assemblage (n=16,670) with five pieces of ground stone and ochre also recorded. Charcoal (164.5 g) and European materials (metal, glass, clay pipe and ceramics) were prominent alongside large vertebrate bone (37.6 kg) and

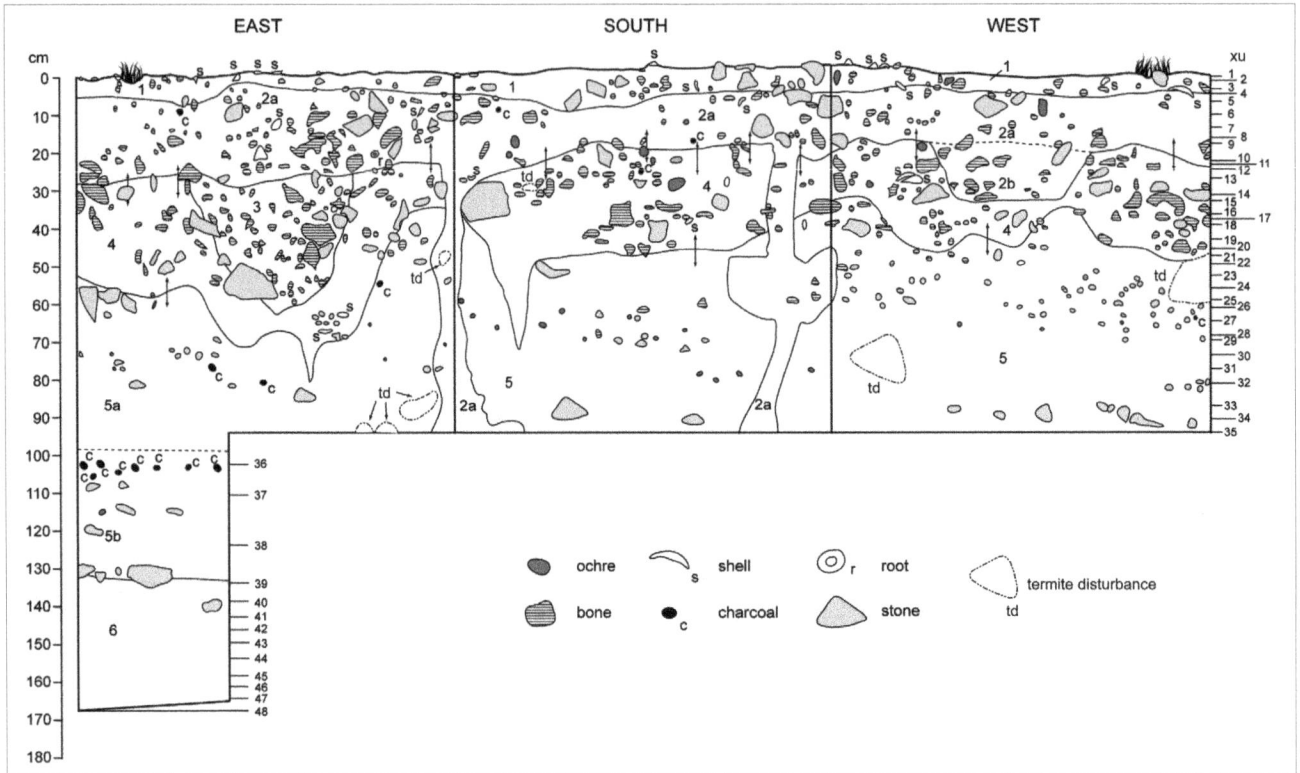

Fig 5.5. Stratigraphic drawing, Square A.

Fig 5.6. East wall of Square A including SU 3 feature.

SU	XU	Sediment description
1	1-3	Consolidated, organic sediment. Black (7.5YR, 2.5/1) and mildly alkaline (pH, 6.33-7.0). Very little cultural material observed in this SU.
2	4-12	Considerably less consolidated, friable sediment. Mainly granular coarse-grained sand (90%) with areas of fine-grained silt (often associated with ant disturbance). Colouration remains very dark grey throughout (7.5YR, 3/1) and sediment is alkaline (pH = 6.06-6.61). Considerable areas of ant disturbance.
3	13-24	Similar to SU 2 but becoming more consolidated and mottled. Mix zone between SUs 2, 5 and adjoining SU 4. Sediment remains alkaline (pH, 8.01-8.25) and is slightly lighter in colour (very dark grey to brown (7.5YR, 3/1-4/2). There was extensive termite activity and a large quantity of cultural material in this SU.
4	11-28	Extremely loose, friable silty sediment. Very dark grey to brown (7.5YR, 3/1 to 4/4) and extremely uniform in pH (6.66 – 6.78). Large quantities of fish bone.
5	25-39	Brown, sandy sediment becoming increasingly consolidated and lighter (brown) with depth (7.5YR, 4/2 – 4/4). Extensive termite activity throughout SU and lenses of pumice/ natural beach shell with very little cultural material.
6	40-48	Highly consolidated cemented sand. Colouration is brown to light brown (7.5YR, 5/2 – 6/2).

Table 5.1. Sediment description, Square A.

Laboratory Code	Excavation Unit (XU)	Depth Below Surface (cm)	Sample Type	Sample Weight (g)	δC13 (‰)	C14 Age (BP)	Calibrated Age (calBP, 1σ)	Calibrated Age (calBP, 2σ)
WK24928	9	16-18	Burnt seed	0.43	-23.4±0.2	197±30	282-253 (18.6%) 226-165 (38.3%) 157-143 (8.9%) 80-75 (2.4%)	295-136 (71.3%) 117-59 (14.7%) 29-0 (9.4%)
WK24929	19A	40-43	Charcoal	0.23	-25±0.2	247±30	301-279 (29.0%) 205-195 (11.2%) 187-180 (7.0%) 170-154 (20.9%)	313-265 (35.3%) 222-147 (60.1%)
WK25437	25A	56-59	Charcoal	0.2	-25.4±0.2	142±30	253-226 (12.9%) 142-131 (5.2%) 125-80 (20.6%) 75-53 (10.2%) 45-2 (19.4%)	267-220 (21.1%) 148-0 (74.3%)
OZM308	30	70-73	Charcoal	0.2	-24.9±0.1	175±40	276-238 (16.8%) 233-212 (8.9%) 152-137 (6.6%) 116-59 (23.3%) 28-0 (12.6%)	281-167 (40.0%) 155-0 (55.4%)
WK25438	35	90-93	Charcoal	0.46	-25.4±0.2	4510±30	5274-5182 (33.4%) 5172-5169 (0.7%) 5122-5110 (3.9%) 5067-5031 (13.5%) 5018-4975 (16.6%)	5288-5155 (41.7%) 5145-4959 (50.8%) 4928-4909 (1.8%) 4901-4888 (1.2%)
OZM309	36	102	Charcoal	0.3	NDA	5530±100	6401-6182 (67.2%) 6137-3132 (1.0%)	6468-5996 (95.4%)
OZM310	39	124-131	Charcoal	0.3	-23.6±0.3	5510±45	6299-6208 (68.2%)	6396-6367 (2.8%) 6351-6178 (89.6%) 6148-6120 (2.7%) 6037-6033 (0.3%)
WK28931	46	162-164	Burnt bone	8.0	-9.8±0.2	6005±30	6416-6299 (68.2%)	6492-6262 (95.4%)
OZM311	48	166-169	Charcoal	0.2	NDA	6160±80	7156-7094 (15.9%) 7087-7076 (2.4%) 7071-7043 (6.5%) 7030-6886 (43.4%)	7239-7218 (1.2%) 7176-6775 (93.2%) 6765-6750 (1.0%)

Table 5.2. AMS radiocarbon dates, Square A. NDA = no data available. Calibrated using OxCAl 4.1 (Bronk Ramsay, 2009).

dugong bone (5.2 kg). Small vertebrates (183.4 g), fish (156.3 g), shark (19.3 g), ray (0.7 g), turtle (40.9 g) and shellfish (308.5 g) were also recovered.

Marine vertebrate bone
Of the 43.1 kg of marine vertebrate bone excavated, 85 % was large vertebrate (36.6 kg) and 12 % dugong (5.2 kg). The majority of large vertebrate bone and all dugong bone were excavated from XUs 1-25 (Fig. 5.7). A conservative MNI estimate of three dugongs was made based on ear-bones excavated from XUs 4, 6 and 9. No identifiable dugong bone was recorded below XU 25, corresponding with the stratigraphic transition from SUs 4 to 5. Significant quantities of dugong bone (7.5 kg) were recovered from the "pit feature", including one ear-bone (raising the total MNI count to four dugongs).

Excluding SU 3 ("pit feature"), the majority of dugong elements (by weight) are ribs (58 %), vertebrae (17 %) and humeri (11 %). Minor quantities of skull fragments (9 %) and scapula (3 %) were recorded (Table 5.3). There are similar proportions of ribs, vertebrae and scapula in the "pit feature" (58 %, 18 %, 3 % respectively); however, skull fragments occur in significantly higher quantities (19 %). While most elements were distributed evenly through this "pit feature", skull fragments, tusks and scapula were restricted to the upper XUs.

Identification of turtle was based on characteristic pitting and linear groves on the surface of osteoderm (carapace/ plastron) plates. Four fragments of osteoderm were excavated from XUs 5 and 19 (6.1 g). A further 34.8 g of turtle bone was dispersed through the SU 3 "pit feature". Recent examination of large vertebrate fragments below XU 30 suggests, "everything with enough morphology to be at all diagnostic is turtle" (Ken Aplin pers. comm., July 2014). DNA tests of the same samples suggested "potential turtle", although conclusions could be affected by sampling contamination.

Bone from small vertebrates and fish (including sharks and rays) made up less than 1% of the total assemblage of marine vertebrates. Not taking into account the "pit feature" a total of 106.8 g of fish bone was excavated as well as 85.0 g of unidentified small vertebrate bone. Fifty eight percent of fish bone came from the upper nine XUs and 96 % from the upper 25 XUs. A similar trend exists for small vertebrate bone (54 % and 95 % respectively) indicating that fish bone makes up a large component of this category. There was also 24.6 g of shark (both reef and tiger shark were observed) and 0.7 g of ray bone. Bone from tiger, reef sharks, and rays were restricted to the upper six XUs, while unidentified shark was recorded down to XU 16 and unidentified shark/ray down to XU 28. Large amounts of fish bone (49.5 g) were excavated from the "pit feature" along with 98.4 g of small vertebrate bone and 1.6 g of shark/ray bone. This small feature contained 32 % of the total fish bone and 86 % of the total small vertebrate bone for Square A. It further contained small quantities

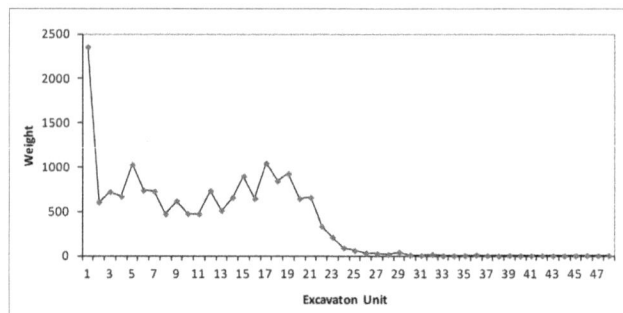

Fig 5.7. **Vertical changes in large vertebrate and dugong bone, Square A (grams per 10 l deposit).**

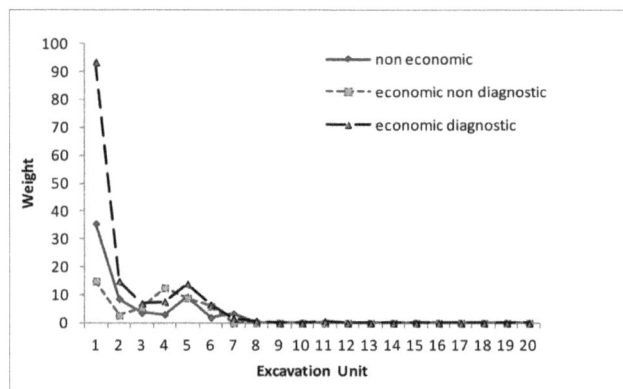

Fig 5.8. **Vertical changes in marine shell, Square A (grams per 10 l deposit).**

of unidentified shark/ray vertebrae. No identifiable shark bone (e.g., Tiger or Reef) was observed. The majority of bone had a blue discolouration consistent with burning.

Bird bone was excavated in very small quantities (1.0 g) in the upper 16 XUs of Square A. One other fragment (0.2 g) was identified in the SU 3 "pit feature". The only mammal bone recovered was a single rodent femur from SU 3.

Marine invertebrates
Shellfish over 15 mm long (maximum dimension) that did not show signs of natural kills (i.e., bore holes) were classed as economic (see also Claasen 1998: 111). At Dhabangay, 231.0 g of shells were classified as economic (both MNI diagnostic and non MNI diagnostic pieces), almost all of which (98 %) came from SU 1 and the top of SU 2 (XUs 1-7) (Fig. 5.8). No MNI diagnostic taxa were identified in the "pit feature" (SU 3).

Of the 39 MNI diagnostic shellfish the most common targeted species were *Nerita* sp. (MNI=26), *Anadara antiquita* (MNI=6) and *Melo amphora* (MNI=4) (Table 5.4). This suggests a focus on littoral zones (rocky/ muddy environments) with reef flats (e.g., *Cypraea* sp.) and sandy littoral zones (e.g., a single *Paphies striata* valve in XU 6) targeted occasionally.

Charcoal
The majority of charcoal (78 % of total, 12.6 g per l of deposit) was excavated from XUs 41-48 (Fig. 5.9).

Charcoal was then present in significantly reduced quantities up to the surface. In the "pit feature" a total of 9.6 g of charcoal was recovered (with an average of 0.2 g per litre of deposit). This was slightly greater than the quantities in XUs immediately above the feature (0.1 g per litre of deposit).

Material culture

Quartz (n=15,165) and igneous (n=1,505) stone artefacts dominate this assemblage (Fig. 5.10). There were a further 51 glass flakes/ flaked pieces and five fragments of ground stone and ochre (Fig. 5.11). A significant vertical change occurs in stone artefact discard, from 2,585 in XUs 26-38 (55-167 cm below the surface) to 14,110 in XUs 1-25 (0-54 cm below the surface). Flaked artefacts were present at the base of Square A with an increase after XU 39 (Fig. 5.10). A single ground stone fragment was also excavated in XU 38. The upper deposit contains 95 % of quartz and 93 % of igneous, flaked stone artefacts (including 109 igneous and 887 quartz artefacts excavated from the "pit feature"). All glass artefacts came from the top seven XUs (within 20 cm of the surface) with

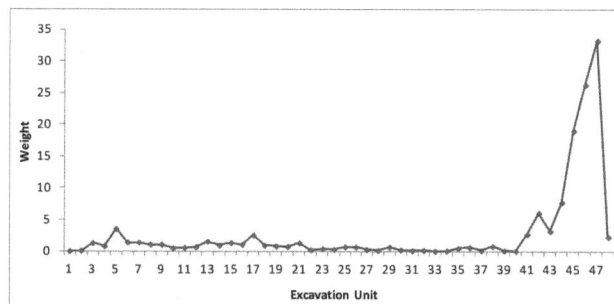

Fig. 5.9. Vertical changes in charcoal, Square A (grams per 10 l deposit).

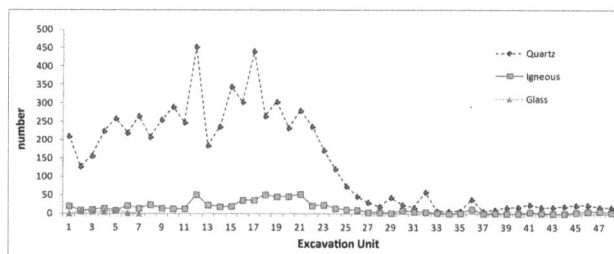

Fig. 5.10. Vertical changes in flaked stone artefacts, Square A (number per 10 l deposit).

XU	Rib	Ear	Vertebrae	Humerus	Scapula	Skull (other)	Condylus	Temporale
1	0	0	0	0	0	0	0	0
2	0	0	0	0	0	0	0	0
3	0	0	0	0	0	0	0	0
4	0	3.7	90.9	0	0	0	0	0
5	106.6	0	0	0	0	0	0	0
6	130.8	3.2	74.7	0	0	88.8	0	0
7	160.2	0	108.5	0	33.9	43.6	0	0
8	19.04	0	39.8	0	0	0	0	0
9	183.8	32.1	31.2	0	0	0	0	0
10A	87.3	0	13.3	80.2	0	0	0	0
11A	167.5	0	0	0	0	0	21.6	0
12A	0	0	12.5	0	14.7	0	6.9	0
13A	141.3	0	189.4	0	0	0	24.7	0
14A	72	0	19.2	66.2	23.4	0	0	21.1
15A	140.4	0	0	0	19.8	0	0	0
16A	254.9	0	0	59.5	0	106.8	0	0
17A	122.01	0	14.2	0	0	0	0	0
18A	233.4	0	0	56.2	0	0	0	0
19A	174.2	0	15.8	119.7	0	0	0	0
20A	0	0	0	28.8	0	0	0	0
21A	0	0	0	0	0	0	0	0
22A	0	0	0	0	0	0	0	0
23A	55.1	0	0	0	0	0	0	0

Table 5.3. Vertical distribution of dugong bone elements (grams), Square A.

	Reading 9	Mode Soil	LiveTime 134.7	Sample kok2	Type standard	Analysis LEAP	Specimen arc
K (LEAP)	K +/- (LEAP)	Mn	Mn +/-	Ti (LEAP)	Ti +/- (LEAP)	Zr	Zr +/-
32934	566	18009	211	3721	124	552	6
Cu	Cu +/-	Sr	Sr +/-	Pb	Pb +/-	Zn	Zn +/-
15041	137	507	6	127	5	58	11
Ca (LEAP)	Ca +/- (LEAP)	Fe (LEAP)	Fe +/- (LEAP)	Mo	Mo +/-	Rb	Rb +/-
163522	2138	15036	165	34	4	75	3

Table 5.4. XRD analysis of glass artefact, Square A by Prof. Shepherd (17th February 2009).

Taxon	Tidal zone	Substrate	MNI	
			SU 1	SU 2
Gastropods				
Nerita spp.	Littoral	rocky	5	21
Cyprae sp.	littoral + sublittoral	coral reefs	0	1
Melo sp.	littoral + sublittoral	sand/ mud	1	3
Bivalves				
Chama sp.	littoral + sublittoral	rocky/ coral reefs	1	0
Paphies striata	Littoral	Sand	0	1
Anadara antiquita	Littoral	sand/ mud	1	5

Table 5.5. Shellfish (MNI), Square A.

the exception of a single bipolar glass flake in XU 17 at a depth of 38 cm. Prof. Peter Sheppard at Auckland University provided XRD analysis for this bipolar artefact. This revealed uncharacteristically high levels of copper (see Table 5.5), suggesting that it may have belonged to an early (non-European) glass vessel. The high levels of copper are likely to have poisoned the contents suggesting this was not used as a serving or storage vessel. After XU 26 there was a significant reduction in the mean weight of lithics, which may indicate in part the movement of smaller materials into SU 5 deposits. Between XUs 41 and 44 the mean weight increased for both quartz and igneous artefacts with many examples of the latter being substantially larger than those recorded in SUs 1-4 (Figs. 5.12 and 5.13).

European materials included glass, metal, lead-shot, ceramics, clay pipe and four beads. These were restricted to the upper nine XUs with the main concentration between XUs 1 and 7. Two beads were made from glass

Fig 5.11. Ground ochre and stone artefacts from Square A (XU 1A; 18D; 38A from right to left and top to bottom).

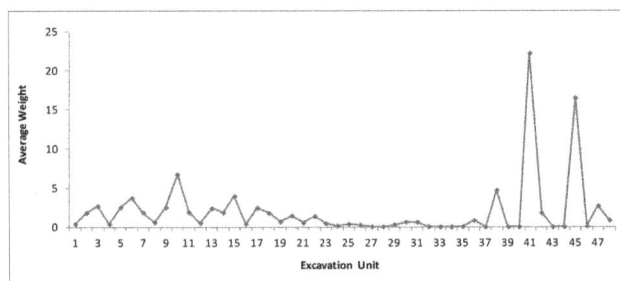

Fig 5.12. Vertical changes in mean weight of flaked igneous artefacts, Square A.

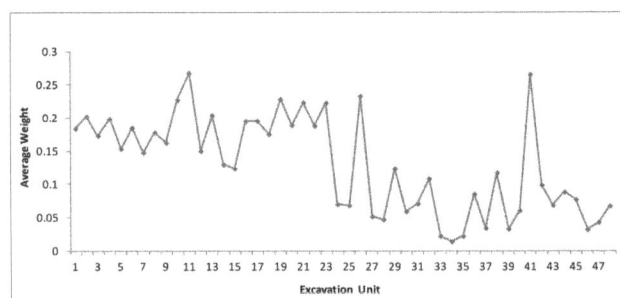

Fig 5.13. Vertical changes in mean weight of flaked quartz artefacts, Square A.

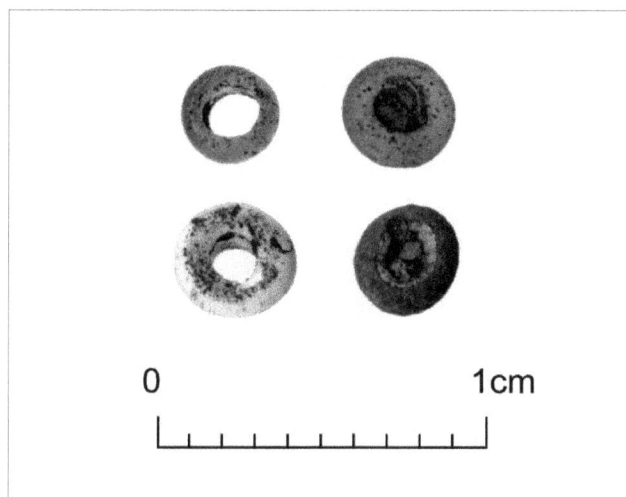

Fig 5.14. Beads from Square A (XU 2 and 5, left to right).

with another two made out of material not yet conclusively identified. The beads were recovered from XUs 2 and 5 (Fig. 5.14). Both ceramic fragments belong to a white ware, were under-glazed and probably manufactured in the UK during the 19th or early 20th century (Ash *et al*. 2008: 476). The larger of the two fragments (XU 3) belongs to an unidentified hollow vessel (probably a cup or bowl) and was decorated with a transfer print (unidentified blue). The motif appears to be a sailing frigate. A second fragment (XU 6) belongs to a plate, also under-glazed with a transfer print.

5.3   Square B

Square B (1 m x 1 m) was located 13.5 m north of Square A, situated deep in the embayment (Fig. 5.2). Excavation methodologies were consistent with Square A with the exception that large sediment samples were collected for sediment size and pollen analyses and that wet sieving occurred on the island (using a fresh water tank), rather than in the Monash laboratory. Excavation units averaged 3.1 cm, with the square discontinued after 105 cm below surface, before culturally sterile deposits were reached. This was due to further termite disturbance, time constraints and the poor preservation of cultural materials. Analysis of Square B remains incomplete and so results should be viewed as preliminary.

Stratigraphy

Five stratigraphic units were observed, with minimal variation in sediment colour and texture (Fig. 5.15). With the exception of a fine layer of dark, organic top-soil, compacted clay continued to the excavation base, grading from fine-grained, patchy clay (SUs 3 and 2) to clay and gravel (SU 4). PH results demonstrate that sediment was mildly acidic (4.14-5.46). There was no visible trend in pH with depth. Compacted sediment and lenses of sandstone

gravel, granite rocks and charcoal suggests stratigraphic integrity. Localised disturbance was observed in SU 2, with sediment from a termite burrow (SU 2b) excavated separately and discarded.

Radiocarbon dates and chronology

Four AMS samples were sent to ANSTO and Waikato Dating laboratories using methods previously described (Table 5.6). Results suggest three phases of human activity. Phase 1 (base of SU 4; prior to 3398 cal. BP) was associated with charcoal and (less securely) lithics; Phase 2 (SU 4-SU 3; 3398-1815 cal. BP) was marked by reduction in cultural materials and Phase 3 (SU 2-1; 1815 cal. BP-PEC) contained the bulk of cultural materials, including 99 % of large vertebrate bone and 97 % of fish bone. A major peak in large and small vertebrate bone occurs above XU 4 (associated with European materials) suggesting the majority of the cultural material postdates 200 years ago.

Cultural materials

Preliminary analysis suggests large marine vertebrate bone (4.49 kg) and flaked stone artefacts (2.1 kg) dominate the assemblage. Small quantities of dugong bone (86.3 g), fish (59.6 g), non-economic shellfish (18 g) and European materials (0.4 g) were recorded. Detailed analysis of stone artefacts has not been completed for Square B. Preliminary results suggest the assemblage consists entirely of flaked quartz and igneous artefacts, with no grinding stones or anvils excavated. By weight, artefacts cluster between XU 9-2 (1.785 kg; 85 % of total by weight; 1815 cal. BP-PEC) and XU 25-XU 23 (130 g; 7 %; 3211 cal. BP +; Fig. 5.16). Whether this is a genuine pattern or reflects the rudimentary nature of the current analysis remains uncertain.

Marine vertebrate bone
The faunal assemblage contains large vertebrate (4573.81 g) including dugong and turtle, and smaller quantities (59.56 g) of fish bone. No terrestrial vertebrate bones were recovered from Square B. Fish and dugong bone were compressed within the upper 20 cm (XUs 5-1) of deposit (PEC) in Square B (Figs. 5.17 and 5.18). Fish bone was prominent above XU 11 (1815-PEC), continuing in small quantities to the base of excavation. Bone preservation is best between XUs 4-1, with poor preservation, and increased burning observed below this.

Charcoal
Small quantities of charcoal (29.5 g) were excavated from Square B. Two peaks occur, the first between XUs 3-1 (11. 51 g; PEC) and a second between XUs 25-23 (9.21 g; 5907-3211 cal. BP) at which stage large fragments occur (Fig. 5.19). Charcoal was observed in reduced quantities in SUs 3 and 2.

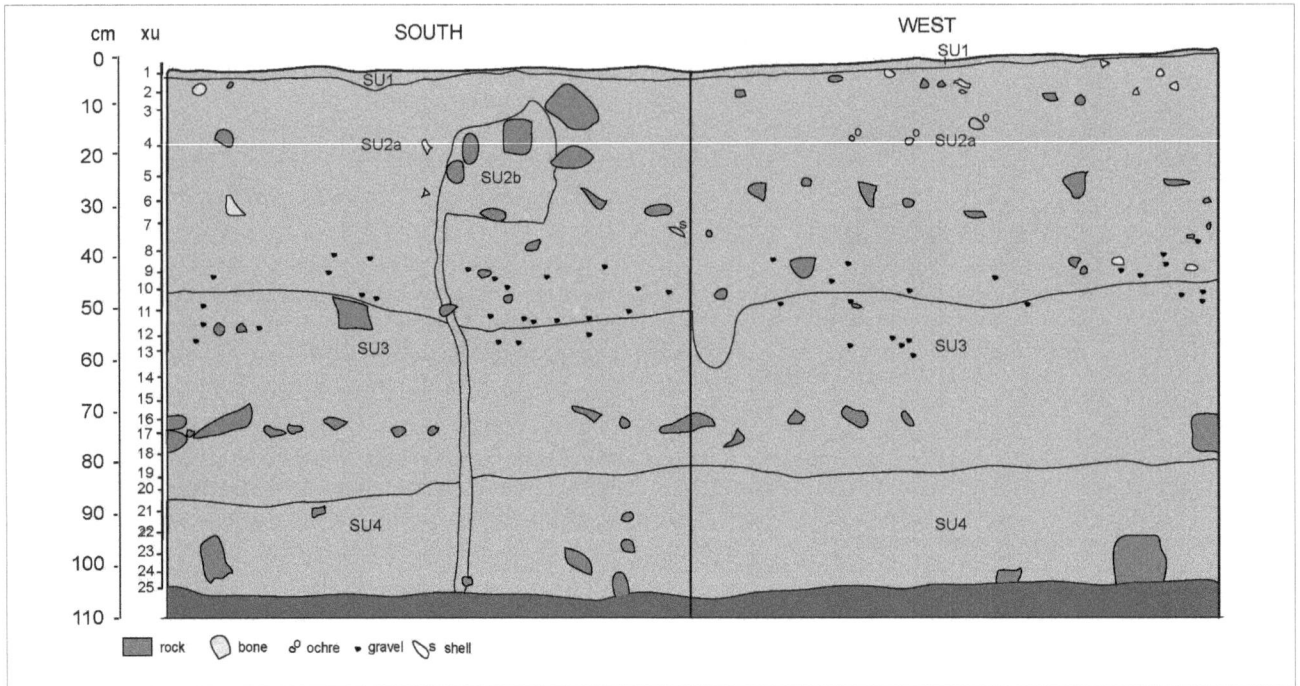

Fig 5.15. Stratigraphic drawing, Square B.

Lab Code	XU	Depth below surface (cm)	Sample/ weight (g)	δ13 (‰)	C14 Age BP	Calibrated Age BP 68.3%	Calibrated Age BP 95.4%
OZP159	4	13-17	Charcoal/ 0.1	-26.2+/-0.2	95 +/- 25	238-232 (4.2%)	252-227 (9.8%)
						137-115 (23.9%)	142-82 (34.6%)
						60-27 (40.0%)	74-5 (50.9%)
WK32909	12	51-55	Charcoal/ 0.2	-23.3+/-0.2	1833 +/- 25	1736-1687 (35.0%)	1815-1611 (95.4%)
						1674-1621 (33.2%)	
OZP161	20	83-85	Charcoal/ 0.6	-28.2 +/- 0.3	3150 +/- 35	3367-3317 (38.1%)	3398-3211 (95.4%)
						3308-3264 (30.1%)	
WK32904	25	101-103	Charcoal/ 0.1	-24.6+/-0.2	5115 +/- 25	5891-5842 (30.6%)	5907-5728 (95.4%)
						5832-5804 (17.7%)	
						5794-5783 (6.2%)	
						5770-5748 (13.6%)	

Table 5.6. AMS radiocarbon dates from Square B.

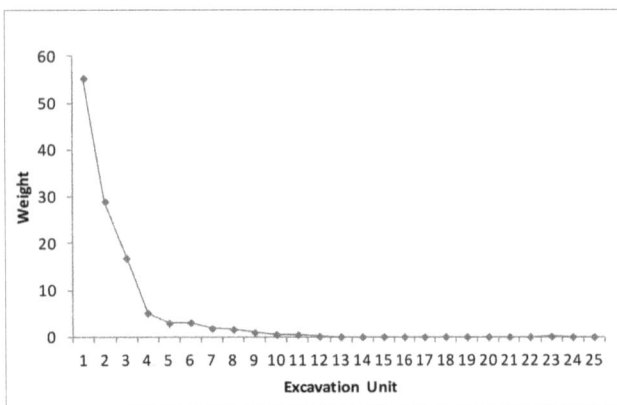

Fig 5.16. Vertical changes in large vertebrate, Square B (grams per 10 l deposit).

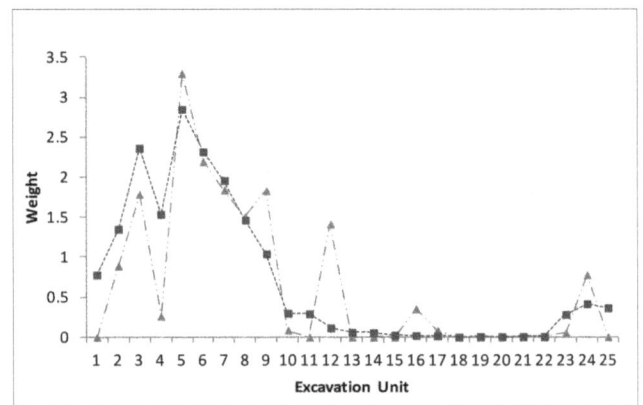

Fig 5.17. Vertical changes in quartz (diamond markers) and igneous (square markers) lithics, Square B (grams per 1 litre deposits).

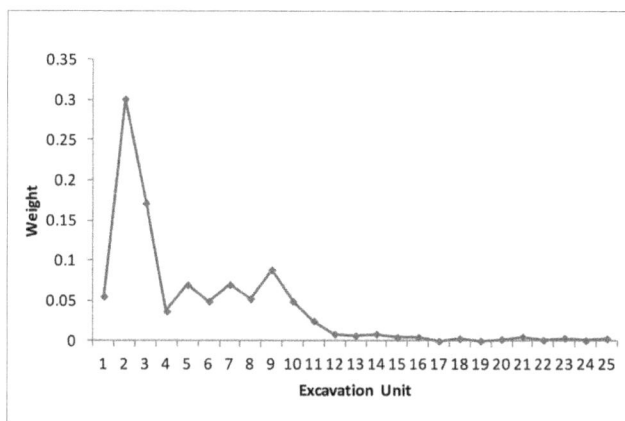

Fig 5.18. Vertical changes in fish bone, Square B (grams per 10 l deposit).

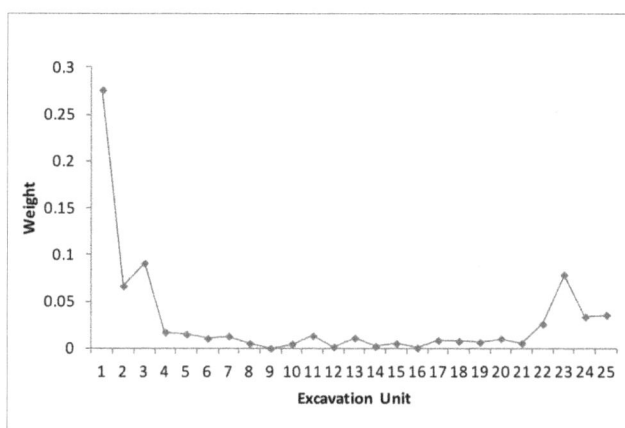

Fig 5.19. Vertical changes in charcoal, Square B (grams per 1 l deposit).

Cultural materials

Analysis of lithics from Square B has not been completed and so results are not reported. Preliminary observations suggest presence of igneous and quartz stone artefacts throughout excavated deposits. European materials were restricted to the upper three XUs. Three fragments of glass and four seed beads were recorded. The glass fragments (MNV = 1) were identified as body sherds from wine or beer bottles of uncertain provenance (Wright and Ricardi In press). The *Cornaline d'Aleppo* "white heart" trade beads were provisionally dated to 1830-1860 (Jamey Allen pers. comm., 24 April 2012).

5.4   Square C

The observed disturbance and paucity of cultural materials from Square B meant that this was discontinued and a third excvation completed. Square C was located 5 m west of Square A and 18 m from current high tide line. It was excavated to a depth of 197 cmbs including 15 cm of culturally sterile, basal deposit. Excavation units (XUs) were guided by natural changes in stratigraphy and averaged 3.4 cm in depth, not including the preliminary

sweep of top-soil (XU 1). All sediment was wet-sieved through a 2.1 mm mesh, with samples collected for sediment size and pollen analyses from excavation units and a column sample in the west wall (Fig. 5.20).

Stratigraphy

Two major and four minor stratigraphic units (SUs) were identified, with a change from very dark grey, humic soil (Munsell = 7.5YR 3/1) to brown-pinkish grey (Munsell = 7.5YR 5/4 to 7.5YR 6/2), calcareous sand (Fig. 5.20). A gradation was observed between mottled, silty sand (SU 3-4) to coarse-grained, cemented, white-yellow sand (SU 5-6). A pH test showed that sediments were mildly acidic (4.14-5.13), with increased acidity in the basal cemented sand.

Clear stratigraphic boundaries and intact lenses of pumice, ochre, stone and bone suggest overall stratigraphic integrity. In contrast to Square A, termite activity was not observed, with disturbance restricted to a single, small pit feature at the interface between SU 2 and SU 3. This SU 2b feature was excavated separately along with a 3 cm-wide buffer (Fig. 5.20). A small, glass flake was excavated from XU 20. We suggest this specimen fell from the wall during excavation and does not indicate substantial vertical movement of material within the deposit. This is supported by the absence of further European materials in mid-Holocene layers, the sequential radiocarbon dates and horizontal orientation of many bones and stones.

Radiocarbon dates and chronology

Thirteen *in situ* samples of wood charcoal and hardwood were submitted to The University of Waikato and Australian Institute for Nuclear Science and Engineering laboratories for radiocarbon (AMS) dating. Six samples (between 170-150 cmbs) could not be dated as the material did not survive treatment, most likely a result of chemical weathering associated with ground-water infiltration (Jim Peterson pers. comm., 2006; Fiona Petchey pers. comm., November 2010).

Three phases of settlement were observed (Table 5.7). Phase 1 (SUs 6-4; 6938-3349 cal. BP at two σ) was characterised by large quantities of charcoal and moderate quantities of lithics and faunal remains. Phase 2 (SU 3; 3349-1684 cal. BP) was represented by sparse cultural remains, albeit sufficient to indicate ongoing human presence. Phase 3 (SUs 2-1; 1684 cal. BP-0) was characterised by a marked increase in all cultural materials. The upper part of Phase 3 contained European materials (nails, ceramic, glass, beads, clay pipe), which clustered between XU 2-6 but were recovered in low numbers down to XU 9, probably reflecting downward movement of heavier fragments of metal (the main component of XU 9) during PEC.

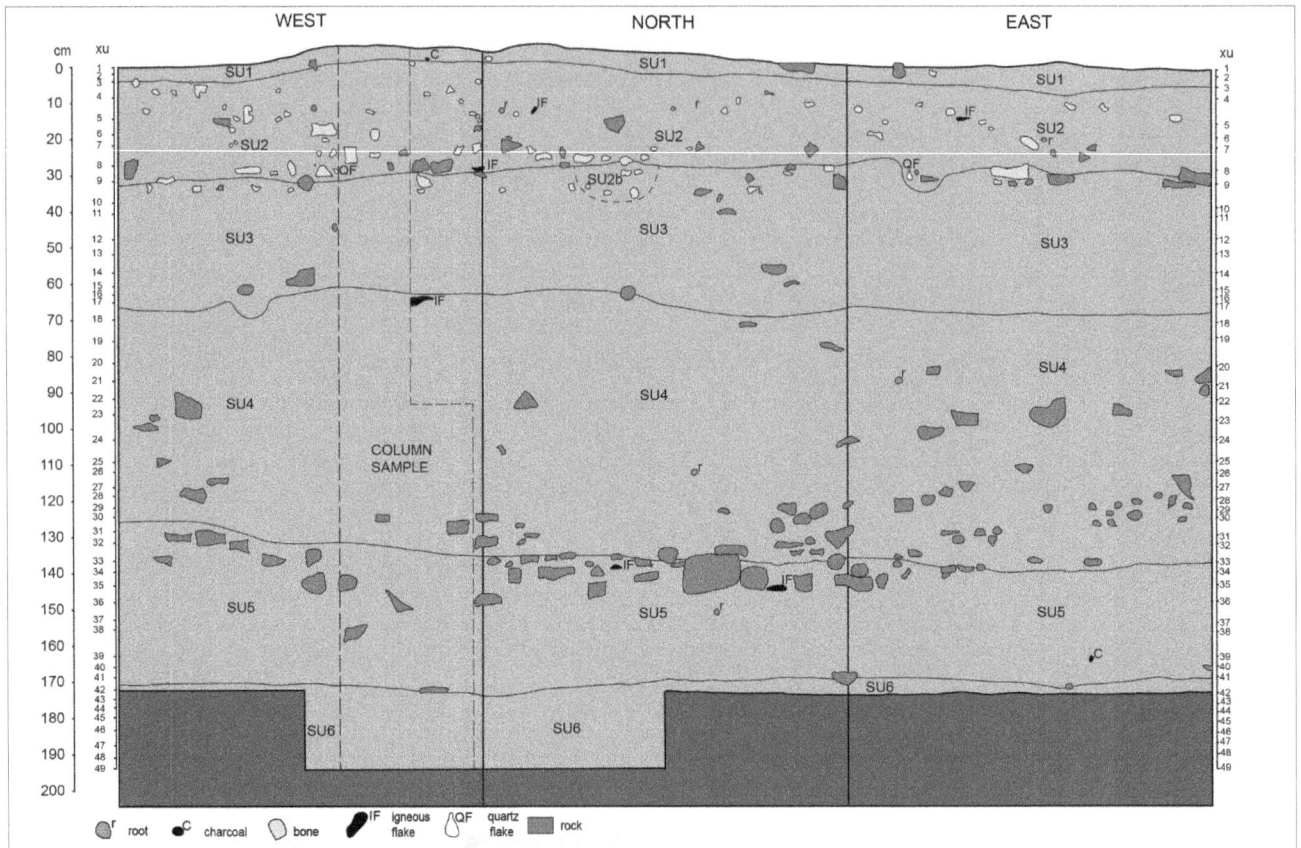

Fig 5.20. **Stratigraphic drawing, Square C.**

Lab Code	XU	Depth below surface (cm)	Sample/ weight (g)	δ13 (‰)	C14 Age BP	Calibrated Age BP 68.3%	Calibrated Age BP 95.4%
OZP159	3	2-4	Charcoal/ 0.16	-25.8 +/- 0.1	240 +/- 25	296-279 (23.1%)	306-271 (29.9%)
						205-195 (12.9%)	219-148 (65.5%)
						187-180 (8.1%)	
						171-154 (24.1%)	
WK32909	10	27-31	Charcoal/ 0.21	-26.9 +/- 0.1	1695 +/- 30	1600-1583(7.7%)	1684-1678 (0.8%)
						1570-1515 (49.5%)	1615-1415 (94.6%)
						1459-1443 (7.6%)	
						1431-1423 (3.4%)	
OZP161	18	67-70	Charcoal/ 0.18	-24.5 +/- 0.1	3250 +/- 30	3446-3383 (68.2%)	3480-3349 (95.4%)
WK32904	23	100-104	Hardwood/ 0.22	-24.9+/-0.2	3924 +/- 32	4406-4367 (17.4%)	4415-4223 (83.7%)
						4357-4323 (16.0%)	4205-4157 (11.7%)
						4317-4311 (2.7%)	
						4304-4240 (32.1%)	
WK32905	29	120-125	Hardwood/ 1.64	-23.3+/-0.2	4454 +/- 33	5037-5007 (15.4%)	5268-5222 (3.1%)
						4980-4875 (52.8%)	5215-5186 (4.2%)
							5120-5112 (0.5%)
							5064-4855 (87.6%)
WK32906	31	130-132	Hardwood/ 0.2	NDA	4359 +/- 34	4958-4832 (11.4%)	5028-5021 (0.7%)
						4883-4832 (56.8%)	4974-4825 (94.7%)
WK32909	41	173-177	Acacia?/ 0.55	-24.6+/-0.2	6052 +/- 29	6889-6786 (68.2%)	6938-6742 (95.4%)

Table 5.7. AMS radiocarbon dates from Square C. NDA = no data available.

Cultural materials

Flaked stone artefacts dominate the assemblage (n = 8522) with two igneous hammer stones and one anvil also recorded. In addition, Square C contained large amounts of dugong bone (11.5 kg) and charcoal (1.4 kg) and smaller quantities of fish bone (109.3 g), turtle (1.07 g), molluscs (13.7 g) and European materials (mainly metal and glass).

Marine vertebrate bone
The faunal assemblage consists of a substantial quantity (11.55 kg) of highly fragmented bone from one or more large marine vertebrates, and smaller quantities of fish bone (109.29 g) and turtle (1.07 g). No terrestrial or volant (e.g., birds, bats) vertebrate remains were recovered from Square C.

The large vertebrate remains from Square C are highly fragmented and only a small proportion can be assigned to anatomical elements and taxa. With the exception of two fragments of what appear to be turtle carapace (XUs 6 and 2) all diagnostic pieces of large vertebrate bone derive from dugongs. We are confident that at least the large majority of the remains can be assigned to this taxon (Wright et al. 2013).

All small vertebrate bone from Square C is derived from fishes, including representatives of at least four families, with Labridae (wrasses) and Scaridae (parrot fishes) dominant throughout the sequence, and Carangidae (jacks) and Lethrinidae (emperors) only sporadically represented. Most are small to medium-sized fish, with the exception of occasional large labrids. The degree of fragmentation of the fish remains precludes meaningful estimation of relative abundances, as the majority of dentigerous elements are fragmented. Shark teeth occur sporadically through the profile. The majority derive from small sharks. A more detailed analysis of the fish remains will appear in a future publication.

Dugong bone was restricted to XUs 19-2 (maximum span = 4223 cal. BP-PEC) with only small quantities (total = 20.53 g) found below XU 13 (Fig. 5.23). By contrast, the vertical distribution of fish bone shows two well-separated peaks, one broadly spread across XUs 29-20 (maximum span = 5268 cal. BP-3349 cal. BP) and a second concentrating between XUs 10-2 (maximum span = 1684-PEC), but continuing to XU 13 (Fig. 5.24). Only small quantities (total = 1.66 g) of bone were recovered in XUs 19-14 and between XUs 29-31.

In Square C, bone from XUs 10-2 (SUs 2-1) appears well preserved and includes a high proportion of unburnt remains. Between XUs 26-11 (SUs 4-3) the unburnt remains are visibly degraded and a higher proportion of the bone is burnt, both good indicators of microbial degradation of the organic components of bone. Below XU 27 (SU 5) virtually all of the remains are calcined. Calcined bone is the product of prolonged burning at very high temperatures (>800°C; Brain 1993) and is normally only produced through cultural activity. Its persistence when all other bone has degraded is due to the complete destruction during firing of organic content, thereby rendering it stable in most environments.

Marine invertebrates
The Square C mollusc assemblage (13.7 g) was highly fragmented, with no MNI diagnostic taxa observed and this meant that no shellfish could be classified as economic. Most shellfish (13.6 g of total) came from the top of SU 2 and SU 1 (i.e., XUs 7-1) with two small fragments located in XU 28 and XU 16. In addition, three crab claws were excavated, one in XU 23 and two in XU 8. The small size of the crabs suggests a non-cultural origin.

Charcoal
Large quantities of charcoal (1.4 kg) were excavated at Dhabangay, the majority of which (1.36 kg) occurred between XUs 41-26 (SUs 6, 5 and base of 4; Fig. 5.25). Charcoal was present in significantly reduced quantities in SUs 3, 2, 1 and in basal XUs, 49-42. In SU 6 (XU 49-37) the weight of some charcoal samples was observed to have increased due to absorption of calcite. Removal of these samples through careful analysis and floatation does not substantially alter results with 1.22 kg excavated between XUs 41-26 (Fig. 5.25). The consistently large size of many charcoal fragments suggests localised rather than landscape burning.

Cultural materials
Crystal and good quality vein quartz dominate the Dhabangay assemblage (94 % of total; n = 8019). In addition there were 506 artefacts (totalling 6 %) made from local igneous rock and 17 glass flakes. With the exception of 2 igneous hammers and one igneous anvil the assemblage consisted of flakes, cores and flaked pieces. Bipolar hammers and anvils were found in XU 6 and XU 30 respectively. Pounding surfaces were deeply pitted suggesting repeated use. Retouched flakes were rare, totalling only 8 out of 8517 flaked artefacts. A large number of cores were identified in the collection: 137 quartz cores and 13 igneous cores. The majority of cores are bipolar (see Wright et al. 2013).

Artefact discard is highest between XU 11-XU 2 (90 % of total), with major peaks in XU 2, XU 7 and XU 9 (41 % of total; Fig. 5.21). Lithic quantities decline steadily below this until a "background" level is reached in XU 16. Less than 6 % of the total artefact assemblage (relative to amount of material excavated) occurs between XUs 41-16, typically between 9 and 30 artefacts per XU. Numbers are particularly low between XU 27-XU 16 with a slight increase between XU 38-XU 28. No lithics were recorded below XU 41.

There is evidence for both consistency and change in the vertical distribution of artefacts. Quartz and igneous lithics continue throughout the assemblage, with quartz flakes

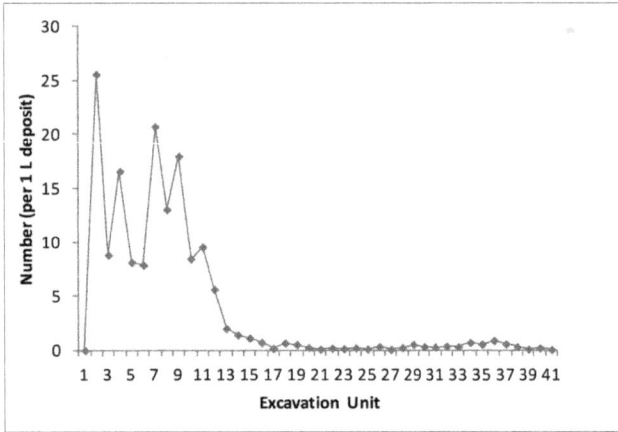

Fig 5.21. Vertical changes in stone artefacts, Square C (number per 1 l deposit). Data labels reduced to 2 decimal places.

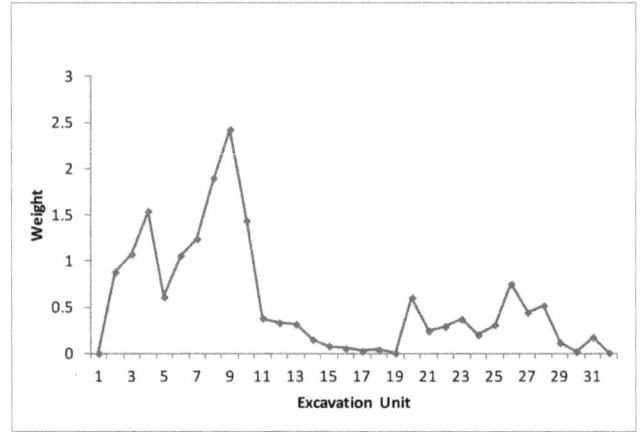

Fig 5.24. Vertical changes in fish bone (diamond) and turtle (square), Square C (grams per 1 l deposit). Data labels reduced to 2 decimal places.

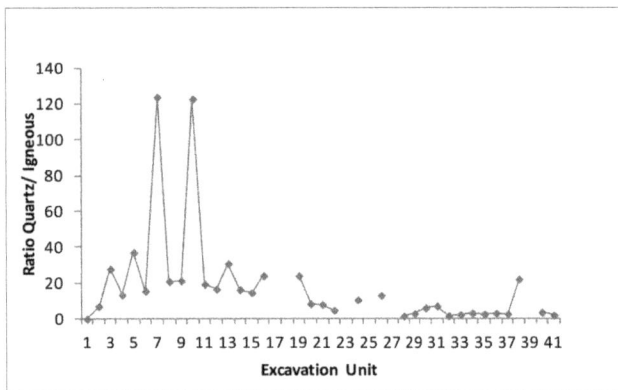

Fig 5.22. Ratio of quartz to igneous artefacts from Square C.

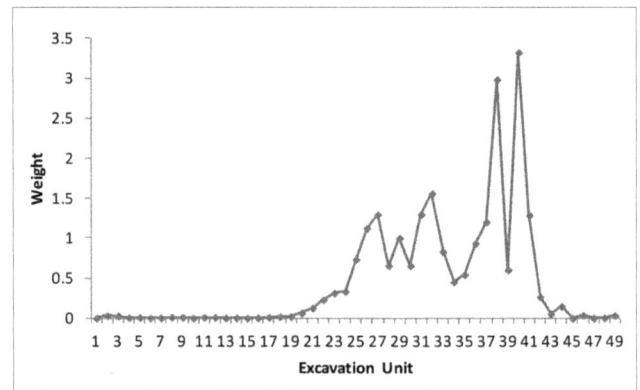

Fig 5.25. Vertical changes in charcoal with (square markers) and without (diamond markers) removal of concretions through floatation, Square C (grams per 1 l deposits). Data labels reduced to 2 decimal places.

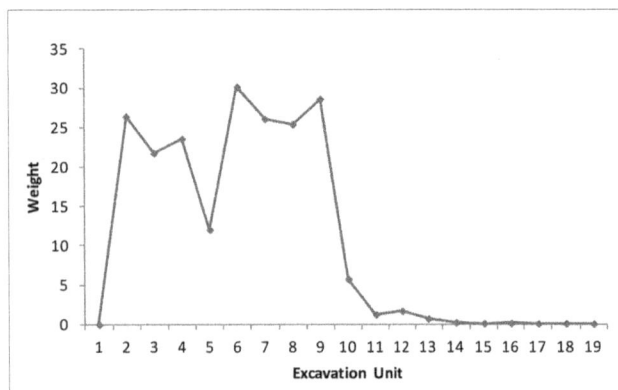

Fig 5.23. Vertical changes in dugong bone, Square C (grams per 1 l deposit). Data labels reduced to 2 decimal places.

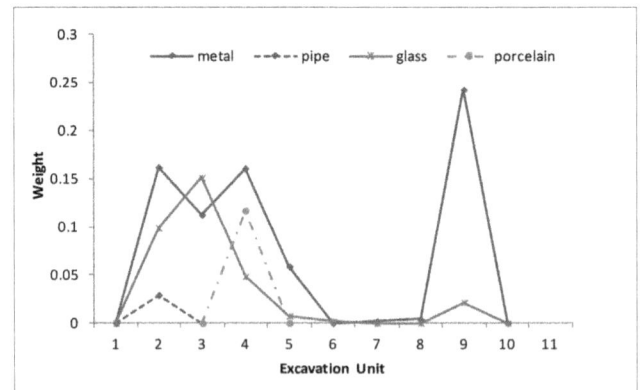

Fig 5.26. Vertical changes in European materials, Square C (grams per 1 l deposit). Metal (diamond marker), clay pipe (square marker), glass (triangle marker), porcelain (circle marker). Data labels reduced to 2 decimal places.

consistently small, highly reduced and lacking cortex while igneous flakes were often larger with cortex present. Quartz flake size increased marginally in the upper layers, although this may reflect the larger sample size in these layers. Analysis indicates consistent use of hand-held

reduction for quartz and igneous artefacts, followed by bipolar reduction as core size diminished. Bipolar techniques continued throughout the sequence with varying levels of reduction. The lowest level with a bipolar core is XU 37. Small numbers of retouched flakes (made through opportunistic flake removal) occurred in upper and lower layers of Square C. Detailed lithic analysis (e.g., materials, size variation and reduction processes) will be reported in a future publication. Raw material abundance shows a distinct chronological trend, expressed in the ratio of Quartz: Igneous (Fig. 5.22). Igneous is relatively common below XU 20 (with the exception of XU 38) and in XU 2, whereas XUs 19-3 have proportionally more quartz to igneous artefacts (Fig. 5.22). A 67 % reduction in the quantity of igneous artefacts occurs between SU 5 and SU 4 while quartz reduced by 23 % in these SUs.

All glass artefacts came from the top 6 XUs (16 within 20 cm of the surface) with the exception of a single, intrusive glass flake at a depth of 80 cmbs (XU 20). This is consistent with other non-artefactual European materials, suggesting the major phase of European activity occurred during the build-up of sediments between XU 6-XU 2.

European materials included fragments of glass, metal, ceramics, clay pipe and beads. Excluding one specimen that we conclude was displaced during excavation (see previous section on lithics), these were restricted to the upper nine XUs with the main concentration between XUs 6-1 (Fig. 5.26). Artefacts below XU 6 were: 2 small pieces of glass and 3 unidentifiable fragments of iron alloy and lead.

Most glass fragments (5 out of 6, MNI = 1) were identified as body sherds from wine or beer bottles (Wright and Ricardi In press). In addition there were two near spherical seed beads (in XU 3), a two-toned German marble (in XU 4), two fragments of unidentified clay pipe (XU 2, XU 4), one piece of glazed white stoneware (XU 4), 2 bird size pellets of lead shot (XU 2, XU 3) and iron alloy and steel nails (XU 2, XU 3).

Clay pipe fragments were consistent with examples recorded during a surface collection that date from mid to late 19th century. Steel patent machine cut nails are likely to post-date 1890 (Burke and Smith 2004: 378) while stoneware was consistent with British ceramics from Mua which dated to from late 19th-early 20th century (Ash and David 2008: 476). One of the two beads was classified as "*Cornaline d'Aleppo*, white heart". This form was devised by the Venetians in about 1825 and appeared in the North American archaeological horizon from ca. 1830 (Jamey Allen pers. comm., April 2012). The Dhabangay bead has been provisionally dated to between 1830-1860 (Jamey Allen pers. comm., 24 April 2012); however, it may have been curated for many years prior to arrival on Mabuyag.

Pumice and ochre

Unworked, red ochre was recovered from all SUs, reaching a depth of XU 36. The majority of ochre clustered between XUs 10-2 (90.5 % of total weight), with a further 8.8 % between XUs 36-27. Pumice was found in all layers, with the greatest density between XUs 10-2 (73.6 % of total weight). A lens of pumice in XU 16 contained 14 % of the total weight (9.1 g).

5.5 Summary

Excavations within the Dhabangay embayment suggest two phases of human activity. An initial phase of sustained settlement occurred between 7239-3349 cal. BP. This involved substantial burning events, the manufacture of large igneous and quartz lithics and varied subsistence practices including predation of turtle, fish (and possibly also dugong). A radiocarbon date from burnt large vertebrate bone (most probably turtle), confirms that marine vertebrates were not intrusive and therefore represent the earliest direct evidence of marine subsistence recorded for Torres Strait. The same integrity was presumably also the case for stone flakes (and a single bipolar, stone hammer), considered too large to have trickled down into the cemented (and apparently undisturbed) sediment in all three excavations. The discovery of a worked/ ground fragment of stone in the lower layers of Square A may also date to this period. Excavations of Square B and C suggest that a major shift in subsistence and technology may have occurred

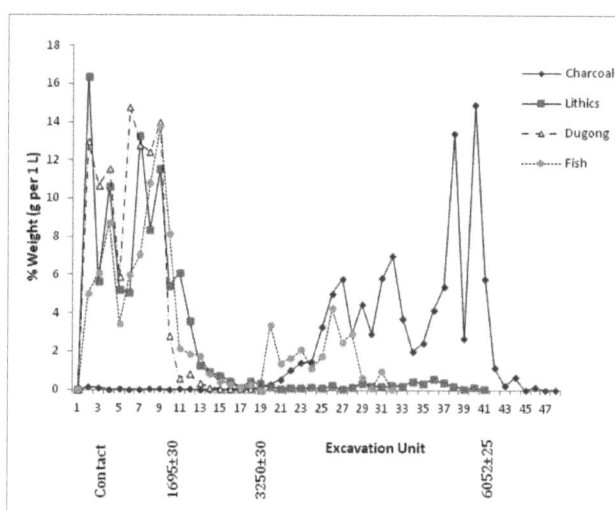

Fig 5.27. Distribution and chronology of cultural material (percentage of total for each) excavated from Square C.

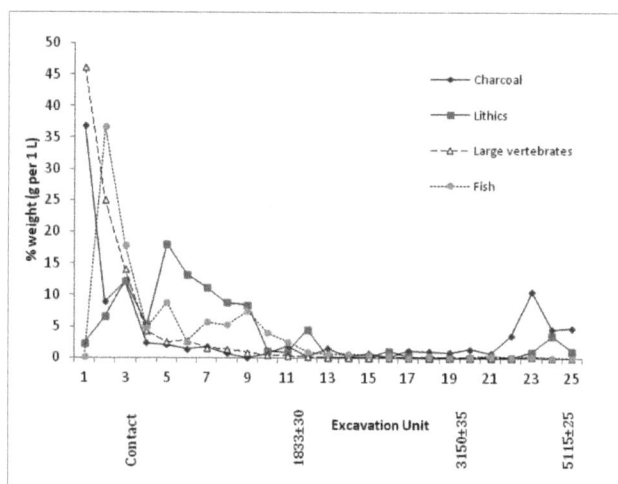

Fig 5.28. Distribution and chronology of cultural material (percentage of total for each) excavated from Square B.

after 4200 years ago. At this stage, people started to exploit dugong in addition to nearshore fishes, and simultaneously showed an increased preference for production of quartz lithics. It has been argued elsewhere (Wright *et al.* 2013) that changes in lithic technologies and subsistence strategies reflect innovations in hunting and/ or butchery by increasingly specialised maritime communities.

After a hiatus in activity between 3349-1815 cal. BP (a period associated with very minimal activity), there is evidence for substantial increase in activity during the late Holocene. Initial results (Square A) suggested this may have occurred after 300 cal. BP, however, more recent excavations suggest onset of human settlement may pre-date this by up to 1500 years. In line with European and Goemulgaw histories, all excavations suggest a significant spike in activity (consistent with a large settlement) immediately prior to or after European arrival on the island (Gill 1876: 202; Moresby 1876: 13). After 1800 cal. BP there is evidence for a substantial increase in marine subsistence with dugong and turtle hunting, fishing and shell fishing prominent at this time. Tiger sharks and rays were also added to the subsistence economy and a pit feature containing large quantities of fish bone dug into the site. Technological shifts include further increase in the ratio of quartz to igneous artefacts and increased use of specialist artefacts (including hammer stones, anvils and worked stone/ ochre) (see Wright *et al.* 2013).

Based on a model of regionalisation and fissioning it is evident that features associated with the Goemulgal (marine specialised activities including varied subsistence, targeted hunting of dugong and ritual activities e.g., bone mounds and totemic stone arrangements) dates to within the past 300-400 years at Dhabangay (see also McNiven and Bedingfield 2008). Totemic stone arrangements may be a particularly recent addition with the stone crocodile attributed to Amarama Bani while the stone dugong on the adjacent headland apparently constructed by Cygnet Repu (the current head of the Goemulgaw *kod*), albeit copying other arrangement seen elsewhere on the island (Edwards and Edwards 1997: 4-5). It is evident, however, that characteristic elements of the Goemulgal (aptitude for fin-fishing, turtle and dugong hunting) were present many thousands of years prior to this.

6

Muyi

Although the original methodology involved excavation of the four principal ancestral villages, the Goemulgal were reluctant to conduct excavations at Maydh. After consultation with the Mabuyag community it was decided to move excavations to Muyi. This village lies on the foreshore between Goemu (to the south), Baw New Village (to the north) and Maydh (to the north west), at the eastern end of the Dhadhakul valley. Muyi is reputed to have been totemically affiliated with the adjoining village of Maydh. European and Indigenous histories identified this as a garden area for Missionaries and Islanders (Dimple Bani, pers. comm., September 2006; anonymous sketcher 1914 cited in Mooke 1972: 17). Muyi may have also been used as a small, seasonal camp, although it is reputed "not to have been as important in the past as the 'villages' of Maid and Goemu to the north and south of it" (Ghaleb 1990: 163; also Young Bani, pers. comm., 1 December 2006; Dimple Bani, pers. comm., September 2006). The southern margins of this site continue to be used as a graveyard for the Goemulgal, while a large dam is located at the western extent of the village. This site was chosen for archaeological survey and excavation, due to its position (adjacent to Maydh, a village that shared the same totem) and to test the interface zone between the LMS settlement, Baw and the large Goemulgaw village, Goemu.

6.1 Surface survey and excavation

Previous surveys in the area overlooking Maydh identified a stone arrangement shaped like a crocodile, and fragments of *bu* (*Syrinx aruanus*) and *akul* (*Polymesoda erosa*) shells, also mound-and-ditch fields in the Dhadhakul valley (Harris and Ghaleb 1987: 32). No archaeological features were observed at Muyi (Harris and Ghaleb 1987: 20; Ghaleb 1990: 163). Surveys in 2005 and 2006 revealed stone piles and walls and field systems in the interior recesses of Maydh (Dhadhakul valley). No cultural materials were observed on the surface or in recent house foundations and drainage cuts (see also the UCL test excavation – Harris *et al*. 1985: 48). It was observed that Maydh had experienced extensive clearance during the expansion of the modern village of Baw. A surface survey conducted by Ian McNiven and surveyor Lynden McGregor in November 2006 revealed 166 surface features at Muyi, covering an area of 0.45 km². The discrepancy between the two surveys may well be explained by the low-lying nature of archaeological features in a landscape that is normally covered in long grass. This had been burnt prior to the 2006 survey.

Mounded middens represent 45 % of all recorded features mapped in 2006 (Fig. 6.1). In keeping with traditional histories (which identified mounding around the base of coconut trees), 16 % of these mounds had central

indentations or surrounded living/ burnt out trees. Other site forms included dugong bone mounds (4 %); stone arrangements (4 %); *Bu* (*Syrinx aruanus*) shells (4 %), and grave posts (5 %). The bulk of these features were situated in the southern portion of Muyi (Fig. 6.1). Surface survey of this area revealed a variety of European artefacts including clay pipes, bottles and ceramics (Ian McNiven pers. comm., 2006).

6.2 Square A

In September 2006, a 1 m x 1 m excavation (Square A) tested an earthen/ dugong bone mound located next to the cemetery road in the centre of the mapped area (Feature 80 in Fig. 6.1). Excavation was located 55 metres away from (and 12 metres above) the current high water mark in an area of abundant midden bone (Fig. 6.2). This low mound was covered by tussock grass, with the surface covered in dugong/ large vertebrate bone, heat-shattered rock and shellfish. Fragments of glass and metal were observed in the immediate vicinity of the mounded midden and a large piece of *Syrinx aruanus*, which rests on the seaward slope of the mound.

Square A was excavated to a depth of 92 cm at which point the area was reduced to 40 cm x 40 cm in the north east corner (Fig. 6.3). This was necessary due to time constraints and the increasingly cemented composition of sediment. The unit continued for a further 77 cm to a maximum depth of 169 cm (36 XUs) before confined space forced discontinuation before culturally sterile deposits were reached. Excavation Units averaged 3.4 cm thick in midden levels becoming slightly deeper (4 cm) in culturally sterile layers with methodology consistent with those already reported for the 2006 field season.

Stratigraphy

Five stratigraphic units (SUs) were observed (not including sub units SU 3a and 3b; Fig. 6.4). The sediment matrix was similar between SU 1 and SU 2, comprising of brown to very dark grey, alkaline, sandy sediment. The main difference between SU 1 and SU 2 was the higher density of large vertebrate bone and rock in SU 1 (Fig. 6.4, Table 6.1). A significant shift occurred in SU 3, with sediment transitioning into gray beach sand, with a corresponding increase in alkalinity and the presence of calcite conglomerate (cockina). At the same time there is a significant drop in all cultural materials and an increase in land snails and pumice. This is indicative of a shift from dynamic beach flat to a more stable terrestrial environment, prior to the onset of mounding activity.

Descending streams of humic soil into SUs 4 and 5 suggest that there has been a certain amount of post-depositional disturbance. Fragments of decayed wood were found in these tracks suggesting root activity. In all cases these features were isolated and excavated as separate SUs/ XUs.

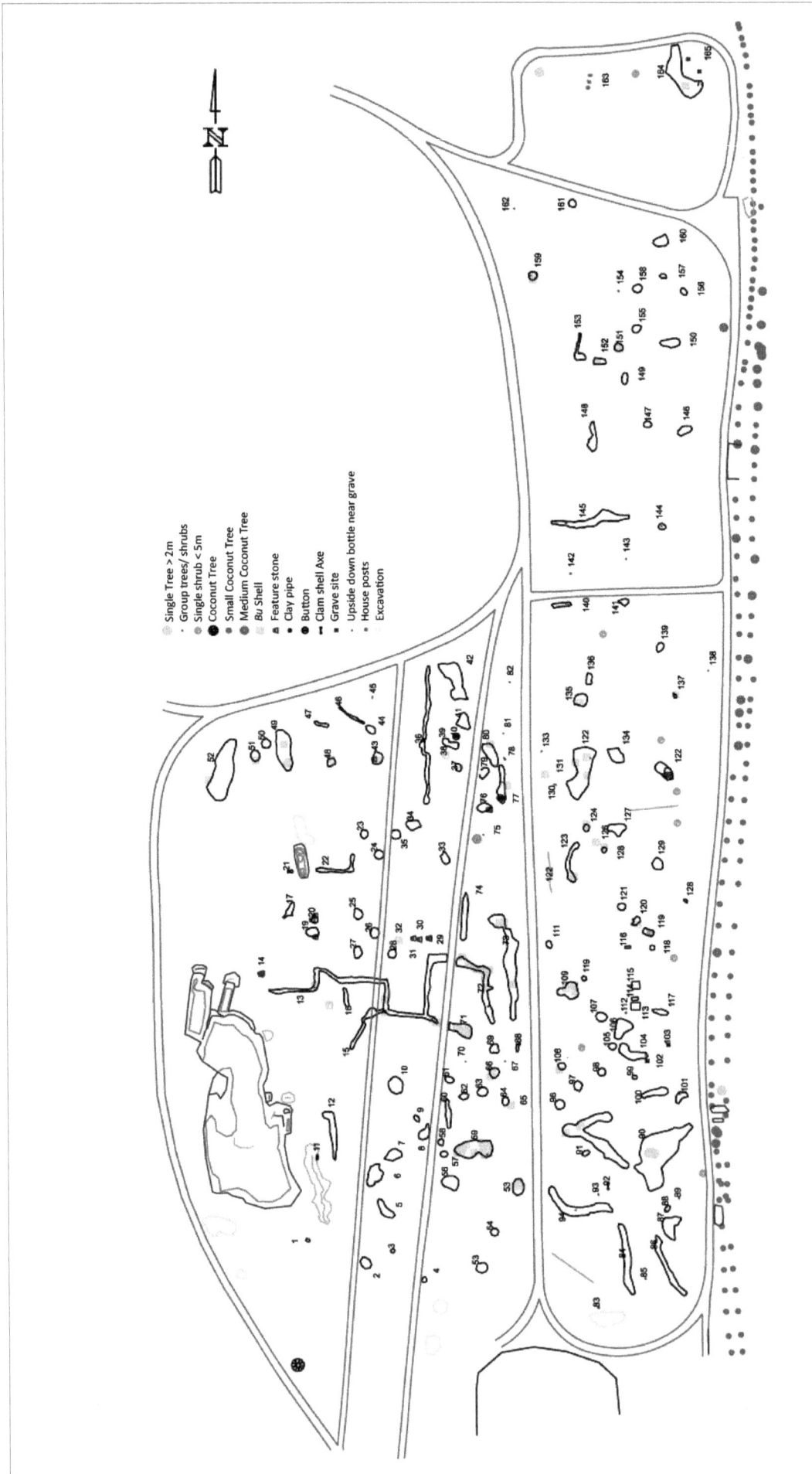

Fig 6.1. Total Station map of Muyi (courtesy of Ian McNiven).

Fig 6.2. Excavation of Square A, Muyi.

Fig 6.3. Thomas Whap excavating SU 5 deposits, Square A.

Further potential disturbance was noted in SU 2 in the form of linear tunnels. These tunnels are consistent with termite activity observed elsewhere on the island. They were restricted in area and are not expected to have compromised the site's stratigraphic integrity. Layers 1, 2 and 5 are considered intact. This is evident through lenses of bone (SU 1), charcoal (XU 36), stone (XU 39) and pumice (XU 41) and the cemented appearance of sediment in SU 5.

Radiocarbon dates and chronology

One shell and three charcoal AMS ages were obtained from Muyi (Table 6.2). Five *Paphies* sp. shell valves (sieve residue) were used to determine the age of the base of the main midden layer (7-9 cmbs, XU 4). This provided an age of 1416-1301 cal. BP (at 95.4 % probability). This age is considered questionable due to the consistent presence of non–diagnostic, European–manufactured materials (metal, glass, roofing slate) within this layer and ethnographic and historical records that suggest that this

was a LMS and Islander garden area. It is expected that initial age was influenced by contamination/ movement of one (or more) of the utilised *Paphies* sp. valves.

Further AMS dates were obtained from near basal deposits in SU 5. These bracketed a sherd of pottery (discussed later) to between 1336-1398 and 1508–1567 cal. BP (at one σ). No dateable material was found in the XUs below the sherd, meaning that that antiquity of the lowest (sparse) cultural deposits remains uncertain.

Cultural materials

Muyi contained a wide variety of cultural material; dominated by marine vertebrate bone (24.2 kg) but also including marine invertebrates (2.9 kg), fire fractured rock (probable oven stones; 5.1 kg) and lithics (1.1 kg; Table 6.3). The majority of all cultural material clustered within upper deposits associate with the mound feature. Deposits between XUs 5 and 1 accounted for 78 % (by weight) of the marine vertebrate bone, with a further 17.5 % recovered in the 5 XUs below this (i.e., above XU 10). Similar patterns were also observed for economic shellfish (74.9 % and 93.2 % respectively). A different situation exists for lithics with 25.9 % (by number) recorded in the upper 5 XUs, with the majority (68.1 %) between XU 5 and XU 15. This mirrored charcoal distributions with 10.1 % (by weight) recovered above XU 5 and 83.2 % between XU 5 and XU 20. Cultural materials (including distributions) will be reviewed in detail in the following sections.

Marine vertebrate bone

Marine vertebrate bone incorporated unidentified large vertebrate (probable dugong; 12 kg); dugong (12.1 kg); turtle (80.6 g); fish (4.6 g); shark/ray (0.7 g) and unidentified small vertebrate bone (1.6 g). As mentioned above nearly all (95.5 %) of the marine vertebrate bone was recovered from layers associated with the bone mound. Two major pulses were observed, the first at the base of SU 2 (XU 10), while a second (less localised) increase throughout SU 1 (XUs 1 to 5; Fig. 6.5). Below SU 2, large vertebrate, dugong and turtle bone continues in significantly reduced numbers until XU 20 at which point weights drop still further (average = 2 g per XU). While this may reflect taphonomic processes, consistency in pH levels suggests this was not the case.

A correlation was noted between the trajectories of dugong and unidentified large vertebrate suggesting turtle bone is negligible in this archaeological assemblage. It also highlights the prominence of the pulses discussed earlier. Using right and left ear bones (periodicals; front periodical; rear periodical - see Appendix 3 for details) a MNI of six dugongs was calculated, with a broad range of dugong bone elements represented (see Table 6.4). Significantly, however, the bulk of the assemblage consists of ribs (61 % by weight) and skull parts (32 % by weight). A further 6 % is connected with the skull (i.e., tusks and

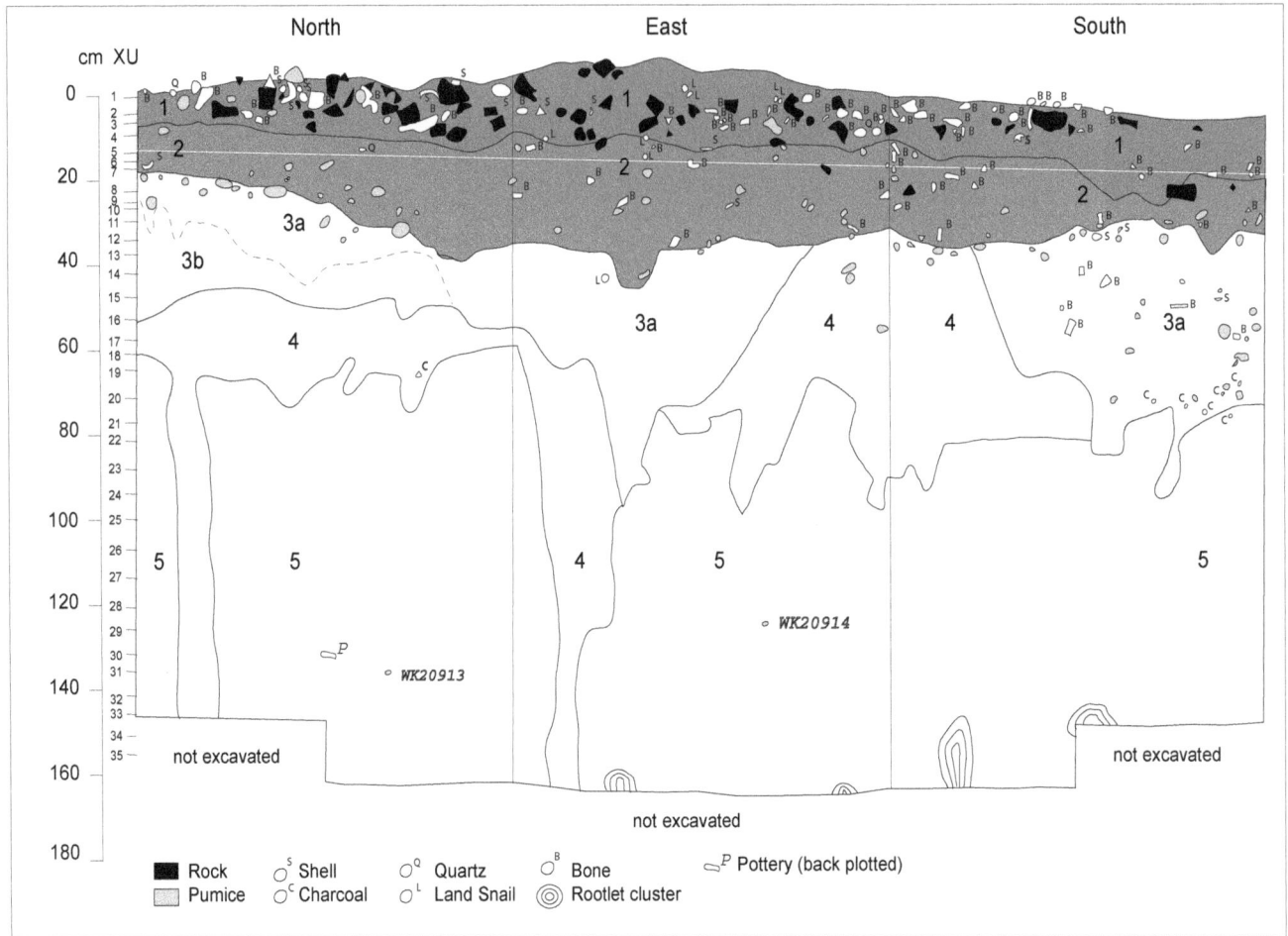

Fig 6.4. Stratigraphic drawing, Square A.

ear bones), which leaves less than 2 % of bones outside these categories (i.e., scapula, vertebrae).

A total of 80.6 g of turtle bone was excavated from Square A with two localised peaks, XU 10 and XU 2 (Fig. 6.6). Small vertebrate and fish bone provides an added dimension to site history. While similar trajectories are observed to other materials in upper deposits (i.e., a density peak between XUs 10 and 4) there is evidence for a second discrete increase between XUs 26 and 18 (Fig. 6.7). While this may reflect bioturbation of small fish bone into basal deposits it does not fit with the normal bell curve distribution, nor does it explain the apparent hiatus between XUs 16 and 13. During this later period (and particularly between XUs 11 and 7) shark/ ray bones become a consistent feature of the site. A single rodent femur was recovered from XU 8.

Marine invertebrates

A total of 2.0 kg of economic shellfish (both MNI diagnostic and non-MNI diagnostic) and 949 g of non-economic or non-classifiable shellfish was excavated at Muyi. Two density peaks are visible, the first corresponding with SU 1, the second occurring at the base of SU 2 in XU 10 (Fig. 6.8). There were 288 (MNI) economic shells recorded, the majority being *Paphies striata* (51 %);

SU	Sediment description
1	Unconsolidated, coarse-grained organic sediment grading from brown (7.5YR, 4/2) to very dark gray (3/1) with depth. Sediment is alkaline (pH = 8.19-8.47) with numerous fibrous roots and large quantities of cultural material and rocks.
2	Slightly more consolidated, fine-grained sand. Colouration = very dark gray (7.5YR, 3/1); pH = neurtral (7.87-6.67). Fewer roots with lenses of pumice at base
3a	Grades from dark gray/ black (7.5YR, 3/1 to 2.5/1) to gray (7.5YR, 5/1) sandy sediment. At base, sand is mottled with fine-grained sand. pH does not change.
3b	Gray (7.5YR, 5/1), fine-grained sand. Moderately to highly consolidated with depth.
4	Mottled gray (7.5YR, 5/1) to pinkish white (7.5YR, 8/2) sand becoming fine-grained (moderately to highly consolidated) at base. Alkaline (pH = 7.81-8.25)
5	Pinkish white (7.5YR, 8/2 to 8/3) sand becoming more consolidated with depth. Calcification occurs in basal XUs with plates of shellfish/sand. Sediment is alkaline (pH = 8.83-9.06) and minimal root activity observed. No visible cultural materials.

Table 6.1: Sediment description, Square A.

Lab. Code	XU	XU mean depth below surface (cm)	Sample Wt (g)	Sample context	δ13X%	C14 date (BP)	Cal BP (68.3%)	Cal BP (95.4%)
WK21806	4	5-11	3.2	*Paphies* sp.	1.8± 0.2	1681±35	1227-1304	1173-1341
WK20914	28	117-124	0.07	In situ burnt wood (SF)	-27.2± 0.2	1538±30	1336–1398	1301–1416*
								1469-1483
WK20913	31	135-139	0.08	In situ burnt seed (SF)	-25.9± 0.2	1686±37	1418–1466	1410–1615*
							1489–1498	1677-1684
							1508-1567*	

Table 6.2. List of Radiocarbon dates from Muyi excavation. Reservoir effect calculation for WK21806 uses Delta R of -30±20 (Ulm et al. 2007). Calibrations calculated using Calib 5.0.2 (Stuiver and Reimer. 1993). * = highest probability of calibrated ranges.

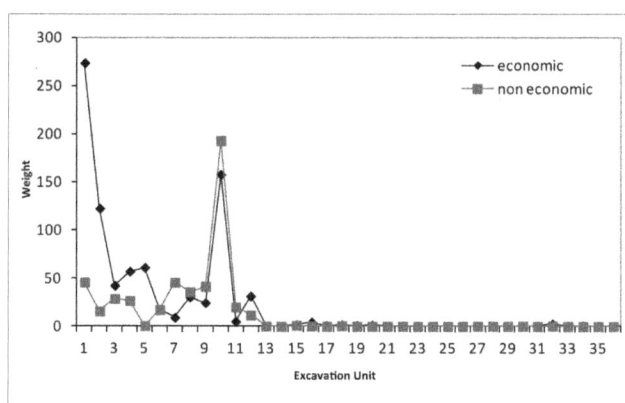

Fig 6.5. Vertical changes in large vertebrate and dugong bone, Square A (grams per 10 l deposit).

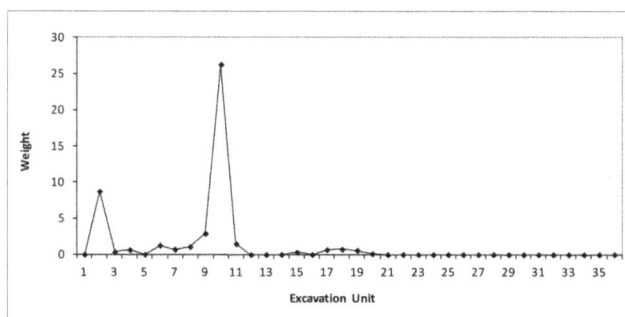

Fig 6.6. Vertical changes in turtle bone density, Square A (grams per 10 l deposit).

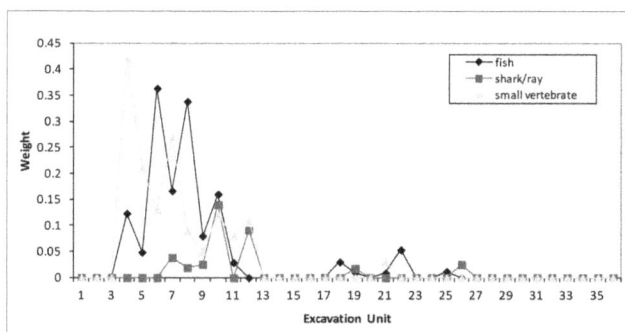

Fig 6.7. Vertical changes in all other marine vertebrates, Square A (grams per 10 l deposit).

Nerita sp. (9 %) and *Chama* sp. (5 %) (see Table 6.5). With the exception of *Paphies* striata and *Dosinia* sp. there is very little shellfish in the basal SUs (4 and 5). At this stage shellfish appears to have been gathered from the easily accessible littoral sand flats (all within the immediate vicinity of the site). SU 3 shows an increasingly varied pattern of shellfish gathering at the site. In addition to near-shore sandy areas the prominence of *Nerita* and *Pinctada* suggests that littoral, rocky zones were also utilised. To a lesser extent muddy, mangrove areas begin to be targeted. Other invertebrates (e.g., limpets and barnacles) also occur in high numbers (13 % and 3 % respectively).

The bulk of shellfish comes from SU 2, at which stage there is also the greatest variety of taxa (17 of the 19 represented species). *Paphies* and *Nerita* continue to be prominent alongside Turbo and Telescopium. During this SU, shellfish were collected from rocky substrates (principally *Nerita* sp.), mud flats (*Polymesoda erosa*), reef tracts (*Tridacna squamosa* and *Cyprae* sp.) and sand banks (e.g., *Paphies striata*). In addition to the previously exploited littoral zones people are now targeting supra-littoral and submerged sub-littoral areas suggesting a more active strategy (e.g., diving) to gather shellfish.

SU 1 contains 15 of the 19 species represented by this excavation. For the first time there is evidence for muddy, mangrove areas (e.g., Cerithidae and *Strombus* sp.). Another taxon, *Chama* (Round Oyster) is also consistently targeted for the first time. A reduced focus on sub-littoral zones and reef species may suggest a return to "snacking" on more accessible species.

Charcoal

A total of 4.5 g of charcoal was excavated from the Muyi excavation, the majority of which was recovered above XU 21 (Fig. 6.9). Numerous density peaks were observed, in particular XU 10 and between XUs 6 and 7.

Material culture

A total of 610 stone artefacts were excavated including 603 flaked artefacts (flakes and cores) and seven implements with use impact. This included two hammer stones (from

SU	XU	pH	weight (kg)	volume (l)	marine vertebrate (g)	economic shell (g)	artefact (#)	stone (g)	pumice (g)
1	1	8.19	25.1	18.0	1606.4	1606.4	3	2421.14	223.39
1	2		40.3	36.5	242.8	242.8	9	9931.08	273.09
1	3	7.47	40.4	26.5	1369.5	1369.5	14	12874.1	396.3
2	4		44.5	33.5	598.0	598.0	55	11067.53	759.31
2	5	7.85	44.7	37.5	397.1	397.1	72	7532.5	1543.25
2	6		28.0	28.0	319.1	319.1	83	730.58	1361.7
2	7	7.87	30.4	31.5	317.6	317.6	83	1215.72	1638.61
3	8		42.7	41.5	235.9	235.9	58	1917.99	2652.27
3	9	7.52	32.9	31.5	246.7	246.7	62	289.72	1447.47
3	10b		30.3	30.0	3112.1	3112.1	56	418.45	1124.76
3	11b	6.67	21.8	19.5	150.6	150.6	36	410.18	1174
3	12b1		13.5	13.0	193.7	193.7	17	129.22	750.08
3	13b1	8.12	14.8	13.5	138.0	138.0	0	102	450
3	14b1		25.6	23.0	28.0	28.0	1	41	208
3	15b	8.01	37.5	43.5	16.4	16.4	3	20.88	199.17
3	16b		57.0	54.0	31.3	31.3	1	71.03	183.53
4	17b1	8.04	16.7	26.0	24.0	24.0	1	8.35	96.43
4	18b2		8.1	8.0	25.7	25.7	2	16.9	112.21
5	19b2	8.04	3.9	4.0	7.6	7.6	1	1.7	45.09
5	20b1		62.4	57.0	8.7	8.7	0	1.02	67.46
5	21b2	8.07	7.3	6.0	0.6	0.6	1	10.1	36.66
5	22b		83.9	70.0	1.3	1.3	0	48.06	2.67
5	23b	8.25	84.5	70.0	0.6	0.6	1	132.11	5.56
5	24b		87.7	70.0	0.1	0.1	0	67.95	5.45
5	25b	7.81	96.9	83.0	0.1	0.1	0	7.95	1.64
5	26		89.8	69.5	0.2	0.2	2	8.79	5.14
5	27	8.95	118.8	108.0	0.3	0.3	0	184.82	3.53
5	28		99.5	84.0	0.4	0.4	1	82.51	0.09
5	29	8.83	87.7	68.0	0.1	0.1	2	29.07	0.22
5	30		99.0	74.5	0.5	0.5	7	414.6	0.7
5	31	8.97	63.0	57.5	0.5	0.5	3	354.58	0
5	32		71.1	59.5	0.1	0.1	8	269.64	0.47
5	33	8.93	54.0	47.5	0.1	0.1	3	141.02	0.01
5	34		31.7	28.5	0.1	0.1	0	5.1	0
5	35	9.06	38.4	35.5	0.3	0.3	0	8.64	0.06
5	36		46.4	40.5	0.1	0.1	0	74.69	0

Table 6.3. Raw excavation data, Square A.

XU 4 and XU 5) and five igneous stones with evidence of grinding. All but one piece in XU 10 were recorded between XU 5 and XU 8. The bulk of the flaked artefacts (n=554) were manufactured from quartz with the remainder (n=24) deriving from other igneous raw materials (i.e., volcanic and granite). All of these raw materials are available locally (e.g., McNiven *et al.* 2006: 62-3). A single glass flake was recovered from XU 6. Two density peaks were observed (XU 33-26 and XUs 12-2) separated by a period of very low (quartz) or no (igneous) artefact discard. Quartz is dominant in the upper assemblage dropping markedly below XU 12 (see Fig. 6.10). A sizable reduction in average weight of igneous lithics was observed (from 10.4 g between XUs 33 and 26 to 0.6 g above the next group of artefacts, XUs in SUs 11-1). Quartz follows a similar (if less dramatic) trajectory decreasing from 1.7 g to 0.2 g (XUs 33 to 26, then 23-1 respectively). It is acknowledged that average weight is not always a useful

XU	Ribs (g)	Scapula (g)	Ear (g)	Tusk (g)	Skull - other (g)	Humerus (g)	Vertebrae (g)	Total (g)
1	1069.5	40.5	26.7	11.9	1219.4	0	0	2368.1
2	3342.4	0	308.8	63.1	1012.7	0	31.7	4758.7
3	997.1	0	82.0	16.1	1080.2	0	0	2175.3
4	733.2	23.6	0	6.3	301.0	0	0	1064.1
5	137.1	0	0	156.7	123.0	20.9	0	437.7
6	225.0	0	0	0	0	0	0	225.04
7	185.9	50.4	0	22.2	10.2	0	0	268.7
8	198.3	28.4	0	18.3	85.3	0	0	330.2
9	148.5	0	0	0	0	0	0	148.5
10	140.4	0	0	0	0	0	0	140.4
11	77.6	0	0	0	0	0	0	77.6
12	45.0	0	0	0	14.5	0	0	60.1
13	8.5	0	0	0	8.1	0	2.5	19.1
14	4.0	0	0	0	2.4	1.2	0	7.6
15	0	0	0	0	0	0	0	0
16	3.5	0	0	1.1	0	0	0	4.6
17	0	0	0	0	6.5	0	0	6.5
18	15.7	0	0	0	0	0	14.4	30.1
19	0	0	0	0	0	0	0	0
20	2.8	0	0	0	0	0	0	2.8
Total =	7335.0	142.8	417.6	295.7	3863.2	22.1	48.5	12125

Table 6.4. Dugong bone elements, Square A.

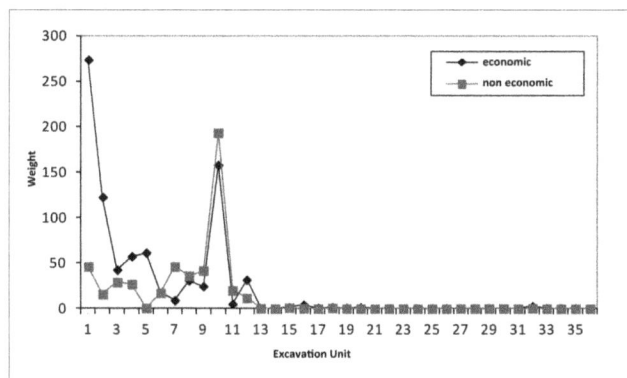

Fig 6.8. Vertical changes in economic and non-economic shellfish, Square A (grams per 10 l deposit).

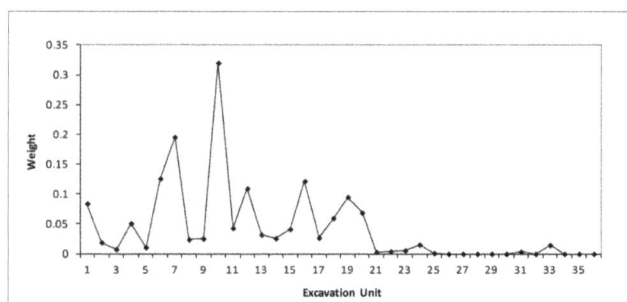

Fig 6.9. Vertical changes in charcoal densities, Square A (grams per 10 l deposit).

measure, affected by sampling complexities including extent of reduction and natural breakage. Considering the visible hiatus (i.e., XUs 13 to 27), this pattern is expected to represent a technological shift between two assemblages.

The location of the Muyi excavation (on a beach flat, far away from the surrounding hills) means that rocks would need to be humanly transported. The same cannot be said for pumice which could easily be transported across the site through natural processes (wind). The bulk of unmodified rock was located in the upper five excavation units, coincident with SU 1 midden. This also made up the majority of heat-affected rocks. Rock continues to be present in small quantities throughout SU 2 before dropping under 23 g per below XU 12. There was a slight increase in rock at the base of SU 5 (between XUs 30 and 33). The similar distributions of pumice, rock and an assortment of other cultural materials is potentially problematic. Two conjoining fragments of pottery were excavated from XU 30 (128 cmbs) cemented within a cockina conglomerate (Fig. 6.11). There was no evidence that these were intrusive to the level with both fragments excavated well outside a root track in the north east corner. Radiocarbon dates obtained from this context suggest an age of between 1508–1567 cal. BP and 1336-1398 cal. BP (at one σ). As there is a gap of at least 6 cm between pottery and the upper AMS sample the latter determination is considered most reliable. Petrographic analysis of a thin

55

Taxon	Tidal zone	substrate	Total MNI					Ranking
Gastropods			SU 1	SU 2	SU 3	SU 4	SU 5	
Nerita spp.	littoral	rocky	1	23	4	1	1	2
Trochus niloticus	littoral	rocky/ coral reefs	1	0	0	0	0	14
Turbo sp.	supra-littoral	rocky/ coral reefs	1	6	1	1	0	5
Melo amphora	littoral + sublittoral	sand/ mud	1	2	0	0	0	12
Cerithidae	mangroves	esturine sandy/ muddy	7	1	0	0	0	6
Strombus sp.	littoral and sublittoral	muddy, sandy, rubble	3	1	0	0	0	11
Syrinx aruanus	littoral + sublittoral	sand/ coral reefs	1	1	0	0	0	13
Cyprae	littoral + sublittoral	coral reefs	0	1	0	0	1	13
Telescopium telescopium	littoral	mud	7	6	0	0	0	4
Bivalves								
Chama sp.	littoral + sublittoral	rocky/ coral reefs	16	1	0	0	1	3
Pinctada sp.	littoral + sublittoral	rocky/ coral reefs	0	3	3	0	1	7
Paphies striata	littoral	sand	17	100	22	11	14	1
Polymesoda erosa	littoral (intertidal)	mud/ mangrove	1	1	2	0	0	11
Anadara antiquita	littoral	sand/ mud	0	2	0	0	0	13
Fragum unedo	littoral	sand/ mud	2	1	2	0	0	10
Gafrarium sp.	littoral	sand/ mud	1	1	1	0	1	11
Tridacna squamosa	littoral	coral reefs	1	0	0	0	0	14
Dosinia sp.	littoral	sand	0	1	1	1	3	8
Telina scobinata	littoral	sand	2	2	1	0	0	9

Table 6.5. Shellfish MNI, Square A.

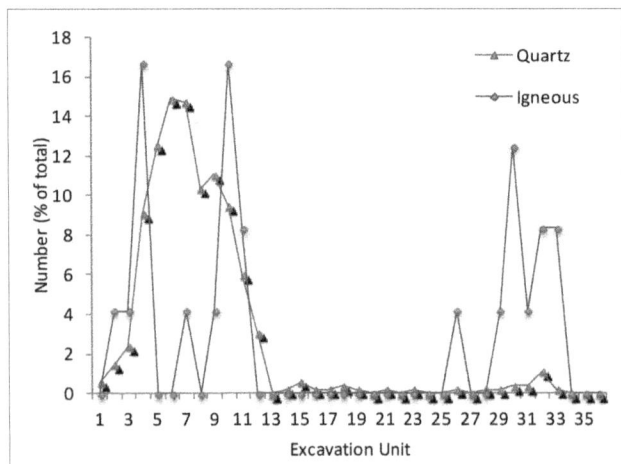

Fig 6.10. Vertical changes in stone artefacts, Square A (grams per 10 l deposit).

grains are also well sorted, but are sub-rounded to sub-angular. This may in part be due to the greater hardness and resistance to abrasion of these silicate grains. A count of terrigenous grains (n=105) present in a thin section documents the following composition:

Grain type	Frequency (%)
Plagioclase feldspar mineral grains	50
quartz mineral grains	15
biotite mica flakes	12
polycrystalline-polymineralic (quartz-feldspar) microgranitic rock fragments	10
K-feldspar mineral grains	8
opaque iron oxide grains (probably magnetite)	3
hornblende (pale green) mineral grains	2

Table 6.6. Terrigenous sand grain composition of Mabuyag sherd, Square A.

section of the Mabuyag sherd identified a high ratio of sand to clay (> 60: 40), with temper predominately calcareous (beach) sand (Wright and Dickinson 2009; Table 6.6). Temper is coarse-grained, rounded to sub-rounded, with an estimated 80 % to 85 % being well sorted. Fragments of reef debris (largely algal in origin) were observed, appropriate for reefs located on the western shoreline of Mabuyag (Willmott and Chertok 1972). The subordinate terrigenous

The nature of the terrigenous grains is also appropriate for derivation from Mabuyag bedrock, in particular the Badu suite of granite exposed in north eastern Mabuyag (Willmott and Chertok 1972; Willmott *et al*. 1973). This explains the high ratio of Plagioclase feldspar as well as the subordinate grains identified in Table 6.6.

Fig 6.11. Conjoining body sherds, Square A (scale in cm units).

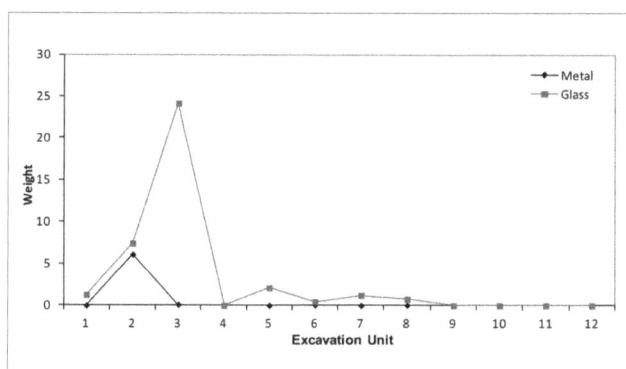

Fig 6.12. Vertical changes in European artefacts, Square A (grams per 10 l deposit).

Non–diagnostic, European–manufactured objects (metal, glass, slate) were interspersed throughout the mound (to XU 8), clustering within the top three XUs (by number, accounting for 64 % of the total glass and 61 % total metal; Fig. 6.12). This included a single glass flake (in XU 7).

6.3 Summary

Ethnography states that Muyi was a small settlement rather than a substantial, ancestral village (Haddon 1904). It was also a garden area and cemetery for Goemulgal and missionaries. This scenario is supported through archaeology with the surface collection revealing large numbers of mounded features (usually piled around coconut trees, or indentations of past trees) and scatters of European-derived materials. No pathways, stone arrangements or other such features (associated with other villages on the island) were observed.

Subsurface examination suggests middens are shallow, restricted for the most part to the upper 15 cm, with European materials prominent throughout these features. While the radiocarbon chronology has not resolved the age of this mound it is expected to date immediately prior to or during the period of European activity on Mabuyag. Midden deposits contain significant quantities of marine vertebrate bone, along with a large range of shellfish. During this period faunal remains appear to be collected from a number of environments and large quantities of rocks are transported to the site. An increase in stone artefacts (and in particular quartz flaked artefacts), charcoal and heat-effected rock suggests that food preparation and cooking may have also occurred.

An earlier archaeological signature was identified in basal XUs (SU 5, XUs 26-33), dated to between 1600 and 1350 BP. During this period human activity is evident through fish, turtle and possibly dugong bone, also the manufacture of locally-made pottery and large igneous and quartz flaked artefacts. Clear technological shifts have been identified at Muyi with an increasing dominance of quartz flaked artefacts and potentially also a decrease in artefact size (particularly igneous lithics). This suggests altering economies or requirements during the past few hundred years. We shall return to this possibility later in this book. This early phase of human activity (involving use of pottery, and minimal evidence for marine specialist activities) compares little with ethnographies for Goemulgaw villages.

Fig. 7.1. The northern margins of Baw village. Note the fish trap near the airstrip and large white washed church (photo's centre).

7

Baw

Baw is the village currently occupied by the Goemulgal. It is located towards the northern end of the main Mabuyag beach, which stretches down the east coast to Goemu. The current residential buildings cluster immediately south of the air-strip, continuing down to "New Village" at the northern margin of Maydh (Fig. 7.1). Historical sources (including oral traditions) suggest Baw was established between November 1873 and August 1874 as a base for the London Missionary Society teachers (see Shnukal In press). The LMS cultivated a "narrow strip of sandy soil about 50 yards wide and two or three hundred yards long" and attempted to encourage Islanders to settle around the church (McFarlane to Whitehouse 1874). According to Chester (1898) the majority of the Mabuyag community were living in Baw by 1897 (see Done 1987 for contrary report). What is less well established is whether Baw was occupied prior to LMS settlement and whether key aspects of Goemulgaw settlement and subsistence practices continued within Missionary jurisdiction. For these reason a small test pit was excavated at the close of the 2006 field season.

7.1   Surface survey and excavation

Detailed archaeological survey was not completed, however, a number of key features were observed.

Remnants of LMS activities include the Anglican Church, built in 1915 and located on the foreshore in the north eastern margin of the village. In the same area (immediately behind the IBIS food store), the foundations survive of the "old gaol house" which dates to a similar period (Fig. 7.2). A round boulder (attributed by Islanders to one of the heads taken by Kwoiam) forms the base of a pedestal for the church font (Done 1987: 17). A large round stone (reputed to have been carried from Goemu by a great Goemulgaw warrior) is located immediately outside the back entrance of the church. The incorporation of these elements of traditional Goemulgaw culture within the Anglican

Fig. 7.2. The Mabuyag Gaol and Court House with the rear wall of the IBIS store in the background.

Church is explained by Reverend Done (1987: 18): "it was appropriate that these two stones, so intimately connected with the dark times, as pre Christian days are called, should be used in the making of the font, the gateway of Christian life". Finally, three standing stones were observed in the open, grassy area outside the council centre.

7.2 Square A

In December 2006 a single, 40 cm x 40 cm test pit was excavated in a grassy area in the northern portion of Baw. Square A was 30 m south of the council centre, approximately 10 m away from a cannon collected from Warrior Reef by Islanders and about the same distance from the three standing stones described previously (Fig. 7.3). No surface materials were observed in this area. The size of excavation was small due to time constraints (a rapidly approaching wet season). For the same reason, excavation units were slightly larger than had been the case elsewhere (averaging 3.5 cm in the upper 50 cm and 5 cm below this). Otherwise excavation methodologies were the same as those described in previous chapters. Excavation reached a maximum depth of 77 cmbs (20 XUs) without reaching culturally sterile sediments or the base of deposits containing European–manufactured objects.

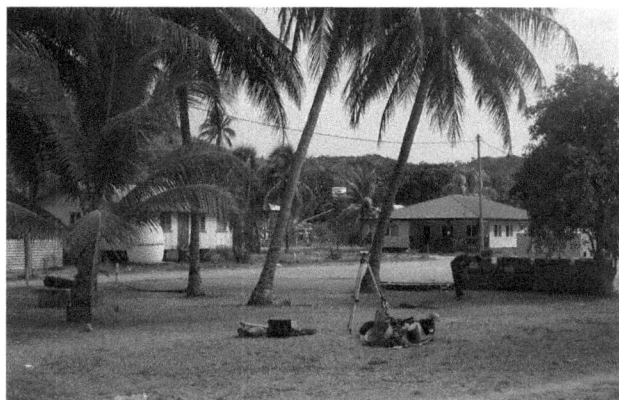

Fig 7.3. Location of Square A in the middle of Baw village.

Stratigraphy and relative chronology

Little stratigraphic variation was observed with sediment consistently sandy and alkaline (Ph = 8.1 to 8.41; Fig. 7.4; Table 7.1). Colour varied from Brown in SU 1 and 3 (Munsell = 7.5YR 4/2 and 4/3 respectively) to light brown in SU 2 (Munsell = 7.5YR 6/2). The four sub-layers were characterised by a shift from fine, loose sand to a much coarser grained deposit, which in SUa adhered in plates. It was noted that the bulk of non-economic

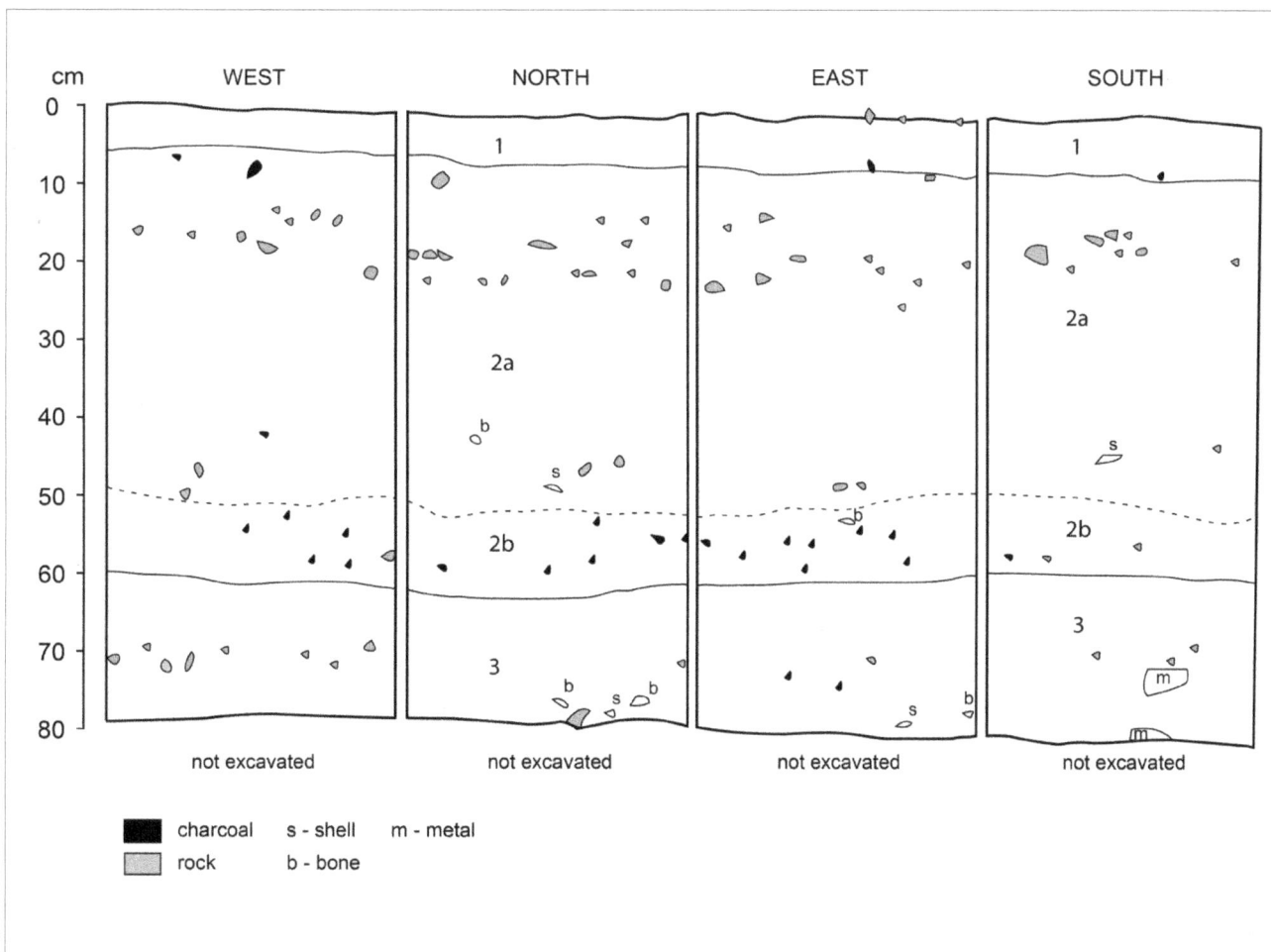

Fig 7.4. Stratigraphic drawing, Square A.

SU	Sediment description
1	Sediment is alkaline (Ph = 8.19-8.41), light brown terrigenous sand (Munsell = 7.5YR 4/2). It is unconsolidated/ brittle and fine grained. This layer is rich in organics/ particularly grass roots, moss etc. Very little cultural material observed.
2a	Light Brown (7.5YR 6/2) medium-grained sand. Variable consolidation throughout with loose, terrigenous sand interspersed with crusty plates of similar sediment. pH = 8.1 to 8.38.
2b	More consolidated, brown sand (7.5YR 6/2). Sediment is coarse-grained calcareous sand and contains a greater quantity of shellfish.
3	Coarse-grained brown (Munsell 7.5YR = 4/3) calcareous sand (pH 8.31 to 8.35). Increasingly unconsolidated and with larger quantities of faunal remains (i.e. shellfish, fish bone). There are more roots in this layer.

Table 7.1. Sediment description, Square A.

material including pumice and unmodified rock focused between XUs 20 and 12. There was little evidence for contamination, with intact lenses of charcoal and stone observed to span the test pit.

No radiocarbon dates were obtained from this excavation however a relative chronology can be established based on the presence of European manufactured artefacts throughout the excavation. This suggests that deposit accumulated within the past 150 years (at least six centimetres of deposit every ten years). Basal XUs (XUs 11-20) were associated with glass trade beads (XUs 13, 14 and 19), which have been dated through formal and chemical analysis to the early-mid 19th century (although presumably curated until the late 19th century; Wright and Ricardi In press). Slate crayons (XU 13) were also in regular use during this period although these continued into the early twentieth century. This is consistent with a pearl-shell button (XU 15) which has a maximum age of 1827 (Lindbergh 1999: 51) but could be considerably more recent. Between XU 5 and XU 1, excavation revealed small quantities of modern bottle glass, house plaster, a metal casing from an electric light bulb and a modern glass bead. We suggest XUs 11-20 span the period from nineteenth century village establishment to early twentieth century, while the upper five XUs date within the past fifty years. European manufactured materials may continue below the base of this excavation meaning that an earlier contact phase is plausible.

Cultural materials

Excavations exposed large quantities of European-manufactured materials including glass, ceramics, metal, trade beads, slate (probable roofing materials), and a marble, pearl-shell button and slate pencil (Table 7.2).

SU	XU	pH	Weight (kg)	Volume (l)	Marine vertebrates (g)	Economic shell (g)	Non-economic shell/rock (g)	Charcoal (g)	European materials (g)	rock (g)	pumice (g)
1	1	8.41	1.9	2	0	0	8.9	0	0.1	0	0.5
1	2		5.9	5	0.1	0	2.5	0.1	14.7	10.0	0.3
2a	3	8.58	6.0	7	0	0.2	7.0	0.1	7.9	72.5	0.6
2a	4		5.6	8	0.4	0	5.0	0.2	2.4	0.5	0.5
2a	5	8.21	9.2	7	0.4	0	6.2	0.1	3.2	116.3	0.4
2a	6		3.5	3	0	0	6.4	0	0	2.6	0
2a	7	8.31	8.5	8	0.3	2.3	17.9	0.1	4.0	26.1	0.1
2a	8		9.0	7.5	0.2	0.9	18.1	0.1	3.4	1.7	0.1
2a	9	8.3	8.7	8.5	0.9	0	16.7	0.1	3.2	0.9	0.3
2a	10		9.4	11.5	0.4	0	12.6	0.1	4.0	6.2	0.2
2a	11	8.48	9.7	13	1.6	2.1	26.3	0.4	7.5	0.7	0.2
2b	12		16.4	14	2.0	2.5	15.3	1.2	15.6	20.5	1.5
2b	13		9.2	8.5	3.6	15.2	25.2	3.0	137.5	28.9	2.4
2b	14	8.51	7.8	7	2.1	14.5	48.7	3.5	15.2	6.6	1.3
2b	15		9.5	8.5	1.6	36.8	70.3	5.3	7.0	7.9	0.6
3	16	8.5	8.7	7.4	0.4	20.4	125.3	1.8	14.2	37.6	4.0
3	17		8.9	7.5	3.2	19.8	110.6	3.4	8.9	38.1	1.1
3	18	8.35	8.9	8.5	2.2	2.7	92.4	4.1	19.7	19.5	1.5
3	19		12.3	11.5	4.4	6.9	181.5	4.8	11.5	417	3.4
3	20	8.34	8.6	8	39.8	6.8	95.0	4.1	19.1	31.2	8.1

Table 7.2. Raw excavation data, Square A.

Marine invertebrates (131.1 g) and vertebrates (176.2 g) were also observed. The latter consisted of unidentified large vertebrate (112.3 g), dugong (33.7 g), fish (28.8 g) and turtle (0.4 g) bone.

Marine vertebrate bone
Only 176.2 g of marine vertebrate bone was excavated at Baw (Fig. 7.5). The majority (64 %) was classified as large vertebrate, with a further 19 % diagnostic dugong bone and 16 % small vertebrate bone. Marine vertebrate bone was recovered throughout SUs 1 to 3 (i.e., XUs 1-20), 90 % of which clusters between XUs 11 and 20 (93 % of the total large vertebrate bone, by weight, was excavated below XU 14). The majority of marine vertebrate bone (28 % of the total) was excavated in XU 20. This excavation unit also contained all diagnostic dugong bone (a rib and tusk fragment), also the only identified fragment of turtle (carapace).

A total of 28.8 g of undiagnostic small vertebrate (primarily fish but with 0.4 g of shark and/or ray) bone was recovered, the majority of which (65 %) came from the lower ten XUs (i.e., XUs 11 to 20). Small vertebrate bone (mainly fish) continued to be prominent to XU 9 (95 % of total), with no shark or ray bones excavated above XU 14.

Marine invertebrates
An MNI of 41 economic shellfish (131 g) was obtained from this excavation. The majority (78 % by MNI) of economic shellfish (mainly *Paphies striata*) was excavated between XU 20 and XU 11, with only 3 % of shellfish recorded above XU 8 (Table 7.3). *Paphies* was represented throughout the assemblage, with the exception of SU 1. While *Paphies* sp., accessible today in the intertidal zone adjacent to Baw village, was represented to XU 3, most species from non–local habitats (e.g., *Chama* sp., *Anadara antiquata*, *Nerita* sp. and *Fragum unedo*) only occurred below XU 11 (Table 7.3).

Charcoal
The majority of charcoal was recovered in the basal XUs of this excavation, dropping considerably above XU 13 and negligible by XU 11 (Fig. 7.6). Two peaks exist, initially in the basal XUs (20 to 17) and then a more

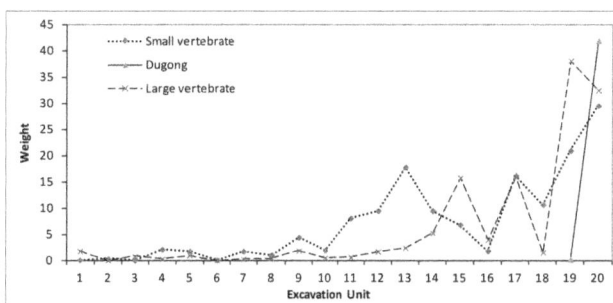

Fig 7.5. Vertical changes in marine vertebrate bone by taxa, Square A (grams per 10 l deposit).

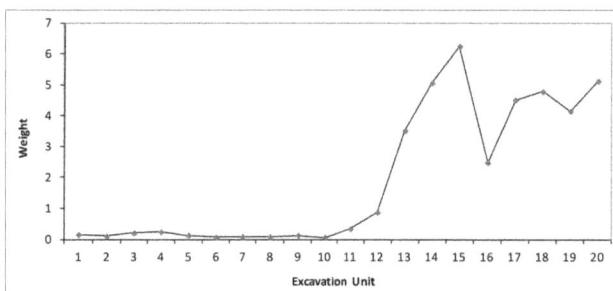

Fig 7.6. Vertical changes in charcoal, Square A (grams per 10 l deposit).

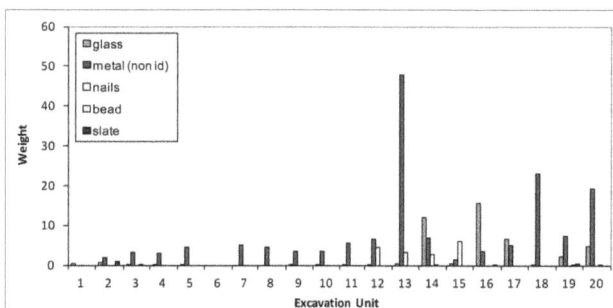

Fig 7.7. Vertical changes in European materials, Square A (grams per 10 l deposit).

localised peak between XUs 15 and 13. This mirrored burnt rock and burnt bone which were only recorded below XU 16.

Material culture
No flaked artefacts were recovered from this excavation. Conversely, European manufactured artefacts/ materials were prolific at Baw (Fig. 7.7). This included building

Taxon	Tidal zone	Substrate	Total MNI				Ranking
			SU 1	SU 2a	SU 2b	SU 3	
Gastropods							
Nerita spp.	littoral	rocky	0	0	3	4	2
Bivalves							
Chama sp.	littoral + sublittoral	rocky/ coral reefs	0	0	0	1	4
Pinctada sp.	littoral + sublittoral	rocky/ coral reefs	0	1	0	1	3
Paphies striata	littoral	sand	0	7	9	13	1
Anadara antiquita	littoral	sand/ mud	0	0	1		4
Fragum unedo	littoral	sand/ mud	0	1	0		4

Table 7.3. Shellfish (MNI), Square A.

Fig 7.8

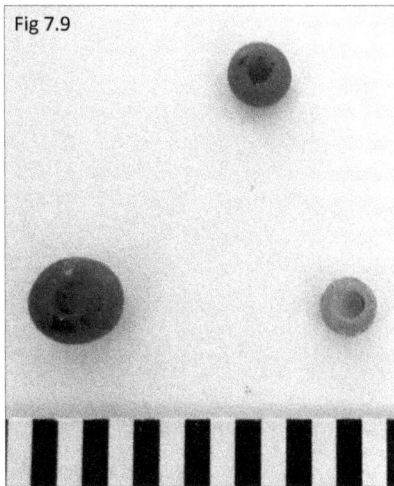

Fig 7.9

Fig 7.8. Crayon and unidentified metal artefact excavated from Square A (scale in cm units).

Fig 7.9. Glass/ ceramic beads from Square A (XUs 14, 19 and 20, left to right and top to bottom. Scale in cm units).

Fig 7.10. Shell button excavated from Square A (scale in mm units).

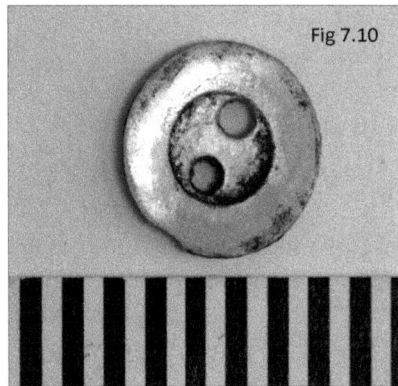

Fig 7.10

XUs 12 and 15 and a rusty, iron (match) box recovered from the east section adjacent to XU 13. Artefacts found close to this object (in XU 13) were a writing crayon and an unidentified metal object. Between XUs 6-10 there were only six fragments of glass ("colourless" and "medium green") of uncertain age. House plaster was also restricted to these excavation units. Between XU 5 and XU 1, excavation revealed small quantities of modern bottle glass (with all colours represented), house plaster, a metal casing from an electric light bulb and a modern glass bead. Between XUs 6-10 there were only six fragments of glass ("colourless" and "medium green") of uncertain age. Three complete and one incomplete bead(s) (Fig. 7.9) were excavated from Baw (XUs 3, 14, 19, 20). This included a "Cornaline d'Aleppo" and two others consistent with 19th century collections. Microscopic analysis revealed significant differences between the machine made, smooth bead from XU 5 and those below it. In addition, a single pearl-shell button was excavated from XU 15 (Fig. 7.10). This measured 1 cm (diameter), with a width of 2 mm, with the irregularity of holes suggesting it had been hand crafted. Pearl-shell went out of regular use after the crash in 1906 so it is unlikely to have a manufacture date subsequent to this period.

7.3   Summary

Surface survey and excavation of Baw provides information about the most recent phase of Goemulgaw settlement, associated with the arrival of LMS. Within the basal SUs 2b and 3 (relatively dated to between mid-19th to early 20th Centuries) there is evidence for localised fires (e.g., burnt bone, burnt stone and charcoal) indicative of earth ovens (*amai*). The possibility that this area was used to prepare feasting events is supported by the large quantities of marine vertebrate bone and photographic evidence from this village (Hurley 1921 cited in NLA). Subsequent reductions in burning (and marine vertebrate bone and invertebrates) occurred in SUs 2a and 1 suggesting altered economy or a shift in the location of food processing. Historical records indicate increased Goemulgal dependence on pearl-shelling captains and missionaries for food, specifically vegetables (Shnukal 1992; see also Gill 1876: 202; McFarlane to Murray 14 September 1876). It is revealing that by 1898 a feast at Baw was described in terms of "flour, rice, jams, tea and sugar, and tinned meats" and "a large pile of food such as could be got from the Thursday Island stores" (Chester 1898; see also Murray to Mullens May 3 1873). While this may well be a contributing factor it is considered likely that food cooking (in *amais*) and processing may have been relocated away from the village centre. This is consistent with Goemulgal ethnography and the current set up for celebrations. Major events (weddings, funeral feasts) continue to occur in the village square and the grassy area tested during the 2006 excavations; however, designated cooking and food processing areas have been set up in the New Village (Fig. 7.11).

materials (roofing slate; plaster, unidentified metal and nails); beverage/ storage vessels (bottle glass, ceramic); clothing/ decoration items (beads, button) and educational/ other artefacts (e.g., a slate crayon, a probable metal matchbox; Fig. 7.8). No clay tobacco pipes were excavated.

Basal XUs (XUs 11-20) were associated with the majority of diagnostic building materials (i.e., nails/roofing slate), diagnostic beverage/storage glass and non–diagnostic metal, ceramic and glass. In these layers, glass was dominated by "medium green" (33 % of total) and "light green" (38 % of total) types, comparable with nineteenth century "beverage bottles" (Wright and Ricardi In press). In addition there were nine nails and four tacks (iron with the exception of one copper tack) excavated between

Fig 7.11. Islanders taking a turtle out of an *amai* at the New Village.

Goemulgaw people who lived inside the LMS–controlled village of Baw may have experienced a lesser level of autonomy. While this village has a large variety of European–manufactured materials with evidence for recreational (marbles), clothing (button), building activities (nails, roofing slate), food consumption (dinner plates, storage and drinking vessels) and education (slate pencil) the absence of traditional technologies (e.g., flaked artefacts) is considered significant. While it is likely that this reflects community avoidance (or LMS discouragement) of traditional activities, at this stage we cannot rule out sampling issues due to the small size of this excavation. It is intriguing, however, that small caches of dugong bone in basal layers of the Baw suggest a certain level of subsistence continuity within LMS jurisdiction.

8

Discussion and conclusions

At the start of this book I explored the feasibility of examining community emergence and development using archaeology. It was demonstrated that a social model of regionalisation (see McNiven 1999) targeting ethnographically-significant sites, offered a useful method for exploring community. A closer examination of archaeology and ethnography in Torres Strait suggested that "village" and "*kod*" sites were appropriate for such a study. Detailed ethnographic and historical records exist for these sites in Western Torres Strait. Research at the Pulu *kod* provided compelling archaeological evidence for socio-political and ceremonial activities. Surviving oral and written histories provided details about the role of ritual installations, further strengthening the cultural heritage values of this study. Torres Strait villages provide an additional, poorly explored, dimension to the late-Holocene history of Torres Strait. Specifically, research had not yet tested whether settlement fissioning, increased territoriality and regionalisation can be observed in the archaeological record. This chapter reviews excavation results from Mabuyag before re-assessing the region's settlement chronology and applications of the regionalisation model for study of small Torres Strait islands.

8.1   Settlement patterns within Goemulgaw territory

This book focused on excavations along the coastal margins of Mabuyag. While it is conceivable that earlier or more substantial settlement areas may yet be found inland, the mountainous, rocky relief and low levels of sedimentation in these areas makes human occupation (and cultural material preservation) unlikely. Furthermore, previous archaeological and anthropological research failed to locate settlement sites (in the form of surface scatters of faunal remains) inland on Mabuyag (Harris and Ghaleb 1987; Haddon 1904; McNiven pers. comm., April 2009). For this reason it is expected that the 2005-2011 excavation results presented here alongside a review of previous research, provide a representatitve indication of settlement on Mabuyag.

Two field seasons of research at Dhabangay suggests sustained human activity on the north coast of Mabuyag between 7239–3317 cal. BP. This period was marked by the development of new technologies (i.e., fishing, turtle and possibly dugong hunting, also large quartz and igneous lithics) potentially supporting increased reliance on marine resources (Wright 2011b; Wright *et al*. 2013). It has not been conclusively established whether people hunted dugong during this period, with a recent re-analysis of large vertebrate bone from basal layers suggesting turtle dominates until approximately 4200-4000 years ago

(Ken Aplin pers. comm., May 2014; see also Wright *et al*. 2013). During this early settlement period Dhabangay experienced significant burning events suggesting an early phase of landscape clearance.

Results suggest there was a major period of re-organisation on Mabuyag after 3317 cal. BP. The reduction in settlement activity at Dhabangay between 3317–1815 cal. BP is unlikely to represent an absence of people on Mabuyag during this period. Burnt dugong bone at this site occurred during a period of alteration in lithic manufacture towards bipolar quartz flakes. This has been used to argue for altered economies involving increased predation of dugong (Wright *et al*. 2013). Concurrent settlement at Mask Cave on Pulu provides further evidence that Islanders were practicing a varied maritime economy, which involved fin-fishing, turtle, and possibly dugong hunting (McNiven *et al*. 2006: 60). At Mask Cave there was evidence for increased cultural activity after 2500-2000 cal. BP. McNiven *et al*. (2006) suggested that pottery technologies (five sherds) may have also come into Torres Strait during this period. The only evidence for simultaneous human activity found during this research on Mabuyag was a cache of dugong bones recovered by Willaim Gizu during building work at Baw, New Village. A dugong bone (rib) returned an AMS date of 2412±31 BP potentially identifying exploitation of a newly formed beach on the eastern coast of Mabuyag (Wright and Gizu 2012). Excavations at Mask Cave and Muyi show that people were manufacturing pottery between 1700–1300 cal. BP (McNiven *et al*. 2006: 13; Wright and Dickinson 2009). I have argued previously that the near identical petrography of all sherds (including those predating 2000 years ago from Pulu) suggests that these may all belong to a single, chronologically discrete period (Wright and Dickinson 2009). Considering that the bulk of sherds from both sites (Mask Cave and Muyi) date between 1700-1300 and observations of intrusive channels at Mask Cave, it is considered more likely that the five older sherds are intrusive (see Wright and Dickinson 2009). This may fit with aceramic human activity at Tiger shark Rockshelter (after 1300 cal. BP) and potentially Dhabangay (after 1684 cal. BP).

The past 1500-1000 years appears to be a period of flux on Mabuyag and Pulu. During this time Mask Cave was abandoned and settlement was observed at Tiger shark Rockshelter (McNiven *et al*. 2008: 28; Fig. 8.1). Ephemeral deposits (primarily fishbone and shellfish) also occurred at Muyi and Dhabangay during this period. The earliest evidence for substantive settlement on Mabuyag involving dugong, turtle and fish bone occurred after 1100 BP at Wagedoegam. Goemu may have also experienced occasional visitation from 1024-726 cal. BP (Ghaleb 1990: 324; McNiven and Wright 2008). Although dugong bone was excavated during this period, quantitative and qualitative analysis of fish, dugong, turtle and shellfish indicates that ethnographically-known levels of marine specialisation had not been attained at either Wagedoegam or Goemu. Alternatively, it may point

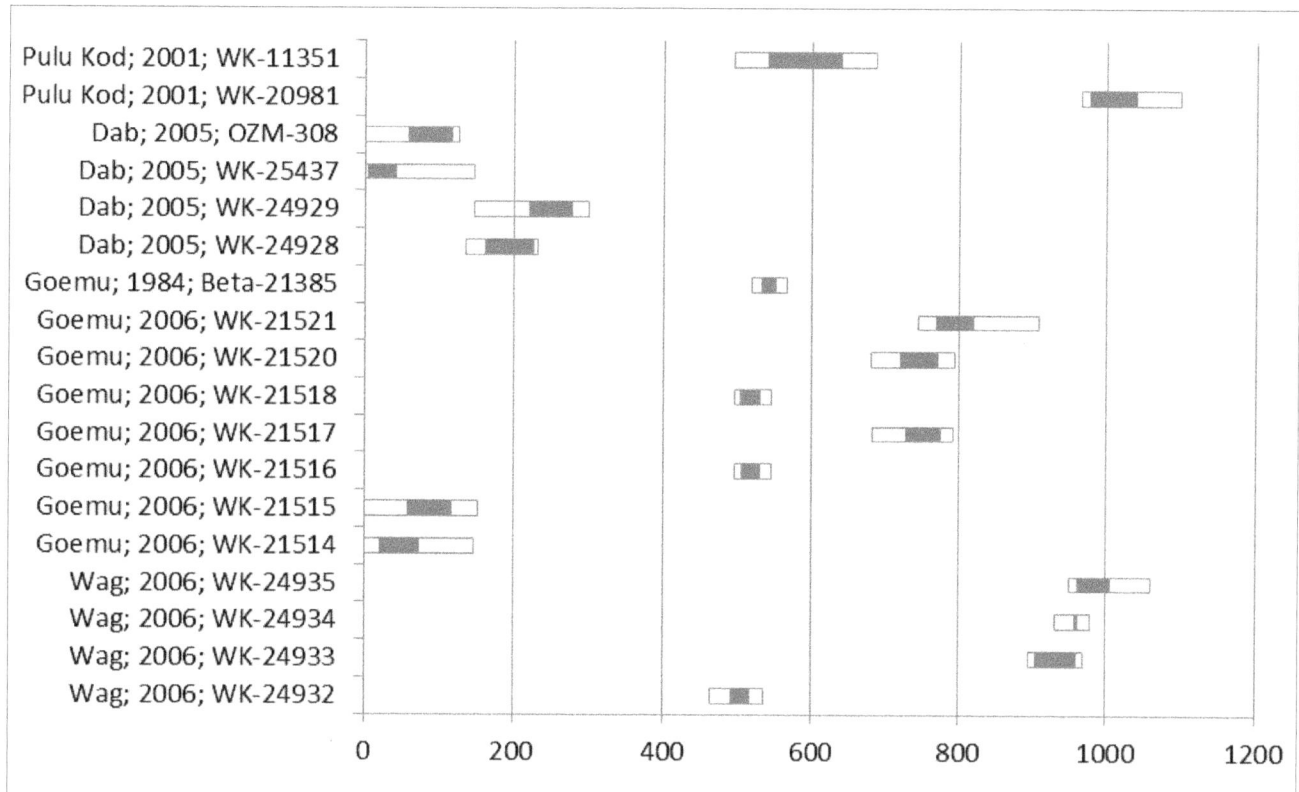

Fig 8.1. Selection of calibrated AMS dates from Goemulgaw villages. Dates marked 2005 and 2006 are from Wright (2010), those marked 1984 are from Barham and Harris (1987) and those marked 2001 are from McNiven *et al.* (2009). Date range represents one and two σ (Reimer *et al.* 2009).

to differential preservation or the reliance on subsistence practices that are yet to be fully established on Mabuyag (e.g., horticulture).

Between 550 and 300 cal. BP archaeology demonstrates significant changes in settlement within Goemulgaw territory. Decreased settlement was observed for small islands off the coast of Mabuyag (Tiger shark Rockshelter), also the north west coast of Mabuyag (Wagedoegam). During this period escalated midden activity (including highly structured large vertebrate bone mounds) occurred along the south east coast of Mabuyag (at Goemu and later Dhabangay). There was also a significant increase in the variety of faunal remains, targeted ecological zones and prominence of small, quartz, bipolar flakes. Archaeological evidence supports a model of population growth, potentially also increased efficiency in dugong/ turtle hunting, fin-fishing and the development of new socio-political engagements with increasingly complex humanly-manipulated landscapes (Wright *et al.* 2013). After 400 cal. BP bone mounds and *bu* shell arrangements were constructed on both Pulu and Mabuyag (McNiven and Bedingfield 2008; McNiven and Feldman 2003; McNiven *et al.* 2009). Although currently undated, the Wagedoegem *kod* appears to fit within a pattern of "profound structural organisation of the people of Mabuyag and surrounding isles" (McNiven *et al.* 2009: 22).

Post–contact layers at Goemu, Dhabangay and Muyi contained large quantities of dugong/ turtle and fish

bone (see also Ghaleb, 1990; McNiven and Bedingfield, 2008; McNiven *et al.* In press). There was also evidence for continued use of quartz (and glass) flakes at multiple villages around the island. Conversely, the London Missionary Society (LMS)–controlled village of Baw may have experienced a lesser level of autonomy with a much higher variety of European–manufactured materials but no flaked artefacts (Wright and Ricardi In press). While it is likely that this reflects community avoidance (or LMS discouragement) of traditional activities, at this stage we cannot rule out sampling issues due to the small size of this excavation. An intriguing discovery was small caches of dugong bone in basal layers of the Baw excavation. These dated to the post–contact period and were associated with charcoal and fire–fractured rock suggesting they belong to feasting events/ use of an earth oven (Wright and Ricardi In press). This points to a certain level of subsistence continuity within LMS jurisdiction.

8.2 Reassessing the Western Torres Strait settlement chronology

An important aspect of the Mabuyag research is how it contributes to settlement and subsistence models for Western Torres Strait. The following section presents this information within its broader context, including evidence for increased human movement involving other Torres Strait Islanders, also people from Papua New Guinea and Island South East Asia.

Settlement and subsistence histories

Dhabangay is the second oldest site (after Badu 15) so far discovered in Torres Strait. It also provides the earliest direct evidence for subsistence and sustained settlement through large quantities of lithics, faunal remains and charcoal across the Dhabangay site. The Badu 15 Rockshelter (Badu) revealed "human presence" (small quantities of charcoal and stone artefacts) dating prior to marine transgression, between 8000 and 6000 BP (David *et al*. 2004c: 72; See Appendix 1). David *et al*. (2004c: 75) suggested that this was followed by abandonment of islands with the exception of "sporadic visits" from Cape York. This corresponded with an earlier model which suggested Islander communities were "ill equipped to deal with insularity" and perished or abandoned their island homes (Rowland 1985: 131). Dhabangay provides evidence for ongoing and sustained habitation during the period of sea level high stand, including Barham's (2000: 291) "high energy window" (6500–5000 years ago). This suggests settlement of Western Torres Strait continued through the isthmus to island transition or people returned to Torres Strait soon after its formation. It is conceivable that earlier settlement existed on/ near present day Mabuyag, however, it is unlikely that sites survived rising seas.

Results support major demographic expansion within Western Torres Strait after 4200-4000 years ago. While it has now been established that turtle and fish were exploited at Dhabangay by 7200 years ago, dugong hunting may post-date this by approximately 3000 years. This corresponds with the appearance of dugong bone at Berberass (Badu) and Mask Cave during this period (Crouch *et al*. 2007; McNiven *et al*. 2006). The high nutritional value of dugong (Kwan *et al*. 2006) suggests improvements in dugong hunting would have major socio-demographic repercussions for Torres Strait Islanders. While this has not yet been fully established (with few sites dating to this period), it is intriguing that a shift towards bipolar, quartz lithic technologies corresponds with the first dugong bones at Dhabangay. This may suggest innovations in hunting and/ or butchery, water craft technologies by increasingly specialised maritime communities (Wright *et al*. 2013).

McNiven *et al*. (2006: 49; see also Carter 2002b; McNiven *et al*. 2011: 5) suggested a migration of "Papuan maritime, horticultural and pottery-making peoples to the Eastern and Western islands of Zenadh Kes [Torres Strait]" after 2600 years ago. This period was also associated with the emergence of a "Torres Strait Cultural Complex", which involved increasing maritime specialisation, a shift in cosmology towards the sea, and fluid links between islands through exchange, warfare, intermarriage and maritime voyaging (Barham 2000: 228). As noted above, archaeological excavations on Mabuyag provide little evidence for this event. Sustained settlement by pottery using people is likely to have occurred considerably later (most likely between 1700 and 1300 cal. BP; see below for details). This corresponds with increased consumption of dugong (after 1684 cal. BP, at Dhabangay) and potentially also the onset of midden dugong and turtle bone at Totalai on Mua after 1621-1384 cal. BP (Ash and David, 2008; Ash *et al*. 2008; 2010). The extent to which Western Torres Strait and Papua New Guinea were connected during this period remains uncertain (see below).

Midden materials, dating after 800 and 600 cal. BP have been recorded throughout the Torres Strait and Cape York (Barham 2000; Barham *et al*. 2004: 36; Carter *et al*. 2004; David and Weisler 2006; Ghaleb 1990; McNiven 2006: 9; Moore 1979: 15; Rowland 1985: 130). This has been interpreted as evidence for widespread cultural changes "in settlement, demography, mobility, rituals, seascape construction, social alliances and exchange relationships" (McNiven 2006). The Mabuyag excavations demonstrate midden formation after 1100 cal. BP (at Wagedoegam), increasing substantially at Goemu (after 800 BP, then again after 600 BP). As will be explored later, it is plausible that these socio-demographic shifts were enabled by increased proficiency in maritime economies (including improved dugong hunting) and the development of delayed production systems (fish traps).

Elsewhere, it has been shown that increased ceremonial activity occurs within the past 550-400 years. This included the formation of highly structured dugong bone mounds, shell and stone arrangements (David and Mura Badulgal 2006; David *et al*. 2004b; 2005: 71; 2009: 10; McNiven 2003; McNiven and Feldman 2003; McNiven *et al*. 2009). Current evidence from Mabuyag supports this with the bone mounds at Dhabangay, Goemu and Wagedoegam likely to post-date 400 cal. BP (see McNiven and Bedingfield 2008; McNiven and Wright 2008). At Dhabangay it has further been argued that a 400-300 year old fish bone pit was "ritually capped" using dugong skull bones (Wright and Jacobsen In press).

Subsistence shifts during the past 300 years (specifically an increased prominence of shellfish) have been suggested for Gerain, Urakaraltam and Turao Kula on Mua (Ash and David 2008). On Mabuyag, the variety of shellfish does appear to increase at many sites during this period. Eight new species of fish were added to the Goemu and Muyi assemblage and the entire economic assemblage from Dhabangay (Squares A and B) date to this period. Foraging patterns become more diverse, ranging from sub-littoral, reef/ mud/ sand areas to littoral rocky-shores and beaches. The taxonomic range of fish bone also increased, with tiger shark one of many newly targeted taxa.

Trade and exchange

The Torres Strait lies between the highly diverse economies of New Guinea and mainland Australia, with its role as "bridge" or "barrier" between these regions frequently questioned (Haddon 1890: 339-41; 1904: 293-97; Harris 1995; McCarthy 1940; Walker 1972).

Historical and ethnographic sources suggest complex exchange relations existed between Mabuyag, other Torres Strait Islands and New Guinea (Haddon 1890: 342-343; 1904: 293-97; 1908: 186-7; McCarthy 1940; Moore 1972: 333; Vanderwal 2004). This included a trade route which connected Mabuyag to Badu, Muralug and coastal New Guinea (Lawrence 1998: 14; Moore 1979: 301). Trade involved the movement of cassowary feathers, bird of paradise plumes and canoes into the Torres Strait from New Guinea and spears and spear throwers from Cape York, which were exchanged for pearl shells, cone-shell breast pendants and dugong harpoons (Laade 1973; Moore 1979: 301).

While a number of linguistic, ethnographic and historical indicators have been proposed in support of interaction, "few archaeological insights into either trans-Strait prehistoric trade or inter-island social interaction have been made" (Barham et al. 2004: 5). The most convincing studies to date surround petrographic studies of club-heads and axes obtained from museum collections. These suggest late-Holocene movement between Torres Strait and Papua New Guinea (McNiven 1998; McNiven and von Gnielinski 2004; McNiven et al. 2004b). Exotic lithics have also been recorded from Saibai (possibly from the Papua New Guinea coast) (Barham and Harris 1987: 94-5). In addition, a small number of pottery sherds (radiocarbon dating to 2500-700 cal. BP) from Eastern Torres Strait have been sourced to Papua New Guinea (Carter 2001; 2002b; 2010; Carter et al. 2004).

A tenuous connection has been made between New Guinea and Mabuyag/ Pulu through ceramics. The Western Torres Strait pottery dates to at least 1700-1500 BP (McNiven et al. 2006; Wright and Dickinson 2009), with a possible earlier period of manufacture at 2400-2500 cal. BP (McNiven et al. 2006: 67). It has been established that pottery is locally manufactured, however, the technology of pottery manufacture is expected to have come from pottery using communities known to occupy the south coast of Papua New Guinea during this period (see McNiven et al. 2011). Whether or not early dates for the Pulu ceramics are accepted, it is important to examine the extent to which this reflects trans Torres Strait interactions. The composition of Mabuyag and Pulu sherds is revealing in this respect. Petrographic study identified significant quantitities of sand used for temper, near maximal for the retention of plasticity and workability and well beyond the normal ratio for other Oceanic sherds (which rarely exceeds 30 % sand to clay; Dickinson 2006: 21). According to Bill Dickinson (pers. comm., March 2006) it would be difficult for any pot to survive the firing process. While the Pulu pottery consists entirely of terrigenous sand and therefore may reflect natural inclusions in the clay, the Muyi example included both terrigenous and calcareous sand suggesting that this was a deliberate decision by the potter. This may demonstrate experimentation by an individual who had minimal knowledge of pottery manufacture or a different (as yet unresolved) motivation

for firing clay to the potters from New Guinea and Eastern Torres Strait. Should we accept the former hypothesis then it is plausible that Western Torres Strait Islander voyagers to Eastern Torres Strait or Papua New Guinea brought back ideas but not detailed knowledge of pottery manufacture technologies. It is considered highly unlikely that this represents an incursion from Papua New Guinea. Alternatively, Western Torres Strait Islanders were using technologies that were not connected with either Eastern Torres Strait or Papua New Guinea. While new sites (with rim sherds) are required to establish the antiquity and role of pottery/ baked clay in Torres Strait, I suggest that the Mabuyag and Pulu sherds do not necessarily demonstrate a link between Papua New Guinea and Western Torres Strait. It is plausible that the Western Torres Strait history of interaction with Papua New Guinea was very different (and much later) than Eastern Torres Strait.

McNiven (2006) has suggested that the onset of increased midden activity after 800 years ago across Western Torres Strait, suggests an increase in population and human mobility. While increased midden activity may support increased mobility and Papuan expansion, without well-dated, exotic artefacts (e.g., pottery, lithics) or definitive, well-dated and shared rock art traditions this connection remains problematic.

Based on the Mabuyag results, the main phase of inter-action between Western Torres Strait and New Guinea/ South East Asia most likely occurred within the past 400 years. At Dhabangay, a single glass flake was found in deposits dating after 317 cal. BP, separated from 19th century, European glass by over 20 cm of deposit. The flake contained dangerously high levels of copper that would be highly unusual for 19th century European glass. While detailed analysis was unable to resolve provenance of this artefact it may be part of an earlier phase of contact. This would fit with discoveries of South East Asian ceramics likely to date to approximately 300-400 BP, from excavated deposits at Goemu and Pulu (Grave and McNiven 2013).

Haddon (1904: 4-5; see also David and Mura Badulgal 2006: 127; Landtman 1927: 329) linked the Western Torres Strait kod with the Horimu grounds and Kwadi in Northern Torres Strait and Papua New Guinea. Based on archaeological results the Torres Strait kod is likely to date within the past 400 years. Brady (2010: 163, 255-56) demonstrated striking similarities between rock art from the Pulu kod and immediate vicinity (e.g., the Mask motif from Mask Cave) and material culture objects from New Guinea. In addition, ethnographic records suggest that yellow pigment used on Pulu may have been imported from Saibai and/ or Kiwai Island (McNiven and David 2004: 219). The kod at Wagedoegam provides further insight into increased connectivity between Mabuyag and Papua New Guinea. Rock art from this site includes distinctive Papuan (spikey haired) figures, one of whom wears a Torres Strait (dhoeri) headdress. This figure closely compares to material culture objects and art in Papua New Guinea (Brady 2010: 361; Paul Taçon pers. comm., November 2014). The only comparable, x-ray style figures recorded for Torres Strait are those from Dauan (off the coast of Papua New Guinea) (Brady 2010: 352, 361; McNiven *et al.* 2004c). Oral histories from this site suggest that one phase of rock art was conducted by Kiwai raiders during an attack on Dauan (McNiven *et al.* 2004c: 248-249). The Wagedoegam *kod* has recently been re-excavated and rock art re-analysed, with a detailed discussion to follow (Wright *et al.* In prep).

8.3   Goemulgaw fissioning and regionalisation

The regionalisation model predicts that socio-demographic pressure will lead to the formation of new groups occupying increasingly restrictive territories (McNiven 1999). Excavations have revealed ephemeral visitation (at Dhabangay) from 7200 BP and at Muyi after 1600 years BP. Archaeological materials from these early assemblages provide little comparison to ethnography of the contemporary Goemulgal. Specifically, pottery does not appear in oral histories nor is there evidence for ethnographically-known settlement and subsistence patterns (i.e., sustained settlement at village sites and the prominence of dugong). The socio-political and ceremonial dimensions of the contemporary community (i.e., totems and ceremonies connected with the sea) also appear to be lacking. That is not to say that an earlier connection does not exist, rather we have moved beyond the point where such a connection can be made through archaeology.

Both archaeology and ethnography suggest that Wagedoegam was the earliest Mabuyag village and the origin for fissioning on the island. Excavations reveal an early phase (1057–896 cal. BP) of sustained settlement by people who ate large marine vertebrates and manufactured quartz and igneous flaked artefacts. This corresponds with oral histories, suggesting that people who possessed economies similar to contemporary Islanders emerged at least 1000 years ago. Earlier (or overlapping) settlement may have also occurred on Pulu, with cultural materials underlying the *kod* (1160–894 cal. BP) and Tiger shark Rockshelter (1300–700 cal. BP) (McNiven *et al.* 2008; 2009). Substantial decline in cultural activity at Wagedoegam (after 900 BP) coincides with initial settlement at Goemu (Fig. 8.1). During this period midden activity occurs at Tiger shark Rockshelter and in deposits underlying the Pulu *kod* (McNiven *et al.* 2008, 2009) supporting increased socio-demographic pressures on the resident population.

A key aspect of the Goemulgaw ethnography is affiliation with multiple, totemically-organised villages. Archaeology suggests that sustained settlement of multiple villages (Dhabangay, Goemu and Muyi) by advanced maritime specialists occurred within the past 500-300 years. This appears to coincide with reduced activity/ abandonment of the north western side of Mabuyag (Wagedoegam) and Pulu (Tiger shark Rockshelter, also settlement pre-dating the *kod*) after 535-464 cal. BP. During this period increased settlement activity (including substantial dugong bone mounds) occurred at Dhabangay and Goemu on the north and east coast of Mabuyag. McNiven *et al.* (2008: 15) suggest this marked a settlement shift towards "larger more communal settlements (i.e., open villages)". It is argued here, that it represents an increasing focus on the east coast of Mabuyag, specifically Goemu. I suggest that Goemu became increasingly central to Islander (Goemulgal) cosmologies during this period, marking the point at which "Mabuiag became a residential island and a separate people (i.e., the Goemulgal) with their own identity" (McNiven *et al* 2006: 75).

The most recent stage of Goemulgaw fissioning was the historically-documented move to Baw (<150 BP). Historically, this represents the final stage of "centralisation" towards localised settlement of the east coast of Mabuyag. Archaeology provides an alternative narrative with midden activity, maintenance of traditional economies and construction of totemic stone arrangements continuing at many traditional villages well into the twentieth century (see also Ghaleb 1990: 234, 301; McNiven and Wright 2008; McNiven *et al.* In press). This included visitation of the remote village, Wagedoegam, by people who used flaked stone and glass artefacts. As explored earlier, less autonomy was observed inside the LMS–controlled village of Baw (Wright and Ricardi In press). Ongoing links between past and present were further evident at Baw through the use of two stones from Goemu (connected with Kwoiam) in the pedestal of the church font. Reverend John Done (1987: 18) recognised that "it was appropriate that these two stones, so intimately connected with the dark times, as pre Christian days are called, should be used in the making of the font, the gateway of Christian life".

McNiven (1999) suggested that the formation of increasingly large, congregative settlements may require support from new, delayed production systems. This is firmly supported by the Mabuyag results. Harris *et al.* (1985: 47) observed that fish traps on Mabuyag are invariably found close to villages (e.g., Goemu, Panay, Awbayth and Wagedoegam), suggesting a late Holocene antiquity for these sites. As they are located near multiple ancestral villages (i.e., not just associated with Wagedoegam) it is probable that fish traps were continuing to be made long after establishment of multiple residential centres on the east coast of the island (i.e., after 500-300 cal. BP). An intriguing study for research will be to assess whether fish traps reflect fissioning patterns observed for associated villages. While this can not yet be confirmed, it was observed that the appearance and size of fish traps on north/ west and east coasts were very different. Those adjacent to Wagedoegam (and surrounding islets) are substantial (both size of rocks used and circumference), involving multiple, overlapping fish traps. Those on the east coast were compact, small and utilised smaller rocks. Whether this reflects a chronologically discrete pattern or different ecologies on both sides of the island will be an interesting study for further research. It is unresolved whether horticultural practices were also necessitated by increased demographic pressures during the late Holocene. While field features were observed to underlay stone-bone-shell mounds at Dhabangay (Harris and Ghaleb 1987: 27), excavation of this site suggest that midden layers in some parts of this village date to within the past 300 years. Resolution to this question would be of great value to our understanding of settlement activities in Western Torres Strait.

The expectation that fissioning may necessitate new political and ceremonial activities to negotiate change does fit with the Mabuyag results. McNiven *et al.* (2009: 314) hypothesised that "the [*K*]*od*, and by association the Goemulgal and their totemic clan and moiety system, emerged over the past 400 years". Haddon (1904: 55) observed a spatial division between two moieties, with the *Koey Awgadhaw Khazi* affiliated with the people of Wagedoegam and the *Moegi Awgadhaw Khazi* affiliated with most of the villages on the east and south side of the island. As midden activity was initiated at Wagedoegam and Goemu between 1000-800 years ago, it is plausible that the two moiety systems developed during this period. A subsequent expansion, involving site (re)establishment or increased activity at existing sites, on the east coast of Mabuyag, occurred approximately 550-400 years ago. This coincided with the onset of installations associated with the *kod*, including those situated in more distant, liminal spaces (e.g., adjacent islets and the west coast of Mabuyag) (see McNiven *et al.* 2009; Wright *et al.* In prep). This corresponds with the appearance of ethnographically-significant bone mounds at Pulu (*Moegi sibuy*) and Mabuyag (Dhabangay and probably Wagedoegam), also *bu* shell arrangements (Koey *Awgadhaw khazi*, Kwoiam's grave) (McNiven *et al.* 2009: 314). This is interpreted as a recent period of settlement/ clan fissioning, with new spatial and spiritual boundaries negotiated through ritual activities at ethnographically-significant villages. Archaeological research at Wagedoegam and Pulu suggested that strong connections were maintained with ancestral village locales despite the absence of settlement activity at these sites (Wright 2011c).

The regionalisation model predicts that fissioning events may be physically expressed through unique sites and/or cultural materials. Goemulgaw Traditional Owners confirm this to be the case, designating totemic associations to human-made sites (e.g., dugong bone mound at Dhabangay), cultural materials (crocodile carvings, *kuthibu* and *giribu*) and intangible markers (e.g., culture hero sites, *wiway* shrine at Goemu). Archaeological surveys identified physical (and often monumental) features that were distinctive to villages. These included the large complex of midden mounds at Goemu, rock

art panels at Wagedoegam and a network of stone-lined paths at Dhabangay. All villages (with the exception of Maydh) contained midden and circular bone mounds; however, platform and ridge midden mounds were unique to Goemu. In addition to unique monumental sites and site combinations, Goemu, Dhabangay and Maydh were associated with stone arrangements "out of respect" for the primary and occasionally secondary totem animal (Tim Gizu, pers. comm., 10 November 2006).

In keeping with the regionalisation model restrictions appear to have been lowered at prescribed places. The Pulu *kod* appears to have been one such site, ethnographically-recorded to be a nexus for sacred and secular activity involving all Mabuyag clans. This scenario is supported by archaeology through the quantity, variety and spatial division of cultural features. The Pulu *kod* was observed to contain numerous sites that are otherwise unique to individual villages on Mabuyag (i.e., bone mounds, stone arrangements, rock art). Pulu also contains the highest density of rock art sites (*n*=14) and motifs (*n*=103) within Goemulgaw territory (Brady 2010: 127, 163). The variety of rock art is high with "a close correspondence between Pulu's painted Zoomorphs and the known Goemulgal totemic animal species" (Brady 2010: 164). This includes a red ochre bird and anthropomorphic figures wearing headdresses, not dissimilar to those recorded at the Wagedoegam *kod*. While totemic associations rely to a large extent on ethnography, the scale and nature of the Pulu *kod* rock art and surface archaeology support the classification of this site as the "national Kwod of the Goemulgal" (Haddon 1904).

8.4 Conclusions

Archaeological research confirms human settlement on Mabuyag from the mid Holocene. To answer the original question set by McNiven *et al.* (2006: 75), extensive human settlement of the Mabuyag Islands appears to originate at Wagadagam after 1057 cal BP. This may have been preceded by 100–200 years at two sites on adjacent Pulu. Archaeology identifies multiple fissioning events (approximately 800 BP, 550 BP, 150 BP) with each stage marked by new (and frequently monumental) sites. In keeping with ethnographic expectations of fissioning, increased congregative settlements required new production systems (fish traps, and potentially agriculture), most likely within the past 550 years. There is also evidence that spatial shifts resulted in the development of new cosmologies (the origin of moiety and clan affiliations) during this period. Altered socio-political identies were negotiated across Goemulgaw territory, and more broadly through western Torres Strait, by the establishment of new ritual centres (including the *kod*) after 400 years ago. The positioning of *kod* sites at ancestral (most likely unoccupied) villages on Pulu and Mabuyag suggests communities were places of power and significance, a connection maintained through stories and song. In keeping with ethnographic expectations of fissioning, the Goemulgal cement identity through social gatherings at the Pulu *kod*, physically marked by the amalgamation of sites otherwise unique to individual villages. In contrast to previous work this study has looked at the fissioning process from a fine-grained perspective, with all events within the past 1000 years. Very few Australian archaeologists have looked in detail at changes over this short time period yet there is increasing evidence that major changes did take place at this time. While some attempts have been made to relate changes to responses to environmental changes, such as the Little Ice Age (e.g., Williams *et al.* 2010), it is also possible to explore the social dimensions of these changes. The fissioning model allows archaeology and oral histories to intersect providing a history that is meaningful to both academic and Indigenous communities. The archaeology of villages on Mabuyag provides a microcosm of the dynamic, variable and complex community that is Goemulgal. The results presented in this book indicate that social change and social divisions can be observed in the Torres Strait despite vibrant inter-relations, trade and exchange. It remains to be seen whether the same fine-grained perspective can be successfully applied to other contexts in the Australia/ Pacific region.

Appendix 1: Further archaeological context for Torres Strait (adapted from Wright *et al.* 2013)

To date, the earliest direct evidence for human settlement in Torres Strait is found on Badu. Excavations revealed charcoal and stone artefacts indicative of sustained human activity, between 8000 - 6000 years ago, during a period of shallow shelf inundation and island formation (David *et al.* 2004c: 72). This was followed during the interval 6000 – 3500 cal. BP by sparse lithics indicative of sporadic visitation. Based on the lack of early sites in the Eastern Islands or southern New Guinea, as well as the significant sea distances between the latter and Western Torres Strait it was posited that this early to mid-Holocene occupation was an Australian incursion (David *et al.* 2009: 74).

Low intensity occupation by marine specialists is recorded between 3800–2400 years ago on two small islets, Berberass and Pulu (Crouch *et al.* 2007; McNiven *et al.* 2006). This coincided with a period of "sustained settlement" of Badu 15 (David *et al.* 2004c: 74). Swamp cores identify an increase in landscape burning and vegetation management during this period (Rowe 2005: 328). David *et al.* (2004: 74) speculated that these events might reflect widespread Austronesian migration but others have postulated a "major demographic expansion of local populations" within Torres Strait and mainland Australia (McNiven *et al.* 2006: 66; see also Carter 2002b; Carter and Lilley 2008).

Mask Cave, Berberass and Badu 15 experienced "a dramatic burst" of activity after 2600 - 2500 cal. BP, interpreted as evidence for a migration of "Papuan maritime, horticultural and pottery-making peoples to the eastern and western islands" (McNiven *et al.* 2006: 49; see also Crouch *et al.* 2007: 61-62; David *et al.* 2004c)[6]. This fits with a wider pattern of island settlement throughout the Torres Strait (Barham 1999; Barham *et al.* 2000: 227-8, 272; 2004; Golson 1972). It is also associated with the formation of a 'Torres Strait Cultural Complex' (Barham 2000: 227). This involved increasing marine specialisation, a shift in cosmology towards the sea and fluid links between islands through exchange, warfare, intermarriage and maritime voyaging (Barham 2000: 228). During this period pottery may have been introduced to Pulu (in the Western Islands) and Ormi and Sokoli (in the Eastern Islands). McNiven *et al.* (2006; see also Carter and Lilley 2008) associate the 2500 BP settlement expansions with a "Papuan influx".

Finally, after 800 years ago there emerged a number of ethnographically-known social and ceremonial arrangements including stone, bone and shell ritual places and totemically-organised villages (McNiven 2006 see also David *et al.* 2004a; 2005; McNiven *et al.* 2009; Moore 1979). It has further been suggested that a "higher frequency of basal site ages [occur] within the period 550-850 BP" (Barham *et al.* 2004: 36; see also Rowlands 1985: 130). This includes the first settlement of the Kaurareg archipelago in the South Western Islands (Moore 1984: 153) and Dauan in the Top Western Islands (McNiven 2006).

Is there evidence for changes in lithic technology during the mid to late Holocene?

Barham *et al.* (2004: 53) observed that "[a]rchaeological data offers little to supplement ethnographic accounts of lithic trade movements…Almost all evidence for lithic use and manufacture is non-stratigraphic". A detailed record was recently provided for a late Holocene stratified assemblage at Dauan 4, in the north western islands (McNiven 2006); however, long term change in artefact technologies remains poorly understood.

At Badu 15, "the only definite cultural materials" were lithics, with 17 definite and 11 likely stone artefacts excavated from layers predating 5966 ± 39 BP and a larger number (46 definite and 24 likely) excavated from layers postdating 3317 - 3310 cal. BP (David *et al.* 2004c: 70-71). Detailed analysis of this lithic assemblage remains unpublished; however, David (*et al.* 2004c: 71) observed overall consistency through time in size (small) and material ("quartz and volcanic rocks").

At Mask Cave, lithics (N = 842) were consistently small (mean weight = 0.6 g), manufactured from quartz (77 %), rhylote ignimbrite (18 %), granite (3 %), microgranite and felsic dikes (1 %) and volcanic (1 %) stone (McNiven *et al.* 2006: 62). McNiven *et al.* (2006: 60) recorded a "major division in cultural items…between lower levels dated to 2900 - 3800 years ago and upper levels dated within the last 2600 years". While rhyolitic ignimbrite and quartz were in predominant use throughout, microgranite and felsic dike rocks (i.e., markers of isolated source outcrops) were more common during the later period (McNiven *et al.* 2006: 63). McNiven *et al.* (2006: 63) were uncertain whether this indicated an initial "lack of familiarity of rock outcrops" or "new functional requirements of stone tools and the need for finer-grained raw materials". Large quantities of lithics were recovered from contexts postdating 1700 years ago, with quartz bipolar flakes the dominant form (McNiven *et al.* 2006: 63).

At Badu 19, little vertical change was observed in lithic size, material or manufacture (Crouch *et al.* 2007). Flaked

---

6 At Woam village on Saibai Island (NW Torres Strait) a bone/ shell midden was radiocarbon dated to 1080 ± 60 BP or (based on one "chronologically anomalous" determination) 2540 ± 60 BP (Barham 1999: 79). No correction was applied for marine isotopic fractionation due to uncertainties surrounding reservoir effects in estuarine areas (Barham 1999: 79). Two charcoal determinations from samples collected at similar depths provided much younger determinations (780 ± 70 BP and 410 ± 80 BP). Due to uncertainties surrounding the chronology of this site we do not include this in our review.

artefacts were consistently small (mean weight = 0.3 g), with quartz (88 %) dominant, and a small igneous component (12 %; Crouch *et al.* 2007: 58). Most quartz lithics were made from "crystal-facet" and "other", suggesting targeted collection from "terrestrial exposures" and "veins within granite outcrops" (Crouch *et al.* 2007: 58). Quartz artefacts "exhibit evidence of bipolar (anvil) reduction", not observed for the 6 igneous artefacts (Crouch *et al.* 2007: 58). The lack of cortex on igneous cores suggested original reduction away from Berberass. Consistent with Mask Cave, the Badu 19 assemblage suggested an increase in lithic discard rates after 2600-2500 cal. BP.

At Dauan 4, little change was observed within the past 700 years, with the assemblage dominated by quartz bipolar micro-cores and flakes (McNiven 2006: 6). Based on ethnographic analogy, McNiven (2006: 6) suggested that "bipolar quartz artefacts may have been used, at least in part, for social (cicatures) and / or therapeutic (bloodletting) reasons". Quartz may also have been used for renewing the edge of bamboo knives and for sawing once hafted onto a handle (McNiven 2006: 6). The small size of flakes and the lack of correlation between distribution of artefacts and faunal remains suggested butchering was not the principal purpose for small quartz artefacts.

In summary, lithic analyses at a range of sites across the region reveal consistent use of locally available raw materials (e.g., igneous, volcanic, quartz) through the past 8000 years but with several changes in raw material selection and reduction technology. After 4000 years ago there is evidence for production of large numbers of small, quartz, bipolar flakes and cores (Crouch *et al.* 2007; McNiven *et al.* 2006). After 2600 - 2500 years ago, a marked increase in lithic discard rates and shift towards fine grained raw materials suggests a major alteration in western Torres Strait settlement and / or subsistence activities (Crouch *et al.* 2007; McNiven *et al.* 2006). Bipolar micro-cores may have become increasingly prominent after 1700 years ago (McNiven 2006; McNiven *et al.* 2006).

Is there evidence for changes in subsistence practices during the mid to late Holocene?

Present Torres Strait Islanders are maritime specialists, the sea "pervading cosmologies, oral traditions, art, material culture, songs, dances, ceremonies, rituals, and subsistence" (Crouch *et al.* 2007: 50; see also Barham 2000; Beckett 1972; Haddon 1904; McNiven and Feldman 2003). The development of these specialised "Islander" economies is expected to have been at least partially dependent on geomorphologic and palaeoenvironmental shifts connected with sea level change (see Barham and Chappell 2005; Lambeck and Chapell 2001; Rowe 2011 for details). Faunal remains within archaeological contexts provide direct insight into the antiquity of environmental changes and the socio-economic responses of Islander

communities (e.g., Barham 2000; Barham *et al.* 2004; Crouch *et al.* 2007; McNiven *et al.* 2006; Wright 2011a). Only two sites (Badu 19 and Mask Cave) provide evidence for human subsistence practices between 4000–2500 years ago (Crouch *et al.* 2007: 57). At Mask Cave, fragments of large marine vertebrates (mainly turtle) and fish were excavated from layers postdating 4000 years ago (McNiven *et al.* 2006). McNiven *et al.* (2006: 62) suggested "a marine subsistence focus on offshore (turtle and to a lesser extent dugong) and near-shore low tide reef pool (small fish) resources throughout the site history". At Berberass layers dating between 4000–2600 years ago produced fauna derived from varied habitats (including sandy, rocky, and coral-reef littoral) but dominated by a gastropod *Nerita* sp. and Emperor fishes (Lethrinidae) (Crouch *et al.* 2007: 57).

After 2600 years ago the Badu 19 sequence shows "a clear chronological difference between the range of fish caught", with sharks and rays (Elasmobranchii), puffers (Tetraodontidae) and wrasses (Labridae) replacing Emperors. Quantities of dugong and turtle bone increased while shellfish decreased suggesting to some researchers the development of "advanced marine subsistence practices" with "a greater emphasis on larger, marine animals" (Crouch *et al.* 2007: 60). At Mask Cave a larger quantity of faunal remains was observed after 2500 years ago, with shellfish/ crustaceans, shark, parrotfish (Scaridae) and puffers added to the diet (McNiven *et al.* 2006: 59). Crouch *et al.* (2007: 57) used the faunal evidence from these sites to infer "long-term importance of inshore resources to Torres Strait Islanders".

In summary, there is evidence that people were hunting dugong and turtle, also fishing on Pulu and Berberass from at least 4000 years ago (Crouch *et al.* 2007; McNiven *et al.* 2006). After 2600 years ago, there is an increase at Badu 19 and Mask Cave in both the quantity and variety of fish species caught, with a transition from littoral reef species (Emperors) to varied deep and shallow water species (Crouch *et al.* 2007).

The European presence in the Torres Strait

In 1606 Luis Vaez de Torres, a Spanish seaman on an expedition from Peru, successfully navigated the Strait between New Guinea and Australia. This was later to be named after him by the Scottish geographer Alexander Dalrymple (Mullins 1995). Further expeditions which skirted the southern and western margins of the Torres Strait involved the Dutch East India Company and Abel Tasman (1623/ 1705 and 1644 respectively) and Lieutenant Cook (in 1770). In 1789 and 1792 Bligh explored the passage through the reefs recording Darnley Island and finally passed between Mabuyag and Badu (Allen and Corris 1977: 7-8). This was followed by exploration voyages by Matthew Flinders in 1802 and Captain Lewis of the "Investigator" in 1836. The first scientific surveys were the "Fly" expedition (between 1842 and 1846) and the "Rattlesnake" expedition (between 1846 and 1850) (MacGillivray 1852). A phased colonial occupation occurred within the Torres Strait with Queensland government officials occupying the settlement at Somerset, on Cape York (Mullins 1995: 31; Lawrence 1998). In 1879 the Torres Strait Islands were annexed by the Queensland Government with the passing of the Queensland Coast Islands Act. By 1871 missionaries and *beche-de-mer* crews had also entered the Torres Strait. This significantly increased the contact between Indigenous peoples and Europeans, Pacific Islanders, Malays and Japanese (Mullins 1995; Shnukal 2004). Samuel McFarlane and A.W Murray from the London Missionary Society (LMS) introduced Pacific Islanders to a number of islands as teachers (Moore 1979: 235-52). This became known by Islanders throughout the Strait as "The Coming of the Light" and Islander communities were encouraged to centralise around the newly formed church (Mullins 1995). In 1914 the LMS withdrew control over the islands due to government pressure. Schooling was handed over to the Queensland government and the Church of England moved into the region (Mullins 1995).

The European presence on Mabuyag

On Mabuyag "The Coming of the Light" occurred at the end of October 1872 with two Lifuan teachers appointed (Eseli *et al.* 1998: 24). Initially a settlement was formed at Dabangai followed by a move to the currently occupied village of Baw in 1877 (Teske 1986: 2). Mabuyag became the head Missionary Station between November 1899 and April 1900, then from 1904 to 1906 and finally between June 1913 to November 1914 (Eseli *et al.* 1998: 26). As part of increasing government involvement in the Strait Mabuyag was gazetted as an Aboriginal Reserve in 1912 before negotiating a handover from the LMS at the end

of 1914 (Eseli *et al.* 1998: 27-28). Reverend John Done arrived on Mabuyag as the first Church of England pastor in 1914 (Done 1987). The first pearl shelling boats to arrive at Mabuyag were the "Pakeha" and "Melanie" in 1870 (Chester 1871). By 1871 Mabuyag had become a central base for the pearl shelling industry with three stations located on the north coast (Mullins 1995: 7-8). By 1873 the entire population was involved with the fishery (Mullins 1995: 8). Although missionary letters in November 1873 suggest that the Goemulgal were unhappy with the working conditions (e.g., Murray to Mullens Nov 19th 1873; see also Ghaleb 1990: 64) a letter in 1876 suggests that this situation remained unchanged (McFarlane to Murray March 1 1876). By the mid 1880s most communities had become heavily reliant on cash incomes (Shnukal 1992). By 1906 a depression in the pearling industry led to the abandonment of pearl shelling stations on Mabuyag. Further historical information will be provided for individual villages on Mabuyag in Chapter 5.

Alfred Haddon and the Cambridge expedition

Much of the ethnographic data (particularly for Mabuyag) comes from the work of zoologist turned anthropologist Alfred Haddon and a team of researchers from Cambridge University. During a number of months in 1888 and 1898 (at a time of significant religious, social and economic upheaval) Haddon collected vast quantities of artefacts and collated large numbers of traditional histories. These were published in six volumes (1901-1935) of the *Reports of the Cambridge Anthropological Expedition to Torres Straits*. While the evolutionary model followed and the desire to "resuscitate" ceremonies is somewhat dated it has to be acknowledged that these volumes represent an unparalleled anthropological asset for those working in the Torres Strait.

Appendix 2: Mabuyag's portable artefacts from ethnographic accounts and museum collections

Gumugal materials	Origin of technology	Origin of manufacture	Citation	Collected?	Purposes
House building					
reed for thatching (*kamug*)	?	local	Moore 1984: 44	1898	multiple
grass for thatching (*magud*)	?	local	Moore 1984: 44	1898	multiple
Cooking					
melon/baler or *bu* shell pot (*alup*)	?	local	Haddon 1890: 386; 1904: 297; 1935: 303; Moore 1984: 23		camp stove
pearl shell cutting implement (*mai*)	?	local	Moore 1984: 43; Philp 2001: 28	1898	dugong cutter?
polymesoda coexans cutter (*akul*)	PNG?	Badu/Moa or PNG	Moore 1984: 43	1898	knife/ladle
earth oven (*amai*)	?	local	Haddon 1935: 303; Moore 1984: 23		village stove
fire-sticks	?	local	Haddon 1935: 302; Moore 1984: 26		
Cleaning					
coconut leaves broom (*piwul*)	?	local	Haddon 1935: 302; Moore 1984: 44	1898	sweeping huts
pandanus drupe paint brush (*abal*)	?	Mabuyag	Moore 1984: 44	1898	painting
Food preparation					
dried dugong skin (*dangal*)	?	Mabuyag	Haddon 1904: 294; Moore 1984: 45	1898?	for long voyages
Sleeping					
coconut leaf mats (*kai; saramud*)	?	Mabuyag	Haddon 1904: 248; Moore 1984: 42	1898	temporary shelters, sleeping
large pandanus mats (*waku, moder*)	?	local	Haddon 1935: 298; Moore 1984: 26-7		shelter, sails, ceremonial (Pulu Kod)
small pandanus mats (*minilai*)	?	Mabuyag	Haddon 1935: 298; Moore 1984: 42	1898	wrapping, sitting, sleeping, serving food
Warfare					
coconut fibre arm guard (*kadig*)	Fly River	Muralug	Haddon 1890: 331; 1904: 294; Moore 1984: 52	1888	bracer for firing arrows
javelin	Cape York	Cape York	Haddon 1890: 332; 1904: 295; 1935: 304		
throwing stick (*kobai*)	Cape York	Cape York	Haddon 1890: 332; 1904: 295; 328		also used to compel approach of enemy (328)
bow	Fly River	local	Haddon 1890: 332		
arrow	Fly River	Fly River/ Daudai/	Haddon 1904: 295; 1935: 304		
stone clubs (*guba guba/ gabagaba*)	Fly River	Fly River/ Murray Islands/ Daudai/ Tugari pirates/local	Haddon 1890: 334;340; 1904: 294; Moore 1984: 52; Wilkin cited in Haddon 1912: 191	1888	

wooden club occasionally with bamboo handle (*gabagaba*)	Fly River	local	Moore 1984: 52	1888;1898	
bamboo sling (*singi*)	Mabuyag?	Mabuyag	Haddon 1904: 301; 1935: 305; Moore 1984: 52	1898	carrying heads
bamboo knife (*upi*);	?	local	Haddon 1904: 301; Moore 1984: 36		cutting off heads

General

Bags/baskets

pandanus basket (*lie*)	Saibaii/PNG	local	Moore 1984: 42; Philp 2001: 32	1888; 1898	food collecting
plaited coconut fibre bags (*kuta*)	PNG	PNG	Moore 1984: 42	1898	yam collecting
small palm leaf bags (*burua iena*)	PNG	PNG	Moore 1984: 42	1888; 1898	for small objects
throw away palm leaf bag (*balboi*)	local	local	Moore 1984: 42; Philp 2001: 32	1898	fish basket
bamboo/ shell water containers	?	local	Moore 1984: 23		

Tools

sharpened pearl-shell scraper/cutter (*wakabi*)	?	local	Moore 1984: 43	1898	pandanus/reed scraper for mat/basket making
turtle shell needle (*ter*)		local	Haddon 1890: 406; 1935: 294		for nose/ear piercing
fish needles for ear piercing		local	Haddon 1890: 406		
clam-shell axes	?	local	MacFarlane cited in Haddon 1935: 302		clearance, canoe making
polished, volcanic stone adze	Lifu/PNG	Lifu/ PNG	Moore 1984: 44	1898	clearance, canoe making
Tridacna gigas/ bamboo water containers	?	local	Haddon 1904: 125, 151		
Tridacna axe	local	local	Haddon 1935: 302		

Rope and Cord

coconut fibre rope (*muti/ mut-umaizinga*)	local	local	Moore 1984: 43	1898	multiple
coconut-fibre string (*arigal kupmani*)	local	local	Moore 1984: 43	1898	multiple (fishing line)

Recreational activity

bamboo tobacco pipes (*sukuba morap*)	European?	local	Haddon 1935: 304; Moore 1984: 51	1888	

Musical instruments

bamboo & clam shell stridulators (*katak*)	European?	local	Haddon 1904: 372; 1935: 314; Moore 1984: 51	1898	dances, rain making
bamboo/ turtle bone castanets (*morap; wanawa*)	European?	local	Moore 1984: 51	1898	

Ball games

sticks used in ball game like hockey (*dabi*)	?	local	Moore 1984: 51	1898	
carved hard-wood ball used in game (*kokan*)	?	local	Moore 1984: 51	1898	
spherical fruits used in hand-ball game (*kai*)	?	local	Moore 1984: 51	1888?	

Tops & Spinners

lead/ hardwood spinning top (*kolapi*)	?	local	Moore 1984: 51	1898	
pandanus spinners	?	local	Moore 1984: 51	1898	

Grinding & Polishing materials

boar tusk scraper (*gi*)	?	?	Moore 1984: 43	1888	smoothing wood (esp. harpoon shafts)
sponge (*gouga*)	?	local	Moore 1984: 44	1898	polishing wood (esp. harpoons)

Appendix 3: Methodology for obtaining MNI count

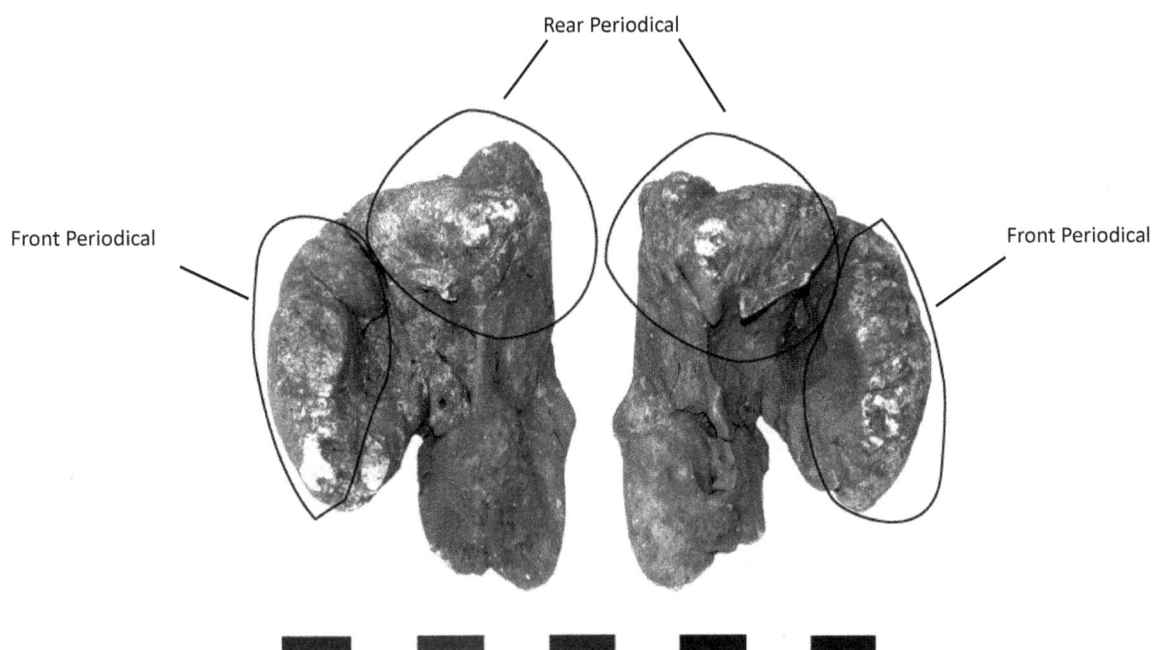

MNI is obtained from danghal ear bone:

1. complete periodical
2. front periodical (including interior groove)

OR

3. rear periodical (including interior groove)

References

Alfred, G. R. (1996). *Heeding the Voices of our Ancestors*. Toronto: Oxford University Press.

Allen, J. and Corris, P. (Eds). (1977). *The Journal of John Sweatman: A Nineteenth Century Surveying Voyage in North Australia and Torres Strait*. St Lucia, Queensland: University of Queensland Press.

Anderson, B. (2006). *Imagined Communities: Reflections on the origin and spread of nationalism*. London: Verso Books.

Ash, J. and David, B. (2008). Mua 22: archaeology at the old village site of Totalai. In B. David, L. Manas and M. Quinnell (Eds), *Gelam's homeland: cultural and natural history of the island of Mua, Torres Strait*, Memoirs of the Queensland Museum Cultural Heritage Series (Vol. 4, pp. 451-472). Brisbane: Queensland Museum.

Ash, J., Brooks, A., David, B. and McNiven, I. J. (2008). European-Manufactured objects from the 'early mission' site of Totalai, Mua (Western Torres Strait). In B. David, D. Tomsana and M. Quinnell (Eds), *Gelam's homeland: cultural and natural history on the island of Mua, Torres Strait*, Memoirs of the Queensland Museum Cultural Heritage Series (Vol. 4, pp. 473-492). Brisbane: Queensland Museum.

Ash, J., Manas, L. and Bosun, D. (2010). Lining the Path: A Seascape Perspective of Two Torres Strait Missions, Northeast Australia. *International Journal of Historical Archaeology*, 14, 56–85.

Barham, A. J. (1999). The local environmental impact of prehistoric populations on Saibai Island, northern Torres Strait, Australia: enigmatic evidence from Holocene swamp lithostratigraphic records. *Quaternary International*, 59, 71-105.

Barham, A. J. (2000). Late Holocene maritime societies in the Torres Strait Islands, northern Australia - cultural arrival or cultural emergence? In S. O'Connor and P. Veth (Eds), *East of Wallace's Line: studies of past and present maritime cultures of the Indo-Pacific Region*, Modern Quaternary Research in Southeast Asia (Vol. 16, pp. 223-314). Rotterdam: A. A. Balkema.

Barham, A. J. and Chappell, J. (2005). Geographic changes of coastal lowlands in the Papuan past. In A. Pawley, R. Attenborough, J. Golson and R. Hide (Eds), *Papuan Pasts: Cultural, linguistic and biological histories of Papuan-speaking peoples*, Pacific Linguistics (Vol. 572, pp. 522-539). Canberra: Research School of Pacific and Asian Studies, Australian National University.

Barham, A. J. and Harris, D. R. (1987). Final Report to the Research and Exploration Committee of the National Geographic Society on Part IIb of the Torres Strait Research Project, July-October 1985. London: Institute of Archaeology, University of London.

Barham, A. J., Roland, M. and Hitchcock, G. (2004). Torres Strait Bepotaim: An overview of Archaeological and Ethnoarchaeological investigations and research. In I. J. McNiven and M. Quinnell (Eds), *Torres Strait Archaeology and Material Culture*, Memoirs of the Queensland Museum Culture Heritage Series (Vol. 3, pp. 1-72). Brisbane: Queensland Museum.

Barker, B. (2004). *The Sea People: Late Holocene maritime specialisation in the Whitsunday Islands, Central Queensland*, Terra Australis (Vol. 20). Canberra: Pandanus Books.

Barth, F. (1969). *Ethnic Groups and Boundaries: The social organisation of culture difference*. Boston: MA, Little and Brown.

Bartlett, M. L. and McAnany, P. A. (2000). 'Crafting' communities: the materialization of Formative Maya identities. In J. Yaeger and M. Canuto (Eds), *The Archaeology of Communities* (pp. 102-122). London and New York: Routledge.

Beck, w. and Sumerville, M. (2005). Conversations between disciplines: historical archaeology and oral history at Yarrawarra. *World Archaeology* 37(3): 468-483

Beckett, J. R. (1963). Rock Paintings of the Torres Straits Islands. *Mankind*, 6(2), 52-56.

Beckett, J. R. (1972). The Torres Strait Islanders. In D. Walker (Ed.), *Bridge and Barrier: The natural and cultural history of Torres Strait* (pp. 307-326). Canberra: Department of Biogeography and Geomorphology. Research School of Pacific Studies. The Australian National University Press.

Beckett, J. R. (1995). The Murray Islands Land Case. *The Australian Journal of Anthropology*, 6(3), 15-31.

Beckett, J. R. (2004). Writing about Islanders: recent research and future directions. In R. Davis (Ed.), *Woven Histories: Torres Strait islander identity, culture and history* (pp. 2-15). Canberra: Aboriginal Studies Press.

Binford, L. R. (1962). Archaeology as Anthropology. *American Antiquity*, 28, 217-225.

Binford, L. R. (1980). Willow Smoke and Dogs' Tails: Hunter-Gatherer Settlement Systems and Archaeological Site Formation. *American Antiquity*, 45(1), 4-20.

Bird, D. W. and Bird, R. B. (1997). Contemporary shellfish gathering among the Miriam of the Torres Strait Islands, Australia: testing of a central place foraging model. *Journal of Archaeological Science*, 24, 39-63.

Bird, D. W. and Bleige Bird, R. B. (2000). The ethnoarchaeology of juvenile foraging: shellfishing strategies among Meriam children. *Journal of Anthropological Archaeology*, 19, 461-476.

Bird, D. W., Richardson, J. L., Veth, P. M. and Barham, A. J. (2002). Explaining shellfish variability in middens on the Miriam Islands, Torres Strait, Australia. *Journal of Archaeological Science*, 29, 457-469.

Birdsell, J. B. (1953). Some environmental and cultural factors influencing the structuring of Australian Aboriginal populations. *American Naturalist*, 87, 171-207.

Bourdieu, P. (1977). *Outline of a Theory of Practice*. Cambridge: Cambridge University Press.

Brady, L. (2005). *Painting Patterns: Torres Strait Region Rock-Art, NE Australia*. Unpublished PhD thesis, Monash University, Melbourne.

Brady, L. (2006). Documenting and analysing rock paintings from Torres Strait, NE Australia, with digital photography and computer image enhancement. *Journal of Field Archaeology*, 31(4), 363-379.

Brady, L. M. (2007). A Different Look: comparative rock-art recording from the Torres Strait using computer enhancement techniques. *Australian Aboriginal Studies*, 1, 98-115.

Brady, L., David, B., Manas, L., Mualgal Native Title Group. and McNiven, I. J. (2004). Rock-Paintings of Mua Island: Initial Results from Torres Strait. *Rock-art Research*, 21(1), 27-46.

Brady, L. (2010). Pictures, Patterns and Objects: Rock-Art of the Torres Strait Islands, Northeastern Australia. Melbourne: Australian Scholarly Publishing Pty Ltd.

Brady, L., and Crouch, J. (2010). "Postcolonial Archaeology with Indigenous Communities: partnership research and ancestral engagement in Torres Strait, NE Australia", in J. Lydon and U. Rizvi (eds.), *Handbook to Postcolonialism and Archaeology*, pp. 413-428. Walnut Creek: Left Coast Press

Brain, C. K. (1993). The occurrence of burnt bones at Swarkrans and their implications for the control of fire by early hominids. In C.K. Brain (Ed.), *Swarkrans. A Cave's Chronicle of Early Man*, pp. 229-242. Transvaal Museum Monograph 8. Transvaal: Transvaal Museum.

Bronk Ramsay, C. (2009). Bayesian analysis of radiocarbon dates. *Radiocarbon*, 51(1), 337–336

Burke, H. and Smith, C. (2004). *The Archaeologists Field Handbook*. Crow's Nest, New South Wales: Allen and Unwin Press.

Byrne, S. (2012). Community Archaeology as Knowledge Management: Reflections from Uneapa Island, Papua New Guinea. *Public archaeology*, 11(1), 26–52.

Caldwell, J. R. (1959). The new American archaeology. *Science*, 129, 303-307.

Carter, M. (2001). New evidence for the earliest human occupation in Torres Strait, Northeastern Australia. *Australian Archaeology*, 52, 50-52.

Carter, M. (2002a). The Murray Islands archaeological project: results of recent archaeological analyses. *Australian Aboriginal Studies*, 2, 75-77.

Carter, M. (2002b). Recent Results of Excavations on the Murray Islands, Eastern Torres Strait and Implications for Early Links with New Guinea: Bridge and Barrier Revisited. In S. Ulm, C. Westcott, J. Reid, A. Ross, I. Lilley, J. Prangnell and L. Kirkwood (Eds), *Barrier, Borders, Boundaries: Proceedings of the 2001 Australian Archaeological Association Annual Conference*, Tempus (Vol. 7, pp. 1-10). Brisbane: The University of Queensland.

Carter, M. (2006). North of the Cape and south of the Fly: discovering the archaeology of social complexity in Torres Strait. In B. David, B. Barker and I. J. McNiven (Eds), *The Social Archaeology of Australian Indigenous Societies* (pp. 287-305). Canberra: Aboriginal Studies Press.

Carter, M. (2010). From humble beginnings: Vanderwal's 1972 fieldwork and recent theories on settlement, subsistence and trade in Torres Strait. *The Artefact*, 33, 109-118.

Carter, M. and Lilley, I. (2008). Between the Australian and Melanesian realms: the archaeology of the Murray islands and consideration of a settlement model for Torres Strait. In J. Conolly and M. Campbell (Eds.), *Comparative Island Archaeologies* (pp. 69-83). Oxford: British Archaeological Reports.

Carter, M., Barham, L. J., Veth, P., Bird, D. W., O'Connor, S. and Bird, R. B. (2004). The Murray Islands Archaeological Project: excavations on Mer and Dauar, eastern Torres Strait. In I. J. McNiven and S. Quinnell (Eds.), *Torres Strait Archaeology and Material Culture*, Memoirs of the Queensland Museum Cultural Heritage Series (Vol. 3, pp. 163-182). Brisbane: Queensland Museum.

Chappell, J. (2005). Geographic changes of coastal lowlands in the Papuan past. In A. Pawley, R. Attenborough, J. Golson and R. Hide (Eds), *Papuan Pasts: Cultural, linguistic and biological histories of Papuan-speaking peoples* (Vol. 572, pp. 525-539). Canberra: Pacific Linguistics, Research School of Pacific and Asian Studies, The Australian National University.

Chester, H. M. (1898). Papua New Guinea. Unpublished Report. National Library of Australia, Melbourne.

Childe, V. G. (1956). *Piecing Together the Past: The interpretation of archaeological data*. London: Routledge and Keegan Paul.

Clarke, A. (2002). The ideal and the real: Cultural and personal transformations of archaeological research on Groote Eylandt, northern Australia. *World Archaeology*, 34(2), 249-264.

Crouch, J., McNiven, I., David, B., Rowe, C. and Weisler, M. (2007). Berberass: marine resource specialisation and environmental change in Torres Strait during the past 4000 years. *Archaeology in Oceania*, 42(2), 49-64.

David, B. (1991). Fern Cave, rock-art and social formations: rock-art regionalisation and demographic changes in south-eastern Cape York Peninsula. *Archaeology in Oceania*, 26, 41-57.

David, B. (2002). *Landscapes, Rock-art and the Dreaming: an archaeology of preunderstanding*. London: Leicester University Press.

David, B. and Ash, J. (2008). What do early European contact-period villages in Torres Strait look like? Archaeological implications. In B. David, L. Manas, M. Quinnell (Eds), *Gelam's homeland: cultural and natural history of the island of Mua, Torres Strait*, Memoirs of the Queensland Museum Cultural Heritage Series (Vol. 4, pp. 427-450). Brisbane: Queensland Museum.

David, B. and Cole, N. (1990). Rock-art and inter-regional interaction in northeastern Australian prehistory. *Antiquity*, 64(245), 788-806.

David, B. and Lourandos, H. (1998). Rock-art and Socio-Demography in Northeastern Australian Prehistory. *World Archaeology*, 30(2), 193-219.

David, B. and McNiven, I. J. (2004). Western Torres Strait cultural history project: research design and initial results. In I. J. McNiven and M. Quinnell (Eds.), *Torres Strait Archaeology and Material Culture*, Memoirs of the Queensland Museum Cultural Heritage Series (Vol. 3, pp. 199-208). Brisbane: Queensland Museum.

David, B. and Mura Badulgal Committee (2006). What happened in Torres Strait 400 years ago? Ritual transformations in an island seascape. *Journal of Island and Coastal Archaeology*, 1, 123-143.

David, B. and Weisler, M. (2006). Kurturniawak (Badu) and the Archaeology of Villages in Torres Strait. *Australian Archaeology*, 63, 21-34.

David, B., Barker, B. and McNiven, I. (Eds). (2006). *The Social Archaeology of Australian Indigenous Societies*. Canberra: Aboriginal Studies Press.

David, B., Crouch, J. and Zoppi, U. (2005). Historicizing the spiritual: Bu shell arrangements on the Island of Badu, Torres Strait. *Cambridge Archaeological Journal*, 15(1), 71-91.

David, B., McNiven, I. J. and Weisler, M. (2008). Archaeological excavations at Gerain and Urakaraltam. In B. David, D. Tomsana and M. Quinnell (Eds), *Gelam's homeland: Cultural and natural history on the island of Mua, Torres Strait*, Memoirs of the Queensland Museum Cultural Heritage Series (Vol. 4, pp. 525-552). Brisbane: Queensland Museum.

David, B., McNiven, I. J., Crouch, J., Mura Badulgal Corporation Committee. Skelly, R., Barker, B. and Courtney, C. (2009). Koey Ngurtai: the emergence of a ritual domain in western Torres Strait. *Archaeology in Oceania*, 44(1), 1-17.

David, B., McNiven, I. J., Manas, L. Manas, J., Savage, S., Crouch, J. (2004a). Goba of Mua: Archaeology working with oral tradition. *Antiquity*, 78, 158-172.

David, B., McNiven, I.J., Mura Badulgal Corporation Committee, Crouch, J. and Brady, L. (2004b). The Argan stone arrangement complex, Badu Island: initial results from Torres Strait. *Australian Archaeology*, 58, 1-6.

David, B., McNiven, I. J., Mitchell, R., Orr, M., Haberle, S., Brady, L. and Crouch, J. (2004c). Badu 15 and the Papuan-Austronesian settlement of Torres Strait. *Archaeology in Oceania*, 39, 65-78.

Davis, S. L. and Prescott, J. R. V. (1992). *Aboriginal Frontiers and Barriers in Australia*. Melbourne: Melbourne University Press.

Dickinson, W. (2006). T*emper Sands in Prehistoric Oceanian Pottery: Geotectonics, sedimentology, petrography, provenance*. Geological Society of America, Special Paper 406. Boulder, Colorado.

Done, J. J. E. (1987). *Wings across the Sea*. Diaries (1915-1926) compiled by B. Stevenson. Brisbane: B. D. Boolarong Publications.

Dortch, C. E. (2002). Modelling past Aboriginal hunter-gatherer socio-economic and territorial organization in Western Australia's lower south-west. *Archaeology in Oceania*, 37(1), 1-21.

Edwards, R. and Edwards, A. (1997). *An Explorer's Guide to Mabuiag Island in the Torres Strait*. Kuranda, Queensland: The Rams Skull Press.

Eseli, P., Shnukal, A. and Mitchell, R. (1998). *Eseli's Notebook*. Aboriginal and Torres Strait Islander Studies Unit Research Report Series (Vol. 3). Brisbane: University of Queensland Press.

Fullagar, R. and Head, L. (2000). Archaeology and Native Title in Australia: national and local perspectives. In I. Lilley (Ed.), *Native Title and the transformation of archaeology in the postcolonial world* (Vol. 50, pp. 24-34). Sydney: Oceania monograph.

Ghaleb, B. (1990). An Ethnoarchaeological Study of Mabuiag Island, Torres Strait, Northern Australia. Unpublished PhD thesis, University College London.

Ghaleb, B. (1998). Fish and Fishing on a Western Torres Strait island, Northern Australia: Ethnographic and Archaeological Perspectives. Internet Archaeology, 4 (http://intarch.a c. uk/journal/issue4/ghaleb/to c. html).

Gill, W. W. (1876). *Life in the southern isles; or, scenes and incidents in the South Pacific and New Guinea*. London: The Religious Tract Society.

Godwin, L. (2005). 'Everyday archaeology': Archaeological heritage management and its relationship to native title in development-related process. *Australian Aboriginal Studies*, 1, 74-83.

Golson, J. (1972). Land connections, sea barriers and the relationship of Australian and New Guinea prehistory. In D. Walker (Ed.), *Bridge and Barrier: The natural and cultural history of Torres Strait* (pp. 375-298). Canberra: Department of Biogeography and Goemorphology. Research School of Pacific Studies. The Australian National University.

Grave, P. and McNiven, I. J. (2013). Geochemical provenience of 16th to 19th century C.E. Asian ceramics. *Journal of Archaeological Science*, 40, 4538-4551.

Gillespie, R. and Temple, R. (1977). Radiocarbon dating of shell middens. *Archaeology and Physical Anthropology in Oceania* 12, 26-37.

Greer, S. Harrison, R. and McIntyre-Tamwoy, S. (2002). Community-based archaeology in Australia. *World Archaeology*, 34(2), 265–287.

Guilfoyle, D. R. (2005). Socializing stone artefact assemblages: Regionalization and raw material availability in northern Queensland. *Australian Archaeology*, 60, 34-40.

Haddon, A. C. (1890). The Ethnography of the Western Tribe of Torres Straits. *The Journal of the Anthropological Institute of Great Britain and Ireland*, 19, 297-440.

Haddon, A. C. (1904). *Reports of the Cambridge anthropological expedition to Torres Straits: Sociology, magic and religion of the Western Islanders* (Vol. 5). Cambridge: Cambridge University Press.

Haddon, A. C. (1908). *Reports of the Cambridge Anthropological Expedition to Torres Strait: Sociology, magic and religion of the Eastern Islanders* (Vol. 6). Cambridge: Cambridge University Press.

Haddon, A. C. (1912). *Reports of the Cambridge anthropological expedition to Torres Straits: Arts and Crafts* (Vol. 4). Cambridge: Cambridge University Press.

Haddon, A. C. (1932). *Head-Hunters: Black, white and brown* (Vol. 26, 2nd edition). London: Watts and Co.

Haddon, A. C. (1935). *Reports of the Cambridge anthropological expedition to Torres Straits: General ethnography* (Vol. 1). Cambridge: Cambridge University Press.

Hall, J. and Bowen, G. (1989). An excavation of a midden complex at the Toulkerrie Oystermen's Lease, Moreton Island, S.E. Queensland. In J. Hall (Ed.), *Queensland Archaeological Research* (Vol. 5, pp. 4-24). St Lucia: Queensland University Press.

Harris, D. (1995). Early agriculture in New Guinea and the Torres Strait divide. *Antiquity*, 69(1), 848-854.

Harris, D. R. and Ghaleb, B. (1987). Archaeological and Ecological Investigations on Mabuyag Island. In A. J. Barham and D. R. Harris (Eds.), Archaeological and Palaeoenvironmental Investigations in Western Torres Strait, Northern Australia. Final Report to the Research and Exploration Committee of the National Geographic Society on Part IIb of the Torres Strait Research Project, July-October 1985 (pp. 5-35). London: Institute of Archaeology, University of London.

Harris, D. R., Barham, A. J. and Ghaleb, B. (1985). Archaeology and Recent palaeoenvironmental history of Torres Strait, Northern Australia. Preliminary Report to the Research and Exploration Committee of the National Geographic Society on Part IIa of the Torres Strait Research Project, July-October 1984 (pp. 1-58). London: Institute of Archaeology, University of London.

Harris, D. R., Barham, A. J. and Kirby (ne Ghaleb), B. (In press). Mabuyag (Torres Strait) in the mid-1980s: archaeological reconnaissance of the island the midden excavations at Goemu. In I.J. McNiven and G. Hitchcock (Eds), *Goemulgal: Natural and Cultural Histories of the Mabuyag Islands, Zenadh Kes (Torres Strait)*. Memoirs of the Queensland Museum Cultural Heritage Series (Vol. 8). Brisbane: Queensland Museum.

Harrison, R. (2000). Challenging the 'authenticity' of antiquity: contact archaeology and Native Title in Australia. In I. Lilley (Ed.), *Native Title and the transformation of archaeology in the postcolonial world* (Vol. 50, pp. 35-53). Sydney: Oceania monograph.

Head, L. (1994). Landscapes socialised by fire: post-contact changes in Aboriginal fire use in northern Australia, and implications for prehistory. *Archaeology Oceania*, 29, 172-181.

Hiscock, P. (1994). The end of points. In M. Sullivan, S. Brockwell and A. Webb (Eds), *Archaeology in the north: Proceedings of the 1993 Australian Archaeological Association Conference* (pp. 72-83). North Australian Research Unit, Australian National University, Darwin.

Hodder, I. (1978). *The Spatial Organisation of Culture*. London: Ducksworth.

Hodder, I. (1986). *Reading the Past: Current Approaches to Interpretation in Archaeology*. Cambridge: Cambridge University Press.

Hodder, I. (1991). Interpretive archaeology and its role. *American Antiquity*, 56, 7-18.

Hope, J. and Littleton, J. (1995). *Finding out about Aboriginal Burials*. Murray Darling Basin Aboriginal Heritage Handbooks. Sydney: Mungo Publications.

Isbell, W. (1997). Household and Ayni in the Andean past. In G. Urton (Ed.), *Structure, Knowledge and Representation in the Andes: Studies Presented to Reinder Tom Zuidema on the Occasion of his 70th Birthday* (pp. 247-305). Urbana: University of Illinois.

Isbell, W. (2000). What we should be studying: The 'imagined community and the 'natural community'. In J. Yaeger and M. Canuto (Eds), *The Archaeology of Communities* (pp. 243-266). London and New York: Routledge.

Jones, S. (1997). *The Archaeology of Ethnicity: Constructing identities in the past and present.* London: Routledge.

Jones, S. (2007). Discourses of identity in the interpretation of the past. In T. Insoll (Ed.), *The Archaeology of Identities* (pp. 44-58). London and New York: Routledge Taylor and Francis Group.

Kroeber, A. L. (1952). *The Nature of Culture.* Chicago: University of Chicago Press.

Kwan, D., Delean, S. and Marsh, H. (2006). Factors influencing the sustainability of customary dugong hunting by a remote Indigenous community. *Environmental Conservation,* 33(2), 164-117.

Laade, W. (1973). Notes on the clans, economy, trade and traditional law of the Murray Islanders, Torres Straits. *Journal de la Societe des Oceanistes,* 29(30), 151-167.

Lambeck, K. and J. Chappell. (2001). Sea Level change through the last glacial cycle. *Science* 292, 679–686.

Landtman, G. (1917). *The Folk-Tales of the Kiwai Papuans.* (Vol. 47). Helsingfors: Finnish Society of Literature.

Larcombe, P., Carter, R. M., Dye, J., Gagan, M. K. and Johnson, D. P. (1995). New evidence for episodic post-glacial sea-level rise, central Great Barrier Reef, Australia. *Marine Geology,* 127, 1-44.

Lawrence, D. (1994). *Customary exchange across the Torres Strait,* Memoirs of the Queensland Museum (Vol. 34, 2, pp. 241-446): Brisbane: Queensland Museum.

Lawrence, D. (1998). Customary exchange in the Torres Strait. *Australian Aboriginal studies,* 2, 13-25.

Lawrie, M. (1970). *Myths and Legends of the Torres Strait.* St Lucia: University of Queensland Press.

Leaversley, M., Minai, B., Kop, H and Kewibu, V. (2005). Cross-cultural concepts of archaeology Kastom, community, education and cultural heritage management in Papua New-Guinea. *Public Archaeology,* 4, 3-13.

Lilley, I. (2000). Introduction. In I. Lilley (Ed.), *Native Title and the transformation of archaeology in the postcolonial world* (Vol. 50, pp. 1-24). Sydney: Oceania monograph.

Lindbergh, J. (1999). Buttoning down archaeology. *Australasian Historical Archaeology,* 17, 50-57.

Lourandos, H. (1993). Hunter-Gatherer Cultural Dynamics: Long-and Short-Term Trends in Australian Prehistory. *Journal of Archaeological Research,* 1(1), 67-88.

Lourandos, H. (1997). *Continent of Hunter Gatherers: New perspectives in Australian prehistory.* Cambridge and Melbourne: Cambridge University Press.

Macgillivray, J. (1852). *Narrative of the Voyage of HMS Rattlesnake commanded by Captain Owen Stanley 1846-1850.* London: T and W Boone.

Marcus, J. (2000). Towards an archaeology of communities. In M. A. Canuto and J. Yaeger (Eds.), *The archaeology of Communities: A new world perspective* (pp. 231-242). London and New York: Routledge.

Marshall, Y. (2002). What is community archaeology? *World Archaeology,* 34(2), 211–219.

McCarthy, F. D. (1940). Trade in aboriginal Australia and trade relationships with Torres Straits, New Guinea and Malaya. *Oceania,* 9(4), 405-438.

McCormac, F. G., Hogg, A. G., Blackwell, P. G., Buck, C. E., Higham, T. F. G. and Reimer, P. J. (2004). SHCal04 southern hemisphere calibration, 0-11.0 cal kyr BP. *Radiocarbon*, 46, 1087-1092.

McDonald, J. (2000). Archaeology, rock-art, ethnicity and Native Title. In I. Lilley (Ed.), *Native Title and the transformation of archaeology in the postcolonial world* (Vol. 50, pp. 54-64). Sydney: Oceania monographs.

McDonald, J. (2005). Archaeological evidence in the De Rose Hill native title claim. *Australian Aboriginal Studies*, 1, 30-44.

McFarlane, S. (August 14th 1874). Voyage of the Somerset. Unpublished Letter to Rev. Whitehouse. Microfilm reel M11. National Library of Australia, Melbourne.

McFarlane, S. (September 14th 1876). Unpublished letter to Rev. Murray. Microfilm reel M18. National Library of Australia, Melbourne.

McIntyre-Tamwoy, S., and Harrison, R. (2004). Monuments to colonialism? Stone arrangements, tourist cairns and turtle magic at Evans Bay, Cape York. *Australian Archaeology*, 59(1), 31-42.

McNiven, I. J. (1998). Enmity and amity: reconsidering stone-headed club (*gabagaba*) procurement and trade in Torres Strait. *Oceania*, 69(2), 94-115.

McNiven, I. J. (1999). Fissioning and regionalisation: The social dimensions of changes in Aboriginal use of the Great Sandy Region, southeast Queensland. In J. Hall and I. McNiven (Eds.), *Australian Coastal Archaeology* (pp. 157-168). Canberra: Research School of Pacific and Asian Studies, Australian National University.

McNiven, I. J. (2003). Saltwater People: Spiritscapes, maritime rituals and the archaeology of Australian Indigenous seascapes. *World Archaeology*, 35(3), 329-349.

McNiven, I. J. (2006). Dauan 4 and the emergence of ethnographically-known social arrangements across Torres Strait during the last 600-800 years. *Australian Archaeology*, 62(1), 1-13.

McNiven, I. J. (2008). Inclusions, exclusions and transition: Torres Strait Islander constructed landscapes over the past 4000 years, north eastern Australia. *The Holocene*, 18(3), 449-462.

McNiven, I. J. and Bedingfield, A. (2008). Past and present marine mammal hunting rates and abundances: dugong (*dugong dugon*) evidence from Dabangai Bone Mound, Torres Strait. *Journal of Archaeological Science*, 35, 505-515.

McNiven, I. J. and David, B. (2004). Torres Strait rock-art and ochre sources: an overview. In I. J. McNiven and M. Quinnell (Eds.), *Torres Strait Archaeology and Material Culture*, Memoirs of the Queensland Museum Culture Heritage Series (Vol. 3, pp. 199-208). Brisbane: Queensland Museum.

McNiven, I. J. and Feldman, R. (2003). Ritually Orchestrated Seascapes: Hunting Magic and Dugong Bone Mounds in Torres Strait, NE Australia. *Cambridge Archaeological Journal*, 13(2), 169-194.

McNiven, I. J. and Russell, L. (2005). *Appropriated Pasts: Indigenous peoples and the colonial culture of archaeology*. Lanham, New York, Toronto, Oxford: Altamira Press.

McNiven, I. J. and von Gnielinski, F. (2004). Stone club head manufacture on Dauan Island, Torres Strait. In I. J. McNiven and M. Quinnell (Eds.), *Torres Strait Archaeology and Material Culture*, Memoirs of the Queensland Museum Culture Heritage Series (Vol. 3, pp. 291-304). Brisbane: Queensland Museum.

McNiven, I. J. and Hitchcock, G. (2004). Torres Strait marine subsistence specialisation and terrestrial animal translocation. In I. J. McNiven and M. Quinnell (Eds.), *Torres Strait Archaeology and Material Culture*, Memoirs of the Queensland Museum Culture Heritage Series (Vol. 3, pp. 105-162). Brisbane: Queensland Museum.

McNiven, I. J. and Wright, D. (2008). Ritualised Marine Midden Formation in Western Zenadh Kes (Torres Strait). In G. Clark, F. Leach and S. O'Connor (Eds.), *Islands of Inquiry: Colonisation, seafaring and the archaeology of maritime landscapes* (Vol. 29, pp. 133-148). Canberra: Terra Australis, Australian National University.

McNiven, I. J., David, B. and Brady, L. (2002). Torres Strait rock-art: an enhanced perspective. *Australian Aboriginal Studies*, 2, 69-74.

McNiven, I. J., Fitzpatrick, J. and Cordell, J. (2004a). An Islander World: Managing the archaeological Heritage of Torres Strait. In I. J. McNiven and M. Quinnell (Eds.), *Torres Strait Archaeology and Material Culture*, Memoirs of the Queensland Museum Culture Heritage Series (Vol. 3, pp. 74-91). Brisbane: Queensland Museum.

McNiven, I. J., von Gnielinski, F. and Quinnell, M. C. (2004b). Torres Strait and the origin of large stone axes from Kiwai Island, Fly River estuary (Papua New Guinea). In I. J. McNiven and M. Quinnell (Eds), *Torres Strait Archaeology and Material Culture*, Memoirs of the Queensland Museum Culture Heritage Series (Vol. 3, pp. 271-289). Brisbane: Queensland Museum.

McNiven, I. J., David, B., Brady, L. and Brayer, J. (2004c). Kabadul Kula rock-art site, Dauan island, Torres Strait. In I. J. McNiven and M. Quinnell (Eds.), *Torres Strait Archaeology and Material Culture*, Memoirs of the Queensland Museum Culture Heritage Series (Vol. 3, pp. 227-256). Brisbane: Queensland Museum.

McNiven, I. J., Dickinson, W. R., David, B., Weisler, F., Carter, M. and Zoppi, U. (2006). Mask Cave: Red-slipped pottery and the Australian-Papuan settlement of Torres Strait. *Archaeology in Oceania*, 41(2), 49-82.

McNiven, I. J., Crouch, J., Weisler, M., Kemp, N., Clayton-Martinez, L., Stanisic, J., Orr, M., Brady, L, Hocknull, S. and Boles, W. (2008). Tigershark Rockshelter (Baidamau Mudh): Seascape and Settlement Reconfigurations on the Sacred Islet of Pulu, Western Zenadh Kes (Torres Strait). *Australian Archaeology*, 66, 15-32.

McNiven, I. J., David, B., Goemulgaw kod, and Fitzpatrick, J. (2009). The Great kod of Pulu: Mutual historical emergence of ceremonial sites and social groups, Torres Strait, Northeast Australia. *Cambridge Archaeological Journal*, 19(3), 92-108.

McNiven, I. J., David, B., Richards, T., Aplin, K., Asmussen, B., Mialanes, J., Leavesley, M., Faulkner, P. and Ulm, S. (2011). New direction in human colonisation of the Pacific: Lapita settlement of south coast New Guinea. *Australian Archaeology*, 72, 1–6.

McNiven, I. J., Wright, D., Sutton, S., Weisler, M., Hocknull, S. and Stanisic, J. (In press). Midden Formation and Marine Specialisation at Goemu village, Mabuyag, Torres Strait, Before and After European Contact. In I.J. McNiven and G. Hitchcock (Eds.) *Goemulgal: Natural and Cultural Histories of the Mabuyag Islands, Zenadh Kes (Torres Strait)*, Memoirs of the Queensland Museum Cultural Heritage Series (Vol. 8). Brisbane: Queensland Museum.

Minar, D. W. and Greer, S. (1969). *The Concept of Community: Readings with Interpretations*. Chicago: Aldine.

Mooke, T. (1972). Mabuiag Lag. Unpublished stories collected by Simpson, B. and Y. Bani. Mabuyag: Mabuyag Island Council.

Moore, D. R. (1972). Cape York Aborigines and Islanders of Western Torres Strait. In D. Walker (Ed.), *Bridge and Barrier: The natural and cultural history of Torres Strait* (pp. 327-344). Canberra: Department of Biogeography and Goemorphology. Research School of Pacific Studies. The Australian National University.

Moore, D. R. (1979). *Islanders and Aborigines at Cape York*. Canberra: Australian Institute of Aboriginal Studies.

Moore, D. R. (1984). *The Torres Strait Collections of A.C. Haddon*. London: British Museum Publications Ltd.

Moresby, J. (1876). *New Guinea and Polynesia: Discoveries and surveys in New Guinea and the D'Entrecasteaux Islands*. London: John Murray.

Morphy, H. (1991). *Ancestral Connections: Art and an Aboriginal system of knowledge*. Chicago: University of Chicago Press.

Moser, S., Glazier, D., Phillips, J., Nasser el Nemr, L., Mousa, L., Nasr Aiesh, R., Richardson, S., Conner, A., and Seymour Source, M. (2002). Transforming Archaeology through Practice: Strategies for Collaborative Archaeology and the Community Archaeology Project at Quseir, Egypt. *World Archaeology*, 34(2), 220-248.

Mullens, S. (1995). *Torres Strait: A history of Colonial Occupation and Culture Contact 1864-1897*. Rockhampton: Central Queensland University Press.

Murray, A. W. (May 3rd 1873). Unpublished Letter to Mullens. National Library of Australia, Melbourne.

Neal, R. A. (1989). An archaeological inspection of alternative Telecom locations on Mabuiag and Yam Islands, Torres Strait. Unpublished report by Pirripoint Pty Ltd to Department of Community Service and Ethnic Affairs, Brisbane.

Orser, C. E. (2007). *The Archaeology of Race and Racialization in Historic America*. Florida: University Press Florida.

Pardoe, C. (1988). The cemetery as symbol. The distribution of prehistoric Aboriginal burial grounds in southeastern Australia. *Archaeology in Oceania*, 23(1), 1-17.

Pardoe, C. (1995). Riverine, biological and cultural evolution in south-eastern Australia. *Antiquity*, 69, 696-713.

Parr, J. and Carter, M. (2003). Phytolith and starch analysis of sediment samples from two archaeological sites on Dauar Island, Torres Strait, northeastern Australia. *Vegetable Historical Archaeobotany*, 12(2), 131-141.

Pate, D. (1995). Stable carbon isotope assessment of hunter-gatherer mobility in prehistoric South Australia. *Journal of Archaeological Science*, 22, 81-87.

Philp, J. (2001). *Past Times: Torres Strait Islanders: Material from the Haddon collection 1888-1905*. Canberra: National Museum of Australia.

Pickering, M. (1994). The physical landscape as a social landscape: a Garawa example. *Archaeology in Oceania*, 29, 149-161.

Postone, M., Lipuma, E. and Calhoun, C. (1993). Introduction: Bourdieu and social theory. In M. Postone, E. Lipuma and C. Calhoun (Eds), *Bourdieu: Critical perspectives* (pp. 212-234). Cambridge: Polity Press.

Preucel, R. (2000). Making Pueblo communities: architectural discourse at Kotyiti, new Mexico. In M. A. Canuto and J. Yaeger (Eds), *The Archaeology of Communities* (pp. 58-77). London and New York: Routledge.

Reimer, P., Baillie, M., Bard, E., Bayliss, A., Beck, J., Blackwell, P., Bronk Ramsey, C., Buck, C., Burr, G., Edwards, R., Friedrich, M., Grootes, P., Guilderson, T., Hajdas, I., Heaton, T., Hogg, A., Hughen, K., Kaiser, K., Kromer, B., McCormac, F., Manning, S., Reimer, R., Richards, D., Southon, J., Talamo, S., Turney, C., van der Plicht, J., and Weyhenmeyer, C. (2009). IntCal09 and Marine09 radiocarbon age calibration curves, 0–50,000 years cal BP. *Radiocarbon*, 51(4), 1111–1150.

Renfrew, C. (1978). Space, time and polity. In M. J Rowlands and J. Friedman (Eds), *The Evolution of Social Systems* (pp. 89-112). London: Duckworth.

Richards, L. (2002). Introduction. In R. Harrison and C. Williamson (Eds.), *After Captain Cook: The archaeology of the recent Indigenous past in Australia* (Vol. 8, pp. 104-112). Sydney: Sydney University Archaeologicial Methods Series.

Ross, J. (2013). A continent of Nations: The emergence of new regionally distinct rock art styles across Australia. *Quaternary International*, 285, 161-171.

Rowe, C. (2005). A Holocene History of Vegetation Change in the Western Torres Strait Region, Queensland Australia. Unpublished PhD thesis, Monash University, Melbourne.

Rowland, M. J. (1984). Archaeological survey and excavations on Moa and Naghi Islands, Torres Strait, November 1st-25th 1981. Unpublished report to the archaeology branch, Department of Community Services, Brisbane.

Rowland, M. J. (1985). Archaeological investigations on Moa and Naghi Islands, Western Torres Strait. *Australian Archaeology*, 21, 119-132.

Rowland, M. J. (1994). The politics of identity in archaeology. In G. Bone and A. Gillam (Eds), *Social Construction of the Past: Representation as power* (Vol. 24, pp. 129-142). London and New York: Routledge.

Rowland, M. J. and Ulm, S. (2011). Indigenous Fish Traps and Weirs of Queensland. *Queensland Archaeological Research*, 14, 1-57.

Shanks, M. and Tilley, C. (1987). *Social Theory and Archaeology*. Cambridge: Polity Press.

Sharp, N. (1980). *Torres Strait Islands, 1879-1979. Theme for an overview*. Melbourne: Department of Sociology, Latrobe University.

Shennan, S. J. (1989). Introduction: Archaeological approaches to cultural identity. In S. J. Shennan (Ed.), *Archaeological Approaches to Cultural Identity* (pp. 1-30). London: Unwin Hyman

Shnukal, A. R. (1992). Pacific Islanders and Torres Strait 1860-1940. *Australian Aboriginal Studies*, 1, 14-27.

Shnukal, A. R. (2004). The post-contact created environment in the Torres Strait Central Islands. In I. J. McNiven and M. Quinnell (Eds), *Torres Strait Archaeology and Material Culture*, Memoirs of the Queensland Museum Culture Heritage Series (Vol. 3, pp. 317-346). Brisbane: Queensland Museum.

Shnukal, A. R. (In press). Marine Industries and Mabuyag, 1870-1980. In I.J. McNiven and G. Hitchcock (Eds) *Goemulgal: Natural and Cultural Histories of the Mabuyag Islands, Zenadh Kes (Torres Strait)*. Memoirs of the Queensland Museum Cultural Heritage Series (Vol. 8). Brisbane: Queensland Museum.

Skelly, R. (2007). Ritual Resource Management at Koey Ngurtai, western Torres Strait: Mediating the place of Dugongs in the Physical and Spirit World. Unpublished Masters, Monash University, Melbourne.

Skelly, R., David, B., Barker, B., Kuaso, A. and Araho, N. (2010). Migration sites of the Miaro clan (Vailala River region, Papua New Guinea): tracking Kouri settlement movements through oral tradition sites on ancient landscapes. *The Artefact*, 33, 16-29.

Smith, L. (1999). *Decolonizing Methodologies: Research and Indigenous peoples*. London and New York: Zed Books Ltd.

Soja, E. W. (1989). *Postmodern Geographies: The reassertion of space in critical social theory*. New York: Verso Press.

Summerhayes, G. (Ed.) (2000). *Lapita Interaction*. Terra Australis (Vol. 15). Canberra: Department of Archaeology and Natural History, and Centre for Archaeology, Australian National University.

Taçon, P. (1993). Regionalism in the recent rock-art of western Arnhem Land, Northern Territory. *Archaeology in Oceania*, 28(3), 112-120.

Taçon, P. (1994). Socialising landscapes: the long term implications of signs, symbols and marks on the land. *Archaeology in Oceania*, 29, 117-129.

Taylor, L. (1996). *Seeing the Inside: Bark painting in Western Arnhem Land*. Oxford: Clarendon Press.

Teske, T. (1986). *Mabuiag Island of Torres Strait*. Cairns: Far Northern Schools Development Unit.

Thomson, D. F. (1939). The seasonal factor in human culture. *Proceedings of the Prehistoric Society*, 5, 209-221.

Tindale, N. B. (1974). *Aboriginal tribes of Australia*. Berkeley: University of California Press.

Trigger, B. G. (2006). *A History of Archaeological Thought* (2nd edition). Cambridge, New York: Cambridge University Press.

Ulm, S., Barham, A. J., David, B., Jacobsen, G., McNiven, I. J., Petchey, F. and Rowland, M. (2007). Marine Carbon Reservoir Variability in Torres Strait: Preliminary Results of AMS Dating of Live-Collected Shell Specimens. Paper presented at the XVII INQUA Congress.

Vanderwal, R. (1973). *The Torres Strait: Protohistory and Beyond*. In P. Lauer (ed.), Occasional Papers in Anthropology (Vol. 2, pp. 157-194). St Lucia: University of Queensland.

Vanderwal, R. (2004). Early historical sources for the top western islands in the western Torres Strait exchange network. In I. J. McNiven and M. Quinnell (Eds), *Torres Strait Archaeology and Material Culture* (Vol. 3, pp. 257-270). Brisbane: Memoirs of the Queensland Museum Culture Heritage Series.

Veth, P. (2000). The contemporary voice of archaeology and its relevance to Native Title. In I. Lilley (Ed.), *Native Title and the transformation of archaeology in the postcolonial world* (Vol. 50, pp. 78-87). Sydney: Oceania Monograph.

Veth, P. and O'Connor, S. (2002). Can archaeology be used to address the principle of exclusive possession in native title? In R. Harrison and C. Williamson (Eds), *After Captain Cook: The archaeology of the recent Indigenous past in Australia* (Vol. 8, pp. 121-140). Sydney: Sydney University.

Veth, P. and O'Connor, S. (2005). Archaeology, claimant connection to sites, and native title: employment of successful categories of data with specific comments on glass artefacts In R. Harrison and J. V. McDonald, P (Eds), *Native Title and Archaeology* (pp. 2-15). Canberra: Australian Aboriginal Studies.

von Gnielinski, F. E., Denaro, T.J., Wellman, P. and Pain, C.F. (1998). Torres Strait Region. In J. H. C. Bain and J. J. Draper (Eds), *North Queensland Geology* (Vol. 240, pp. 159-164). Canberra: AGSO Bulletin.

Walker, D. (Ed.). (1972). *Bridge and barrier: the natural and cultural history of Torres Strait*. Canberra: Department of Biogeography and Goemorphology. Research School of Pacific Studies. The Australian National University.

Webb, S. G. (1989). *The Willandra Lakes hominids*. Canberra: Research School of Pacific Studies, The Australian National University. Williams, A., Ulm, S, Goodwin, I. and Smith, M. (2010). Hunter-gatherer response to late Holocene climatic variability in northern and central Australia. *Journal of Quaternary Science* 25(6),831-838.

Willmott, W. F. and Chertok, I. (1972). *Igneous and metamorphic rocks, Cape York Peninsula and Torres Strait, Queensland and Papua*. Canberra: Australian Bureau of Mineral Resources, Geology and Geophysics map.

Willmott, W. F., Whitaker, W. G., Palfreyman, W. D. and Trail, D. S. (1973). Igneous and metamorphic rocks of Cape York Peninsula and Torres Strait. *Bulletin of the Bureau of Mineral Resources, Geology and Geophysics*, 135, 113-128.

Woodroffe, C. D., Kennedy, D. M., Hopley, D., Rasmussen, C. and Smithers, S. G. (2000). Holocene reef growth in Torres Strait. *Marine Geology*, 170, 331-346.

Woodroffe, C. D., Samosorn, B., Hua, Q. and Hart, D. E. (2007). Incremental growth of a sandy reef island over the past 3000 years indicated by component-specific radiocarbon dating. *Geophysical Research Letters* 34, 1-5.

Wright, D. (2010). The archaeology of community emergence and development on Mabuiag, western Torres Strait. Unpublished PhD thesis, Monash University, Melbourne.

Wright, D. (2011a). The archaeology of community emergence and development on Mabuyag (Mabuiag) in the central western Torres Strait, northeast Australia. *Australian Archaeology*, 73, 49–57.

Wright, D. (2011b). Mid-Holocene maritime economy in the western Torres Strait. *Archaeology in Oceania*, 46, 23–27.

Wright, D. (2011c). Is a village a village if no one lives there? Negotiated histories on Mabuyag in the central Western Torres Strait. In J. Liston, G. Clark and D. Alexander (Eds), *Pacific Island Heritage: Archaeology, identity and community*, Terra Australis (Vol. 35, pp.115–126), Canberra: The Australian National University.

Wright, D. and Dickinson, W. (2009). Movement of ideas not materials: Locally-manfactured pottery on Mabuyag Island, western Torres Strait. *Archaeology in Oceania*, 44(1), 38-41.

Wright, D. and Gizu, T. (2012). What's under Baw village? Dugong hunting on Mabuyag before 2000 years ago. Unpublished report to the Mabuyag community council, Mabuyag, Queensland.

Wright, D. and Jacobsen, G. (2013). Further radiocarbon dates from Dabangay a mid-to late Holocene settlement site in western Torres Strait. *Australian Archaeology*, 76, 79–83.

Wright, D. and Jacobsen, G. (In press). Convergence of ceremonial and secular: The archaeology of Dabangai on Mabuyag in the western Torres Strait. In I.J. McNiven and G. Hitchcock (Eds), *Goemulgal: Natural and cultural histories of the Mabuyag Islands, Zenadh Kes (Torres Strait)*. Memoirs of the Queensland Museum Cultural Heritage Series (Vol. 8). Brisbane: Queensland Museum.

Wright, D. and Ricardi, P. (In Press). Both sides of the frontier: The 'contact' archaeology of villages on Mabuyag, western Torres Strait. *Quaternary International* (corrected proof available online at: www.sciencedirect.com/science/article/pii/s1040618214006764).

Wright, D., Hiscock, P. and Aplin, K. (2013). Re-excavation of a mid-Holocene settlement site on Mabuyag in western Torres Strait. *Queensland Archaeological Research*, 16, 15-32.

Wright, D., Taçon, P., Ulm, S., Fogel, A. and Sutton, S. (In prep). Archaeology of the Wagadagam mens' meeting place (*kod*) on Mabuyag, western Torres Strait.

Wurm, S. A. (1972). Torres Strait - linguistic barrier? In D. Walker (Ed.), B*ridge and barrier: the natural and cultural history of Torres Strait* (pp. 345-566). Canberra: Department of Biogeography and Goemorphology. Research School of Pacific Studies. The Australian National University.

Yaeger, J. and Canutto, M. (2000). Introducing an archaeology of communities. In J. Yaeger and M. Canuto (Eds), *The Archaeology of Communities* (pp. 1-15). London and New York: Routledge.

Index

www.ingramcontent.com/pod-product-compliance
Lightning Source LLC
Chambersburg PA
CBHW061010030426
42334CB00033B/3433